Biblical Epics

This is the first major survey and analysis of the relationship between religion and film in the Hollywood cinema. Within the context of American history, *Biblical Epics* examines the impact of ethnicity, sexuality, gender and religion on this fascinating and complex genre. The authors raise questions of narrative, spectacle, Jewish–Christian relations, authorship, star meanings, the representation of Christ and sexual desire.

Babington and Evans theorise the Biblical Epic in its three main forms: the Old Testament Epic; the Christ film; and the Roman/Christian Epic, which provide the focus for the book. Films analysed include *David and Bathsheba*, *The Last Temptation of Christ*, *The King of Kings*, *The Greatest Story Ever Told*, *Demetrius and the Gladiators*, *Samson and Delilah* and *Ben Hur*.

This book will be of interest to undergraduate and postgraduate students, and lecturers in film studies, media and cultural studies and religious studies.

Bruce Babington is Senior Lecturer in English Literature and Film and Peter William Evans is Professor of Spanish Literature and Film at the University of Newcastle upon Tyne. Their previous books, *Blue Skies and Silver Linings: aspects of the Hollywood musical* (1985) and *Affairs to Remember: the Hollywood comedy of the sexes* (1989), are published by Manchester University Press.

To our families and in memory of Arnold Oscar Babington (1905–92)

BIBLICAL EPICS

Sacred narrative in the Hollywood cinema

Bruce Babington *&* **Peter William Evans**

Manchester University Press

Manchester and New York

Distributed exclusively in the USA and Canada by St. Martin's Press

Copyright © Bruce Babington and Peter William Evans 1993

Published by Manchester University Press
Oxford Road, Manchester M13 9PL, UK
and Room 400, 175 Fifth Avenue, New York, NY 10010, USA

Distributed exclusively in the USA and Canada
by St. Martin's Press, Inc., 175 Fifth Avenue, New York, NY 10010, USA

British Library Cataloguing-in-Publication Data
A catalogue record for this book is available from the British Library

Library of Congress Cataloguing-in-Publication Data
Babington, Bruce
    Biblical epics : sacred narrative in the Hollywood cinema / Bruce Babington & Peter
    William Evans.
       p.   cm.
    Includes bibliographical references.
    ISBN 0–7190–3268–7 (hardback). — ISBN 0–7190–4030–2 (pbk.)
    1. Bible films — History and criticism.   I. Evans, Peter William.   II. Title.
PN1995.9.B53B3   1993
791.43'682 — dc20   92–35884

ISBN 0 7190 3268 7 *hardback*
ISBN 0 7190 4030 2 *paperback*

Photoset in Linotron Janson by
Northern Phototypesetting Co Ltd, Bolton
Printed in Great Britain
by Bell & Bain Limited, Glasgow

Contents

List of stills   *page* vi
Acknowledgements   viii

Introduction **Theorising the Biblical Epic**   1

Part one **THE OLD TESTAMENT EPIC**   25
  1 Jewish questions   33
  2 Questions of narrative   42
  3 Henry King's *David and Bathsheba* (1951)   70

Part two **THE CHRIST FILM**   91
  4 The lives of Christ: the greatest story every screened   98
  5 'Abide with Me': Cecil B. De Mille's *The King of Kings* (1927)   110
  6 'Son of Man': Nicholas Ray's *King of Kings* (1961)   127
  7 An American pastoral: George Stevens's *The Greatest Story Ever Told*
     (1965)   139
  8 From Main Street to mean streets: Martin Scorsese's
     The Last Temptation of Christ (1988)   149

Part three **THE ROMAN/CHRISTIAN EPIC**   169
  9 The poetics of the Roman/Christian Epic   177
  10 *The Robe* and *Demetrius and the Gladiators*   206

Coda **Victor Agonistes; or, justice done to an unconsidered star**   227

Note on sources   239
Index   243

Stills

THE OLD TESTAMENT EPIC

1 Law and orgy in *The Ten Commandments* (1956).
© Paramount Studios   *page* 27

2 Charlton Heston with friend.
© Paramount Studios   28

3 Mother and sons in *The Ten Commandments* (1923).   28

4 Heroic counter-culture in *The Ten Commandments* (1956).
© Paramount Studios   29

5 The antagonists in *Samson and Delilah*.
© Paramount Studios   30

6 In the empire of the senses in *Solomon and Sheba*.   30

7 *David and Bathsheba*.   31

8 The heroine as prisoner and carrier of the look in *David and Bathsheba*.   32

9 David's conscience: Nathan in *David and Bathsheba*.   32

THE CHRIST FILM

10 The great storyteller in *King of Kings* (1927).   93

11 The five ages of feminised man in *King of Kings*, (1927).   93

12 Ray's beautiful rebel with a cause in *King of Kings* (1961).
© 1961 Turner Entertainment Co. All rights reserved.   94

13 Female presences in the Christ film in *The King of Kings* (1927).   95

14 'The shadow of the Galilean' in *King of Kings* (1961).
© 1961 Turner Entertainment Co. All rights reserved.   95

15 On the road in *The Greatest Story Ever Told*.   96

16 Graduate school for alternative values in *The Greatest Story Ever Told*.   96

17 De-iconisation in *The Last Temptation of Christ*.   97

18 Introspective, troubled Jesus in *The Last Temptation of Christ*.   97

THE ROMAN/CHRISTIAN EPIC

19 Judaeo-Christian humanity and Roman discipline in *Ben Hur* (1925).
© 1927 Turner Entertainment Co. All rights reserved.   171

20 The arena in *Spartacus*.   172

21 A balcony of Roman connotations in *Quo Vadis?*
© 1951 Turner Entertainment Co. All rights reserved.   172

22 Hollywood's epic image of the Arab in *Ben Hur* (1959).
© 1959 Turner Entertainment Co. All rights reserved.   173

23 Roman soldier and Christian maiden in *The Robe*.   174

24 The robe as sign in *Demetrius and the Gladiators*.   175

25 Demetrius, the slave, and Messalina.   175

26 Victor Mature in close-up.   176

Acknowledgements

Newcastle University Small Grants Committee; Newcastle University Schools of English and Modern Languages, Combined Studies, and Centre for Continuing Education; Newcastle and Pittsburgh University Libraries; British Film Institute Library and Stills department; John Banks; Lucy Fischer; Susan Davidson; Pamela Bacarisse; George Erdos; Bill Telford; John Sawyer; Isabel Wollaston; Marianne Guillon; Marion O'Connor; Rosalie Novick, Gail Anderson and Gavin Robson; Ron Guariento; Terry R. Wright; Michael Brick; Jerry Patterson. And finally a less fulsome acknowledgement of M. Alain Marchand's proposal to charge us £150 to see the Paris Cinémathèque's copy of *Noah's Ark*. Salut, Alain.

Introduction

Theorising the Biblical Epic

PROBLEMS OF DISCOURSE: BEYOND THE VALLEY OF THE WISECRACK

Loved Ben, Hated Hur — Elliott Stein

Pick up that bible of middle-brow film viewing, *Halliwell's Film Guide*, and turn to Stevens's *The Greatest Story Ever Told* (1965). After the author's comments (for instance 'Solemn spectacular with elephantine pace'), look down the list of review excerpts that support his views.

> George Stevens was once described as a water buffalo of film art. What this film more precisely suggests is a dinosaur. — *Monthly Film Bulletin*

> God is unlucky in *The Greatest Story Every Told*. His only begotten son turns out to be a bore . . . The photography is inspired mainly by Hallmark Cards . . . as the Hallelujah Chorus explodes around us stereophonically and stereotypically it becomes clear that Lazarus was not so much raised from the tomb as blasted out of it. As for pacing, the picture does not let you forget a single second of its four hours. — John Simon

> No more than three minutes have elapsed before we suspect that Stevens' name and fame have been purchased by the Hallmark Greeting Card Company, and that what we are looking at is really a lengthy catalogue of greeting cards for 1965 – for Those Who Care Enough to Send the Very Best.
> — Stanley Kauffmann

> Who but an audience of diplomats could sit through this thing? As the picture ponderously unrolled, it was mainly irritation that kept me awake.
> — Shana Alexander, *Life*

> If the subject-matter weren't sacred, we would be responding to the picture in the most charitable way by laughing at it from start to finish.
> — Brendan Gill, *New Yorker*

> A Big windy bore. — Bruce Williamson, *Playboy*

All but one of the above are American, but the style is Anglo-American, if not International. Thus these English instances (*King David*, 1985): 'Philistines Get Their Own Back' (Derek Malcolm, *Guardian*, 28 October 1959); 'And having begot Beresford, lo! the Lord of Paramount begat Martin Elfand (hoping he would beget as many millions with this film as he has with *An Officer and a Gentleman*) (Alexander Walker, *Evening Standard*, 29 June 1986).

The isolated *bon mot* may evoke an occasional weary smile, but displayed in its unvarying monotony the style is more likely to provoke depression, repetition exposing its too-familiar techniques of laboured wit, condescending hauteur, the assumed veneer rather than the actuality of knowledge, a vulgarity far more vulgar than that it claims to have endured. Once you have grasped its few limited conventions – for instance any anachronistic play with biblical language is intrinsically hilarious; any one of vulgarity, boredom, anaemic good taste may be used as interchangeable accusations – it is a style you can compose by rote. Resolutely unintellectual, it nevertheless claims intellectual superiority to its targets of ridicule. To give one last and representative example, in reviewing Anne Edwards's *The De Milles: An American Family*, an English reviewer, Gerald Kaufman, comments: 'The flavour of Cecil B. De Mille's attitude to the Good Book can best be discerned in his description of Samson's first glimpse of the mature Delilah. "She turns around. He sees who she is. And he cries out, 'Jesus H. Christ, Delilah!' " ' Passing by the offences the passage commits against writerly sensibility (how revealing that anachronistic joviality of 'the Good Book' is), we come to the finale. Here, for the joke against De Mille to work, we are required to believe that De Mille, who had a part-Jewish mother, who had difficult relations with Jewish groups over *The King of Kings*, who made three films on Old Testament subjects, was so crass that he could utter a statement showing not only absolute ignorance of biblical chronology but also of the differences between Christianity and Judaism which are the obsessive material of some of his most significant films.

Consulting Edwards's book, we find that the original anecdote came from an ex-reporter, Phil Koury, who worked for De Mille on the making of *Samson and Delilah*. By the time Kaufman repeats the story, already uncritically accepted by Edwards despite lack of corroboration and its suspicious fit with the most clichéd views of De Mille, it has lost both its source and its particularity, for, as Koury tells it, it must relate to an early screenplay containing material not used in the film, which is why Kaufman, writing about a film he cannot remember, mistakenly implies that Samson has known a younger Delilah.

Two more plausible explanations are not even considered. Firstly, the story may simply be an invention gratifying prejudices about De Mille, Hollywood and the Biblical Epic, allowing tellers and audience an (unearned) feeling of intellectual superiority. Secondly, if actually true, why assume that the joke is on De Mille rather than made by him? For some reason the interpretation of the statement as a comically vulgar moment of iconoclasm – that is, we laugh with De Mille rather than at him – is inconceivable to these writers. The particular case with its simplification of De Mille's complexly symptomatic personality and art is unfortunately representative of most writing about the genre.

In writing a book that approaches the Biblical Epic analytically, as an object of intellectual scrutiny, we could have omitted any reference to such writing as wholly insignificant. But this discourse, though banal, is highly revealing, so that to start without confronting it would have been to neglect the most immediate problem of the subject, the oppressive sense of the way ahead being blocked at every turn by the banality that passes for criticism. Of course there have been exceptions, a minority of reviewers, an even smaller number of analysts, who have approached the films with less limited perspectives, and film makers who have responded more adequately to the traditions of the genre, as Spielberg does when paying homage to De Mille's 1956 *The Ten Commandments* in that scene in *Close Encounters of the Third Kind* when, in the context of the extra-terrestrial mysteries unfolding, Richard Dreyfuss's and Teri Garr's children insist on watching a television replay just at the moment of the opening of the Red Sea.

The critic's role is to analyse, not simply to surrender to such nostalgias, but Spielberg's homage is a salutary reminder that these films were memorable cinema experiences for many viewers. For all that our task is an analytic one, we feel more in common with those naive viewers on screen than with the pseudo-sophisticates who have often so ignominiously mis-judged the films. Between our own naive 1950s childhood pleasures in which this study ultimately originates and the critic's necessarily sadistic (Metz's term) operations on the text, much knowledge has intervened: enough, we hope (unlike the 'little knowledge' of most approaches to the subject) to set the agenda for study of the last of the great Hollywood genres to find its proper level of attention.

THE LIFE AND DEATH OF THE BIBLICAL EPIC

The term 'Hollywood Biblical Epic' is taken to cover three sub-types of film: the Old Testament Epic; the Christ Film; and the Roman/Christian Epic (of the beginnings of post-Christ Christianity). This inherited terminology is not absolutely precise in that the material of the third is not usually strictly biblical. A satisfactory alternative is hard to find. 'The Hollywood Religious Film' fails to point to the historical period and to whatever the term 'epic' is taken to mean, and could include works like *The Song of Bernadette* (1943). Attempts to be accurately inclusive produce unwieldy terminology like 'the Hollywood Judaeo-Christian Epic of Origins' or 'the Hollywood Biblical (and immediately Post-Biblical) Epic'. But even these would struggle to cover *The Last Temptation of Christ* (1988) which in many ways takes leave of the Hollywood Epic style. But if our readers are aware of the problems, we find established usage convenient, preferring not to become sidetracked by the secondary complications of perfect classification. Our plea is that our definitions are serviceable, and that generic theorists' possible improvements on them will not alter their general shape. Equally, we set out for our purposes a workable definition of the 'epic' component in the 'Biblical Epic'. Cinematic 'epic' takes as its subject world-historical events, the distant myths or more recent turning points of the culture. These must be treated 'epically', that is with resources of cinematic style approximating the effects of the epic in literature, great events given the largest scale of treatment; *great* as in *massive*, but also connoting grandeur and overwhelming cultural significance. The Hollywood interpretation of 'epic' cinematic style does not exhaust its possibilities. It is a specific style, different from, but with interesting points of relation to, that of Eisenstein and Pudovkin. It is also (as Scorsese shows, after Pasolini) not the only mode in which a biblical film can be made in the American cinema, though for most of Hollywood's history it has been believed to be.

Like other genres, the Biblical Epic has a complex prehistory, both pre-cinematic and cinematic. In treating nothing earlier than D. W. Griffith's *Judith of Bethulia* (1914) we bypass the importance of religious subjects in the primitive cinema. But our emphasis is on the mature narratives of the Hollywood cinema, rather than progress towards them, narratives which descend from the epic films of Griffith and which fully establish their three sub-types through his successor De Mille's films *The Ten Commandments* (first version, 1923), *The King of Kings* (1927) and *The Sign of the Cross* (1932). Though *Intolerance* (1916) was too radically conceived for mass audiences, these others were major box-office attractions: Findler's American rental figures for the period 1914–31 (though like all such figures they can be taken only as very broad indicators) list *Ben-Hur* fourth ($4.5 million), *The Ten Commandments* eleventh ($2.5 million) and *The King of Kings* twenty-seventh equal ($1.5 million) of all films made in those years. There is evidence too that in its non-commercial format *The King of Kings* was one of the most viewed films of all time.

In a tradition stretching back to spectacular Victorian theatre, including *Ben-Hur* with chariot race on stage (1899 New York; 1901 London), and for which cinematic standards were set first by the epics of the early Italian cinema, and then by Griffith's great reconstruction of Babylon for *Intolerance*, these films established precedents of vast ancient-world reconstruction and matching expenditure. But much as they cost and earned, they also carried significance in excess of box-office as the loci of quintessential Hollywood spectacle. *Ben-Hur* (1925) for instance, brought greater prestige to the new MGM company than profits could measure, while the 'flop' *Intolerance* contributed vitally to the myth of Hollywood's greatness, the enormous Babylonian set becoming the byword for extravagance, the synecdoche bespeaking 'Hollywood epic'.

Although major films such as Curtiz's *Noah's Ark* (1929) and *The Last Days of Pompeii* (Schoedsack, 1935) continued to be made, production in the genre lapsed in the 1930s and 1940s. As Findler notes, financial considerations in the Depression era militated against epic productions. Regarding the Biblical Epic, our speculation is that the crises of the Depression and the Second World War required more domestic inspiration, a Father O'Malley in *The Bells of St Mary's* (1945) or a Bernadette Soubirous in *The Song of Bernadette*, though *The Sign of the Cross* was reissued with a contemporary prologue, which argues for a continuing audience memory of such films.

The second 'golden age' of the Biblical Epic began with the great success of De Mille's return to the genre with *Samson and Delilah* (1949, and the number one box-office film of 1950 with a take of $9 million). It was quickly followed by *David and Bathsheba*, the most successful film of 1951, and by *Quo Vadis?* (LeRoy) which took $11 million, the second most in 1952. The success of these films created the context for the choice of *The Robe* (Henry Koster) as the first Cinemascope film in 1953. *The Robe* was a staggering success, amassing over $17 million in the last months of 1953. Its successor, *Demetrius and the Gladiators* (Daves), released in the following year, was followed by De Mille's *The Ten Commandments* (1956), its immense take of $34 million dwarfing even that of the extravagant Todd AO showpiece of the year, *Around the World in 80 Days*. The success of *Ben-Hur* (Wyler, 1959) was even greater, the biggest box-office draw of the decade 1951–60, with *The Ten Commandments* second and *The Robe* fourth. Three films in the top four is astonishing, demonstrating the popularity of the genre in the 1950s (though significantly these films all belong to our first and third s ib-types and not to the more problematical Christ film).

The year 1959 marked the height of production with the release also of *Solomon and Sheba* (King Vidor) and *The Big Fisherman* (Borzage), but actually proved the prelude to decline. Even at its greatest we can talk only of relatively sustained production (and largely limited to the first and third types). It is part of the meaning of 'epic' cinema that every production is a 'unique', costly, much-advertised affair. Any suggestion of the conveyor-belt is to be avoided. Therefore the genre exists only in the superlative mode, unlike, say, the Western. Here the tip and the iceberg are one. *Samson and Delilah* does not emerge from B epics as *High Noon* emerges from masses of B Westerns. This means that more than other genres it is highly vulnerable to major shifts of the determinants of production (ideological or financial), and that it can, in fact, as has happened, vanish from the screen.

Decline was not immediately apparent, for Kubrick's *Spartacus*, on the margins of the Roman/Christian Epic, was the biggest box-office success of 1960. But from then production declined rapidly. The turnaround is dramatised by the 1963 listings where four of the top five films are epics (*Cleopatra, The Longest Day, Lawrence of Arabia, How the West Was Won*) but all are strikingly secular. Death was not instantaneous, the genre producing a number of distinguished films (for instance Huston's *The Bible: In the Beginning*, 1966) in its terminal throes, including the double revival of the Christ film in Ray's *King of Kings* (1961) and Stevens's *The Greatest Story Ever Told* (1965). In the case of *The Bible*, impressive audience figures were swallowed up by monumental costs, but *Greatest Story* holds an undesired place in the lists of 'all-time box-office disasters', with costs of $20 million and takings of only $6.9 million. Returns like *Greatest Story's* (coupled with the huge unreclaimed expenditure on the ancient-world epics *Cleopatra*, 1963, and *The Fall of the Roman Empire*, 1964) sealed the fate of the genre until the 1980s when the commercially unsuccessful but interesting *King David* (Beresford, 1985) was made, as well as another Christ film, Scorsese's controversial *The Last Temptation of Christ* (1988).

The rest of this book will move away from the kind of production history outlined here towards analysis of questions relatively independent of such considerations. Stevens's film, whatever its box-office trauma, came into being, is still, though almost wholly on television, in circulation, and as a complex text passing into history offers itself to readings irreducible to industrial determinants. Before that move, however, two matters demand brief notation. Firstly, despite long traditions of critical condescension, the Hollywood industry frequently recognised elements of aesthetic merit in these films in its own parochial judgements on itself. Such judgements have no overriding validity, except as an indicator of the industry's (often questionable) views, but they do suggest respect, reminding us of various kinds of admiration these films have elicited. Thus we should not forget – leaving aside the genre's many nominations in most fields – that *Ben-Hur* and *Spartacus* won Best Picture Academy Awards, that Charlton Heston and Hugh Griffith gained acting awards for their roles in *Ben-Hur* and Peter Ustinov for his in *Quo Vadis?*, and that Wyler was given Best Director award for *Ben-Hur*. There is also a substantial pattern of design and cinematography nominations, of which we note here only the awards: *Samson and Delilah*, art and set direction and costume design; *The Robe*, best cinematography, colour design and costume design; the special effects award to De Mille's second *The Ten Commandments*; *Ben-Hur's* awards for colour cinematography, costume design and art and set direction; and *Spartacus's* awards for best cinematography and art and set direction. For all the arbitrariness of the system and the pressures and ideological factors influencing it, these qualify the idea that the critics' contempt for the genre was absolutely matched by the industry's cynicism.

Secondly, various convincing (in no way mutually exclusive) 'subtextual' reasons have been offered for the genre's revival in the 1950s, including its uncontroversial subject-matter during the anti-communist investigations, its suitability as a showcase in the cinema's fight against television, and the parallelisms invited by the new Israel. Such explanations, however, have to be taken in tandem with a large-scale willingness on the part of audiences to view representations of religious texts, that is, a strong attachment to the genre into which these other considerations played.

Equally fascinating is the question why the genre declined after its great popularity. Here the causes seem both numerous and heavily intercalated.

(i) What might seem the obvious answer – steadily increasing secularism producing audiences less interested in the genre – is not in itself absolutely satisfying, for while it is applicable to Britain and most of the 'West', it is far less convincing for America where religious belief has not so markedly declined.

(ii) The genre's survival in the television mini-series (*Moses, Jesus of Nazareth, A.D.*, etc.) suggests that its audience did not vanish but, rather, stopped going to the cinema. By 1979 the proportion of the 12 to 17 age group to the total cinema audience had increased to over 40 per cent, vitally affecting decisions on the kind of film made, at least as regards 'blockbusters'. Whilst an absolute equation of greater age and religious interests is untenable, market researchers were right to guess that religious themes would not be a priority with youthful audiences, at least not in their traditional forms, though there is a strong unconventionally 'religious' element in contemporary Hollywood cinema, from Spielberg's epiphanic *Close Encounters* and *ET* to the ironic saviour parables of the *Superman* series, to the supernatural conceits of a film like *Ghost*, all, in some senses, readable as performing functions analogous to the Biblical Epic.

(iii) The escalating costs of films militated against the risk of reviving a genre whose last outings had been notably unsuccessful.

(iv) The biblical film, in what may in retrospect seem a rather naive symbiosis, was infallibly identified with a vision of the epic involving the hugest costs and display. The idea (to adapt Schrader's terms below) of 'sparser means', suggested by the success of Pasolini's *The Gospel According to Matthew* (1964), seemed impossible until Scorsese's *The Last Temptation of Christ* (1988), and then only for an *auteur* film more argued about than actually seen.

(v) It can be plausibly argued that before the explicit violence and sexuality of 1970s and 1980s Hollywood cinema the Biblical Epic gave release (see our discussion of Neale below) not only to sadistic and masochistic drives repressed in other films but also to displays of sexuality in the orgy and the period-justified semi-nakedness of both male and female bodies. With the diminishing of censorship this function became superfluous.

(vi) The liberalisation of censorship, rather than freeing the genre, affected its future in a complicatedly negative way. One might have thought it would benefit a genre in which pressures towards conformity and an ecumenical blandness were always prominent. But the one film to take uncompromising advantage of the new freedoms, *The Last Temptation of Christ*, aroused such hostility as to demonstrate the deceptiveness of such liberty. A difficult double bind now constricted those films, or the ideas of them. Not to take advantage of the new freedoms in the desire to be acceptable, ran the risk of audiences and critics feeling they had seen it all before. But to take advantage of them would be sure to cause uproar among fundamentalist groups with increasingly sophisticated access to the media, making any future backers of such projects think twice about defying protest campaigns and pressures on exhibitors. The difficulties of a Christ film in such circumstances are obvious, but the other sub-types would hardly be exempt. A mass film which in any real sense presented, say, the Roman view of Christianity would render the Roman/Christian Epic a site of controversy, while any analogous deconstruction of Old Testament texts could stir accusations of anti-Semitism and be read as politically anti-Israel.

TEXTS AND CONTEXTS

The superficiality of most writing about the Biblical Epic has the excuse that this is how Hollywood's rituals of publicity have always talked about them. The old-time vulgarity of these processes recalls a more exuberant and innocent cinematic age: the live prologue to De Mille's *The King of Kings* at Graumann's Chinese Theatre with (among other slightly more than tacky pseudo-spectacles) a Daniel surrounded by drugged lions; usherettes dressed as Vestal Virgins at the London premier of LeRoy's *Quo Vadis?*; the plans for the world premiere of the same at the Coliseum (cancelled because of cold weather); above all, the never-ending stream of newspaper and periodical articles stressing opulent size and cost – '30,000 Extras in *Quo Vadis?*' (*The Times*, 12 January 1952; '15,000 Sandals All Hand-Sewn' (*Daily Sketch*, 28 September 1953), and so on. The kitschy charms of this discourse cannot simply be dismissed as accidental epiphenomena of the texts. They are in some sense part of the greater meaning of the films within the institution of the Hollywood cinema. In limited ways they become determinants not only of audience reaction but of the films themselves, yet they never wholly determine the making of the films nor audiences' experience and uses of them, let alone routes that interpretation and analysis may subsequently take.

In the vacuum left by the failure of analysis, only one type of literature has sprung up, genially but wholly unanalytically, around the genre. In lavish books replete with text-dwarfing stills, sometimes of epic dimensions themselves and vaunting titles like *Great Movie Spectaculars* and *Spectacular! The Story of Epic Films*, the Biblical Epic, in association with other massive productions, is celebrated in a riot of statistics, anecdotes and stuntmen's secrets. Such books register an uncomplicated delight in the most obvious outsize pleasures of the genre but fetishise them into the sole value of the films. For all the enthusiasm informing them, the drive to analysis produces no more than statistics as proofs of the films' impressiveness, while the urge to deconstruction is deflected into exposés of how famous illusions were produced, reducing the multiple possibilities of meaning to the celebration of technology.

Where critical writing exists that has (fragmentarily) addressed the Biblical Epic outside such clichés, it has concentrated on the films' sub-texts rather than their overt subject-matter, largely steering clear of their surface religious content. This approach is ultimately too restrictive, but it is a strategy which manages to uncover a great deal. Michael Wood, in *America in the Movies*, approaches the 1950s Biblical Epics with a twofold argument. Firstly, he suggests that the genre had a special role in the cinema of the day, its spectacle amounting to something approaching an unconscious allegory of meanings central to American mythology. Arguing that 'ingenuity, authority and money quickly become the almost overt subject of these films', he adds: 'The ancient world of the epics was a huge many-faceted metaphor for Hollywood itself, because . . . these movies are always about the creation of such a world in a movie, about Hollywood's capacity to duplicate old splendours, to bring Egypt and Rome to the screen . . .' For Wood the moments of epic destruction so typical of the films become meaningful moments of 'pure excess', 'a ritual expression of a lack of need', at once a correlative of 'the spectacular waste of American life' and an 'oblique expression of faith' in that cinema's and that society's seemingly eternal productivity.

The second part of Wood's argument amplifies a perception about the use of American and British actors across the genre, the clearest example of which is found in the association of the oppressing ruling class with the British, and of the oppressed but ultimately triumphant Israelites or Christians with Americans. This reworks the American Revolution scenario, giving a new inflection to the 'famous old transatlantic story' of American/European relations. Wood's claim that in the final image of De Mille's 1956 *The Ten Commandments*, Moses (Charlton Heston) is posed to resemble the Statue of Liberty is one of the few significant perceptions about the Biblical Epic; once seen in this way the image illuminates the furthest reaches of the genre. Wood's assertion is balanced by his counter-suggestion that much of the attractive energy in the narratives is placed where it should not be, with the Old-World oppressors, the Egyptians, the Romans and the Philistines, expressing the inferiority that bedevils America's sense of superiority to the Old World. Another version of this, which is surely accurate about part of our experience in the cinema, is where Frank McConnell in Storytelling and Mythmaking defines part of the meaning of the epic (writing about *The Iliad* but taking in the 1956 *The Ten Commandments*) as nostalgia for the defeated culture felt amidst the triumphs of the rising one.

Where Wood makes deeper sense of what floats around unanalysed in the discourse of costs and size inseparable from the films, Stephen Neale looks at the films from a psychoanalytical viewpoint, like Wood shaping into meaning other *topoi* that circulate incoherently through the journalism the films have generated, particularly the recurrent fascination/repulsion the genre has held for viewers as a locus of sex and violence. From present perspectives this may seem unlikely, but a kind of fascinated moralism about these films, accusations of hypocrisy and demands for more stringent censorship, is constant even into the 1960s, varied by complaints that the films never deliver what they promise. Often, with spectacular unconcern for contradiction, both attitudes are expressed in the same reviews. With an interesting leap of perception, Neale parallels the Epic with the Musical as a genre centred on spectacle, its games, shows, parades and contests a (Noir) equivalent to the musical numbers' display. These are the focal points of a genre licensing the sado-masochistic drives in displays of power and sub-mission. (Which Alex unabashedly enjoys in his Christ Epic fantasies in *A Clockwork Orange*: 'I could viddy myself taking charge of the tolchocking number nailing in, being dressed in the height of Roman fashion'). Though exceedingly narrow in focus, and almost perversely underdeveloped, Neale's remarks do make possible an approach at a more far-reaching level than usual to generic characteristics that many have vaguely sensed without articulating their significance.

A third, more over-arching, approach is found in Gilles Deleuze's first volume of cinema theory, *Cinema 1: The Movement-Image*. Here we can again see a mind approaching the fundamental questions behind the ephemeral discourse about the films, in this case questions about the genre's treatments and distortions of history, its authenticity or inauthenticity, its seriousness or triviality: real questions but usually handled in a trivial and condescending way. When Deleuze says – extremely gnomically, it must be added – that in these films 'the image remains sublime, and although the Temple of Dagon can trigger off our laughter, it is an Olympian laughter which takes hold of the spectator', we find it difficult to grasp his meaning, yet at the same time are haunted by its striving towards a perception of the sublime and the ridiculous mingled together in a more elevating mode than the bathetic. If the Temple of Dagon incites a kind of laughter, the audience – seen as Olympian – may laugh, but their laughter is godlike. Godlike because in the Biblical Epic they spectate the rise and fall of nations, religions and ideologies, their views sublime in that what are seen are the arising and cessation of the greatest forces of history, comic in that they are seen to subside with so little weight, destroyed in a few moments of screen spectacle. If the viewers possess a Christian view of history, they laugh sublimely at the flight of false gods ('And sullen Moloch fled / Hath left in shadows dread, / His burning idol all of blackest hue', as Milton writes his version of the mode in 'On the Morning of Christ's Nativity'). If, however, they agree with Nietzsche's programme notes, the Judaic and Christian themselves become subject to the same crepuscular perceptions.

The other more local sublime that Deleuze articulates as a governing force over these films is one close to, though more epically conceived than, Wood's second thesis, an assertion of the absolutely pivotal place of the Biblical History film in the American cinema. In the shock of this rearrangement, the previously despised is moved to the centre, since the doublings connoted in the Epics (the Israelites, the Christians as, if not Americans, then the spiritual precursors of America) are the other side of the parallelisms running through the various secular historical genres, especially the Western, with its enacting of America's coming to birth as the Promised Land. Western and Biblical Epic in this interpretation symbiotically command the whole field of American cinema.

Deleuze's vital contribution to thinking about history in the genre and in the American cinema in general is first of all to define it as 'deeply analogical or parallelist', viewing all other periods in their health or sickness in terms of America, a tendency most overtly inscribed in the four epochs under one theme structure of *Intolerance* and the two epochs (ancient and contemporary) structure of De Mille's first *The Ten Commandments*. His further insight is to reject any easy ridicule of this conception of history, and to see it as embodying the three aspects which Nietzsche defines in his meditation on 'the Uses and Disadvantages of History', the 'monumental', the 'antiquarian' and the 'ethical'. He then demonstrates the coherent logic as well as the great limitation ('that of treating phenomena as effects in themselves, separate from any cause') of the Hollywood cinema's 'analogical' interpretation of history, its way of seeing the immense moments of history as (monumental) duels between individuals, their forms recreated down to the most detailed (antiquarian) outward signs of 'the actualisation of the epoch', all seen (ethically) under the judgement of Good and Evil.

> The ancient or recent past must submit to trial, go to court, in order to disclose what it is that produces decadence, and what it is that produces new life, what the ferments of decadence and the germs of new life are, the orgy and the sign of the cross, the omnipotence of the rich and the misery of the poor. A strong ethical judgement must condemn the injustice of 'things', bring compassion, herald the new civilization on the march, in short, constantly rediscover America.

For Deleuze the sub-texts, which Wood and, somewhat differently, Neale discuss without reference to the films' religious content, do not just make contact with but essentially have never left the main text. In our own study we insist on not treating the films' religious content simply as a screen for other preoccupations, real though these may be. It is not a case of either/or, text or sub-text; the Biblical Epic is both. Comprehensive analysis necessitates consideration of the originating site of its most obvious interests, the unique context of American religion.

THAT OLD-TIME RELIGION

In a memorable phrase Berger and Luckmann write about 'the conspicuous Piety of the cis-Atlantic masses'. Their words summarise many sociologists' acknowledgement of the difference of an American Christianity which has resisted becoming peripheral to modern society. Polls as recent as 1987 cite 94 per cent believing in God, 88 per cent believing that the Bible is the inspired word of God, and 90 per cent associating themselves with a denomination. Yet the dominant sociological (and surely correct) view is that this has happened only at the cost of religion itself undergoing a process of secularisation. 'In America secularisation drained the religious content, without too radically affecting the form of religious institutions' (B. R. Wilson, 'Religion in a Secular Society'). 'The cultural, social and religious functions which the churches perform for American Society as a whole as well as for its social groups classes and individuals, would be considered "secular" rather than "religious" in the view the churches traditionally held of themselves.'

These perceptions are not just the views of sociologists but those of critical American theology. Richard Niebuhr's *The Kingdom of God in America* traces the routes by which the originating belief in America as a divinely chosen nation became conflated with 'democracy, Americanism, the English Language and culture, the growth of industry and science, American institutions', with the result that 'As the Christian Church became the protector of the social mores, so its revivals tended to become the instruments for prevailing standards'. The post-war religious revival, still strong in America in the 1950s, was viewed sceptically by writers in the critical tradition of the Niebuhrs – for instance in Roy Eckhardt's description of a kind of utilitarian folk religion in *The Surge of Piety in America: An Appraisal* and in Martin E. Marty's arrival at judgements similar to Niebuhr's about the identification of religion and American democracy in *The New Shape of American Religion*. Similar conclusions were also reached in Will Heberg's *Protestant–Catholic–Jew: An Essay in American Sociology*, where the primary function of religion across the three main groupings is seen not so much as spiritual but as 'the primary context of self-clarification and social location', with faith in American democracy operating as a sort of over-faith, embracing and uniting disparate religions.

To speak of this as the totality of American religion rather than a very dominant tendency would be to over-simplify. After all, we have already cited from the tradition of theological self-criticism. Yet it is certainly one of three unique elements in the American religious scene, the other two being the absence in American history of an established Church and

America's embodying the extreme of Protestantism in its myriads of sects and sub-sects, including offshoot religions invented in America such as Mormonism and Christian Science.

Explicitly and implicitly this book will argue that the peculiarities of the Biblical Epic should not be considered as simply the product of the Hollywood cinema's travestying touch. Rather, even the much criticised ecumenicism of these films, resulting in accusations of blandness, relates intimately to the contexts of American religious life. The Hollywood cinema, a mixture of the highly determined and the semi-autonomous, produced, as the anthropologist Hortense Powdermaker put it in her study of Hollywood, highly significant 'caricatures' (her description is neutral, not pejorative) of American society and ideology and of the interaction of religious ideology with the latter. Made in America, the films were also designed for a universal, or at least world-Christian, consumption. Their transparency for the greater audience owes in part to the 'universality' of the Hollywood 'classical style', in part to the 'universality' of the concepts of America and democracy so foregrounded in them, and to their content of passion and power, the elemental struggles of Good and Evil, the pleasure of spectacles, and so on. But even where they are most rooted in the particularity of the American religious situation, in certain ways so different from that of the rest of the Western world where religion has declined with the advance of secularism, they also communicate as paradigms of a highly secularised society's dramatising of its religious foundations through mechanisms on which secular values have had a profound impact. The explanations for the embarrassment which the genre's secular/religious negotiations sometimes provoke in viewers are also the explanations of some of its most vital interests.

TRANSCENDENTAL AND UNTRANSCENDENTAL STYLES

The classical Hollywood style has had many critics whose aim was to expose the seeming naturalness of the dominant cinema and its ideological power. Though such criticism, had it ever turned its materialist procedures on so obviously 'mystifying' a genre as the Biblical Epic, would undoubtedly have found much to deconstruct, the most developed critique of the genre comes from the different direction of the most obsessively religious director in the contemporary American cinema, Paul Schrader, Scorsese's screenwriter on *Taxi Driver*, *Raging Bull* and *The Last Temptation of Christ* and the director of films like *Hardcore* and *American Gigolo*.

A critic before a film maker, Schrader argued in *Transcendental Style in Film* that the true, as distinct from ersatz, religious cinema is marked by a style whose ultimate aim is to express the encounter with absolute otherness, achieved through techniques that have their sources and/or analogues in the severity of 'primitive' art, in Byzantine icons, Zen gardens and painting and the statues of Henry Moore, among others. In terms borrowed from Jacques Maritain, this style denies the 'abundant means' of most art to embrace the poverty of the 'sparse means' best suited to religious expression. Schrader praises films like Bresson's *Journal of a Country Priest* because their narratives gradually shed 'abundant means' to reach through 'sparse means' the 'stasis' they seek. In absolute contrast he then scornfully addresses the religious art of the mainstream American cinema, in particular fastening on to a moment in *The Ten Commandments* (1956) as a demonstration of the 'false syllogism' by which the Biblical Epic works: 'The film is "real", the spiritual is "on" film, ergo: the spiritual is real.'

> . . .Moses is on Mount Sinai and God is off-screen to the right. After some premonitory thundering, God literally pitches the commandments, one by one, onto the screen and the awaiting blank tablets. The commandments first appear as small whirling fireballs accompanied by the sound of a rushing wind, and then quickly . . . across the screen and collide with the blank tablets. Puff! the smoke clears and the tablet is clearly inscribed.

The naive externality of presentation leaves Schrader in no doubt that as the product of the cinema of 'abundant means' par excellence, this kind of film is a hopeless case.

We cannot wholly dismiss the moment that Schrader picks out, for, though we might argue that his biased rhetoric fixes on a relatively weak example of the style, we have to admit that it is intimately related to other examples of the epic style we might prefer in its insistence on monumentality, externality, the kinetic, and technology as the vehicle of the miraculous. It is undeniably a style often at the furthest extreme from the one Schrader approves, and almost by definition incapable of the effects he values. But even if we agree with Schrader that 'Transcendental Style' is infinitely more capable of expressing what he identifies as religious experience, and what the non-religious might wish to call with Freud 'oceanic feeling', does this mean that his comments exhaust the significance of the Biblical Epic? That the films are valueless?

In refutation, we can point to what has already been mentioned. The films have a sub-textual richness that emerges from the expression of secular concerns in the context of religious ideology, and vice versa. That is, they can be approached in ways to which their overt content is secondary. But in their actual religious content they also dramatise the encounter of religion and secularism in twentieth-century America. Further, the style, the aesthetic system expressing these concerns, is not only far from negligible – like any style it is an intricate network of possibilities and constraints – but has marked resemblances to the single most influential and valued style in the history of Western art, the religious art of the Italian High Renaissance.

This is hardly surprising since the films' visual style is ultimately derived (via many influences from Victorian art) from it. For instance, Correggio's *Nativity* and Raphael's *Transfiguration* both have more in common with the Biblical Epic style than with Schrader's transcendentalism. Their aesthetic power has little connection with interiority or the approach to otherness. Rather, it comes from the paintings finding correlatives within the treatment of religious subjects for emotions, feelings, possibilities of self and society that are dramatically heightened versions of the values of secular life and art.

It would be simplistic to say that the religious subject-matter functions here only as a screen for non-religious interests, for the religious occasion provides conditions for the release of whatever else the work is about. However great the differences between the producing cultures, the aristocratic humanist, proto-capitalist culture of the Italian Renaissance and the populist, individualist–capitalist culture of twentieth century America are alike in their confident accommodation of religious and capitalist (proto-capitalist) ideologies. There are enormous differences, one being that in the Renaissance a great amount of art was directly religious in subject-matter, whereas in the American cinema secular subjects overwhelmingly predominate, so that overtly religious films are few and the production of Biblical Epics is small compared with other genres. But, as regards the central style with which the art images sacred history, the main comparison holds and can be pursued further in that both cultures are ones in which conditions make the artistic expression of religious interiority difficult. But in this they are surely representative of the modern experience – the one at the beginning of the secular era, the other at its point of furthest advance. In this the Biblical Epic is the paradigmatic expression of a secular culture's redefinition of its distant spiritual sources, through an artistic machinery which is the only one not to have its origins in religious usage.

Yet from its beginnings cinema has sought to express the religious narratives of the culture: and what can be seen as the seminal film in the American cinema, *Intolerance*, does it both overtly and obliquely. If when

Griffith took as models Victorian melodrama, the Victorian stage spectacle and ultimately the Renaissance religious tableau, these were already outdated in the dawn of modernism, they must appear even more so as they are re-enacted by Griffith's successors through the century. A difference in the similarities we have been underlining is that what in the earlier period was a dynamic, developing style, in the later period is a retreating, second-hand one. Yet that very lack of new modes of expression forms part of an inbuilt set of problems, an often unconscious, sometimes conscious formal echoing of the deep-structural thematics of the traumatic encounter of traditional beliefs and modernity that underlies the genre.

Returning to Schrader, it seem to us that the contradictions between his theory of religious film and his own film making where, for instance, the allusions to *Journal of a Country Priest* and *Pickpocket* play into the worlds of *Taxi Driver* and *American Gigolo* – express something beyond the obvious fact that Bressonian themes and stylistics can exist only on the margins of a different, kinetic, sexual and commodified film universe. For when Schrader worked on the screenplay of Kazantzakis's novel for *The Last Temptation of Christ*, he downplayed Kazantzakis's mystical concerns, to develop what he calls the Nietzschean 'becoming' theme. The extent of this downplaying is in excess of what it actually needed to be, and suggests the deeprootedness, even within the American film maker who most clearly articulates alternative values in his theorising, of secular pressures (over and above the most obvious commercial ones) on the expression of religious material.

MORNING AND EVENING STAR: RELIGION IN THE 'SECULAR' SECULAR CINEMA

Contiguities

In noting the great body of related cinema from which our subject has been bracketed off – a bracketing we have loosened wherever possible – we pause briefly to focus on that context: religious films of the second order, built around modern or at least post-biblical subject-matter, and the much greater mass of religious films of the third order, predominantly secular subjects touched by religious concerns. We do this by considering two films which represent antithetical yet closely related tendencies in the treatment of religion in the American cinema – on the one hand *The Bells of St Mary's*, standing as the type of the populist religion of sentiment and affirmation; and on the other *Elmer Gantry*, the type of the satiric, critically 'deconstructive' attitude to religion which is a powerful minority voice in American literature and film. These tendencies and others, easier to recognise in a modern setting, are present in more coded forms in the biblical films.

The Bells of St Mary's (1945)

> *The Doctor* (answering a question about praying): Not since I was a little boy and wished what I wanted for Christmas, and got it.
> *O'Malley*: Sort of the same thing.

The mythic nature of *The Bells of St Mary's* is inscribed in cinema itself. When in Capra's *It's a Wonderful Life* (1946) George Bailey (James Stewart) reaffirms his will to live and rushes down the Christmas-decorated streets of Bedford Falls, he passes the Bijou Cinema where, of all possible films, the one actually showing is Leo McCarey's *The Bells of St Mary's*, the film that, beyond any specificities of sectarianism, most speaks for a populist American religious optimism. The film's emblematic status is equally clear in *The Godfather* where it is the movie Michael and Kay have just seen at Christmas 1945, when they discover that Michael's father has been gunned down. If the first example uses the film as a symbol of the restoration of everything decent, the second employs it to mark the illusoriness of that world. In either case, it is aureoled with meaning.

The film is, at one level, a specifically Catholic fantasy, the central figures of its romantic/spiritual love plot a priest, Father O'Malley (Bing Crosby), and a nun, Sister Mary Benedict (Ingrid Bergman). But what interests us here is the way this Catholicism can act not in alienating singularity but as the vehicle of an ecumenical tenor where Bing's parochial crooning of 'Ora pro Nobis' becomes as universal as 'Aren't You Glad You're You.'

A momentary diversion to the subject of Mormonism is revealing. Mormonism, one of the American-invented variants of Christianity, is the subject of two Westerns, *Wagonmaster* (1950) and *Brigham Young* (1940), but in both it becomes a means to the shared providential vision of the epic of American settlement, shedding almost any evidence of distinct religious beliefs and practice. In *Wagonmaster* reference to the specificities of Mormonism goes little further than Ward Bond's joke about having many wives. In *Brigham Young* it extends to a close-up of the Book of Mormon burning, to someone spitting on 'the Mormon Bible', to Brigham Young visiting Joseph Smith, and to a view of the future Salt Lake City, but all these instances fall into the pattern of persecution and visionary future of the mythology of white America's beginnings. At the end of *Wagonmaster* the radiance playing on the faces of the Mormons is the light of the vision of the New Zion of America. Both films also employ a characteristic structure which involves uncommitted outsiders, the wagonmasters in Ford, as well as the theatrical-cum-medicine troupe which, in doubling the Mormons' outcast role, makes the Mormons more outcasts than Mormons. Zina in Hathaway's film has a similar function. Both films also close with promises of marriages (Zina and the Mormon scout; one of the wagonmasters and a Mormon girl), miscegenation without conversion, which underlines the films' project of inclusivity rather than exclusivity.

Similar processes mark *The Bells of St Mary's*. As Father O'Malley, Bing Crosby acts out a secularisation of religious impulses into mundane sentiments touched with a faint religious numinousness – life lived (as his jaunty straw boater affirms) with a practical, but not wholly unidealistic, ease, summoning up all the vaguer pelagian securities without religion's more stringent demands. (The title song tellingly celebrates the sonic reassurance of the old church bells – 'Oh bells of Saint Mary's / We always will love you / With your inspiration / We never will fail'.) O'Malley's *Irish* Catholicism, connoting nostalgia mixed with go-aheadness, happy-go-luckiness, non- (or relatively unaggressive) materialism and optimistic faith in a faithless age, is close enough to the mainstream to act as a generalising synecdoche, an English-speaking, non-alien ethnicity superior to Englishness in being cheerfully marked by a rebelliousness which relates to America's own. On the other hand, Ingrid Bergman's Sister Mary Benedict is, like the actress, Swedish, but since Swedes are associated with Protestantism rather than Catholicism the mix-up of connotations actually aids the ecumenical project.

Equally, the problems solved by O'Malley and Sister Mary are ultimately secular, not those of an estranging realm of the religious but concerned with the preservation of a charitable capitalism (re-achieved in the *Christmas Carol* 'conversion' of the Scrooge-like Bogardis) and the restoration of the family (O'Malley's search for and re-domesticising of Mrs Gallagher's wandering husband and his rescuing her from prostitution). In a pattern of substitutive relationships O'Malley plays a feminised paternal role towards Patsy, the troubled daughter of the broken marriage, while Sister Mary Benedict, acting out her and the film's sense of Christianity as positively feminising (for example her ironic remark about bringing up 'masculine little men'), takes on masculine values in teaching the too-feminised Eddie to box.

These two figures of the priest and nun not only oedipally embody everybody's ideal father and mother but are idealised lovers too, as conveyed in the yearning sweetness of the close-ups at the film's end, their story matching at many points the outlines of romantic comedy and passionate melodrama. Just as the pair represent both the freedoms of a licensed singleness in a marrying society and religion in its softest inflections, so their unconsummatable love enacts a pastoral of sexuality shorn of its difficulties and disillusions, which is not the least of the film's attractions.

The shadow of the sin-killer: *Elmer Gantry* (1960)

Through films like *The Miracle Woman* (Capra 1932), *The Night of the Hunter* (Laughton, 1955), *Elmer Gantry* (Richard Brooks, 1960) and *Wise Blood* (Huston, 1979) moves Father O'Malley's doppelganger, the itinerant preacherman. Heir to the 'Great Awakenings' of the late eighteenth century which initiated a repeated pattern of convulsive populist religious crusades, he presides over the high theatre of enthusiasm with his rhetoric of sin, redemption and damnation. He or she (for the evangelists Florence Fallon in *Miracle Woman* and Sharon Falconer in *Elmer Gantry* are women, based on Aimee Semple MacPherson) takes on two variants. In the first film the character embodies the dubious evangelist who, in a charade of sentimental piety and staged miracles, feeds predatorily on the credulous masses, the sick and the dispossessed. In the second the evangelist turns dysangelist. Here no longer just corrupted by the business ethic, he becomes a site of the darkest spirits, a figure destabilised into psychosis by an inheritance of metaphysical violence reaching back to Salem. His most remarkable figurations are in Robert Mitchum's nightmare of a rogue preacher in *Night of the Hunter* (with the words 'LOVE' and 'HATE' tattooed on the backs of his hands) and his contemporary bloodbrother Max Cady in Scorsese's *Cape Fear*, his body and mind inscribed with minatory biblical quotations.

Understandably, since the monstrousness of such figures can suggest that religion is less a Freudian neurosis than a fullblown psychosis, it is versions of the first who predominate. For whatever their abuses they can finally be seen as an incidental misappropriation of the religious spirit. Thus satire of hypocrisy and materialism need not finally be seen as undermining belief. Even in the grimmest comedy of *Wise Blood* there is perhaps room for a not wholly negative reading in which Hazel Moates's obsessive desire to preach 'The Church of Truth Without Christ' is interpretable as a heroic quest to cancel the Christ of false consciousness purveyed by false prophets like Onnie J. Holie and Asa Hawks.

Brooks's version of the Sinclair Lewis source takes over a pattern already acted out in *Miracle Woman* where Florence's success is dependent on hired cripple-impersonators who pretend that she has healed them, but, having realised the fraud, she is found at the end of the film serving humbly in the Salvation Army. *Elmer Gantry* follows suit. While Burt Lancaster's

Elmer, with his mixture of narcissism, credulity and cunning, dominates the film, at the same time the narrative omits all the novelistic elements tending to compromise Christian belief itself, elements such as Lewis's exposure of the soul-destroying pieties of smalltown religion and the compassionate but trenchant analyses of the disbelieving theologian Dr Zechler and clergyman Frank Shallard, pathetically unable to sever themselves from the Church.

Beneath the satire built around Elmer is a more protective and even redemptive attitude. The reluctant atheist Jim Lefferts's part in this is important. While Jim follows Sharon's evangelical circus, writing newspaper pieces exposing evangelism, in the film he never breaks with Elmer or Sharon, even physically defending both the evangelists when they are attacked by the mob. In the narrative's last phase, following Lulu's recantation, Elmer disappears, significantly for three days, before returning. Where Sharon, just before her death, is allowed what seems to be the genuine faith-healing of a deaf man, Elmer is allowed an ending of extraordinary dignity when, tempted into a recapitulation of his old routine ('What is Love? Love is the Mornin' and the Evenin' Star . .'), he stops and says the words: 'When I was a child I spake as a child, I understood as a child; when I became a man I put away childish things . . . Saint Paul, First Corinthians, 13, 11.' So while the novel ends with a sardonic recapitulation of the anti-hero's incorrigibility, the film allows Elmer a decisive moment of self-knowledge and renewal, a moment which it is not necessary to interpret in terms of religion being the childish thing that the man leaves, only the childish attitudes of evangelism.

That this reversal of the satiric drive is not exceptional can be seen in a film of the same year, Stanley Kramer's *Inherit the Wind*. In this version of the 'Monkey Trial', after Harrison Brady (Fredric March playing a fictionalised William Jennings Bryan) dies at the moment of his pyrrhic victory for fundamentalism over the Darwinian enlightenment represented by Henry Drummond (Spencer Tracy as Clarence Darrow), a conversation takes place between Drummond and Hornbeck (Gene Kelly), the newspaperman who, like Jim Lefferts, represents the journalist H. L. Mencken, who covered the trial and to whom Lewis dedicated *Elmer Gantry*. In this it becomes clear, to Hornbeck's dismay, that Drummond regards his cynicism as even less sympathetic than Brady's reactionariness, accepting the insult Hornbeck throws at him – 'The Atheist who believes in God!'. Leaving the courtroom alone Drummond pensively weighs in his hand first the Bible, then *The Origin of Species*, finally exiting with the one clasped on top of the other, an image of reconciliation that refuses Mencken's voice of satire on religion the final word.

TEXTS AND SUPERTEXTS:
ON THE NECESSITY FOR CLOSE VIEWING

The notes above constitute – hesitantly, cautiously – the framework of a theory, the outline of a perspective making understanding of the genre possible.

This book has not been written from 'committed' religious or socio-political positions. If it has very distant, much transmuted models as regards its attitudes to religion, they are Max Weber's *The Sociology of Religion* and Mircea Eliade's *A History of Religious Ideas*, texts whose dispassionate analysis of religious phenomena and their social interactions are equally of interest to the believer and to the non-believer.

We are aware that within the highly politicised world of academic film criticism the failure to deconstruct religious phenomena along Marxist, Freudian or Marxist–Freudian (Althusserian–Lacanian) lines will be seen as a weakness. In fact we employ related concepts locally, but deliberately stop short of totalistic theorising, as part of a strategy aimed against reductionism. To take one instance: in psychoanalytic terms the divine is reducible to the wish-fulfilment recreation of the childhood father or to the transference of the irrecoverable unity lost to the child in the movement from the 'imaginary' to a fantasised realm of future plenitude. Like Weber's our interest is more in the social and intellectual functioning of religion than in tracing its origins through persuasive but ultimately unprovable hypotheses. This has the advantage that we do not demand a reader who shares our particular beliefs or disbeliefs about such origins, only one conscious of the social and intellectual roles of religion.

Our interest in individual texts, and sometimes authors, is also likely to be labelled by some as a species of 'fetishisation'. One counter-example will serve as a justification for our method.

In an article published by *Screen*, a Hollywood historian, Richard Maltby, recently wrote about De Mille's *The King of Kings*. Much of what this article, '*The King of Kings* and the Tsar of all the Rushes', establishes is of interest, particularly its placing of the film within the ideological crisis of liberal Protestantism in the 1920s and the emergence of newer forms more attuned to the business and consumerist ethos. Maltby's argument is built around the influence upon De Mille of Bruce Barton, one of the founding figures of modern advertising, and his best-selling book *The Man Nobody Knows: A Discovery of the Real Jesus* (1925), which sold 250,000 copies in eighteen months and which provided an up-to-date inflection of the Protestant capitalist ethic through its virtual identification of Christ with the businessman. Maltby's claim that Barton was a major influence on *The King of Kings* is underpinned by De Mille's appointing Barton as a consultant for his film. But the crucial evidence is textual, the indubitable traces of Barton's descriptions of Jesus in a passage of De Mille's *The Autobiography of Cecil B. De Mille*, where the director writes about his conception of Jesus in the film. In Barton's description, the image of the Sunday School Jesus, 'a pale young man with flabby forearms and a sad expression . . . Something for girls – sissified . . . "meek and lowly", a "man of sorrows and acquainted with grief" ', is transformed into 'Jesus pushed a plane and swung an adze; he was a successful carpenter; he slept outdoors and spent his days walking around his favourite lake. His muscles were so strong that when he drove the money-changers out, nobody dared to oppose him!' In De Mille's *Autobiography* the relevant passage reads:

> All my life I have wondered how many people have been turned away from Christianity by the effeminate, sanctimonious machine-made Christ of second-rate so-called art, which used to be thought good enough for Sunday schools. This Man of Nazareth was a man, with a body hard enough to stand forty days of fasting and long journeys on foot and nights of sleepless prayer, a man with a mind as sharp as a razor and balanced as a precision scale.

The case seems watertight. Barton was an important mediator of mass ideology: De Mille read him, employed him, unconsciously quoted him. It is only a short step to the statement that 'The Jesus of *The King of Kings* is a figure derived out of the sensibility of *The Man Nobody Knows* . . .', the sensibility suggested in the quotations above and accompanied by many references to Jesus as an entrepreneurial hero. And it is only a shorter step to referring to Barton's book simply as De Mille's 'source'. Following the logic built up out of quotations from secondary literary, autobiographical and socio-historical texts, the argument reads impeccably. Only one thing contradicts it: the forgotten matter of the concrete film itself. The argument, no doubt so good that it ought to be true, has a fatal flaw that will not be evident to the historian or student of ideologies unless they have actually looked at the film recently enough to have a reliable memory of it. For whatever De Mille thought he was doing, whatever views about Jesus he committed to paper in his *Autobiography*, no observer of the film could do anything but register the absolute disparity between Barton's 'muscular sun-tanned' 'middle-class advertisement executive' of a Jesus (Maltby's own words) and the figure of Jesus played in the film by the 50-year-old H. B. Warner, that 'man of sorrows' who may be many things – gentle, patriarchal, ecumenical, feminised – but 'muscular' and 'suntanned', never. You simply could not make such a statement if the film itself had not been forgotten beneath secondary sources and ideological presuppositions assumed wholly to define it. Once one looks at the 'evidence' in the light of the film, a question arises that is much more interesting. Why does this film not do what the critic thinks it should do, but instead revives (in contradiction to De Mille's stated intentions) another and very pre-Bartonian Christ, much more akin to the world of D. W. Griffith? Later we try to answer this particular question, but the principle at stake goes past the single instance. It constitutes a general warning about reductive readings of multi-levelled texts against the slide rule of an assumed ideological totality, and a justification of our own text-oriented procedures.

THE OLD TESTAMENT EPIC

1 Law and orgy: the culture-hero of sublimation denounces the Israelites' orgiastic apostasy in *The Ten Commandments* (1956)

2 The twinned heroic profiles of Charlton Heston and Michelangelo's Moses encapsulate the genre's ancient/modern parallelisms in an elegant publicity shot for *The Ten Commandments* (1956)

3 The phallic mother and her sons in the modern section of the original *The Ten Commandments* (1923), the New Testament of the family Bible apparently unread

4 Heroic counter-culture: Yul Brynner's Rameses in *The Ten Commandments* learns the despair of the will and the flesh

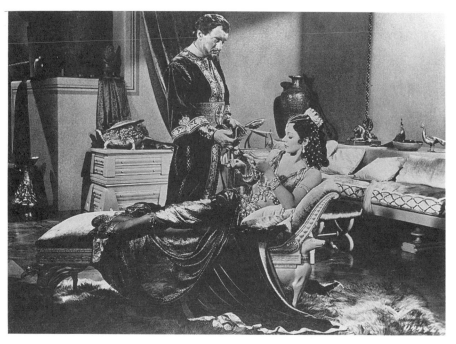

5 *Samson and Delilah:* the culture-hero's antagonists – the flesh (Hedy Lamarr) and the devil of cynical rationalism (George Sanders)

6 In the empire of the senses, the Sheban queen (Gina Lollobrigida) urges her parrot to 'Come! . . . Come!'

7 The heroic star-wearing leader of Israel (Gregory Peck as David) flouts the Law by taking his woman, Bathsheba (Susan Hayward), in adultery

8 The Biblical Epic's Film Noir/Woman's Picture heroine as both prisoner and carrier of the look

9 David's conscience and austere, intolerant adversary, Nathan (Raymond Massey)

1

Jewish questions

COVENANTAL PRINCIPLES

> He had never seen a lobster before; in Jewish dietary law, which his family had observed, lobster was regarded as *trayt* or taboo. But Zukor gladly indulged. He was an American now. — Neal Gabler, *An Empire of Their Own*

While in some contexts it is productive to talk of the Biblical Epic as a genre, more often the distinctiveness of the separate sub-genres demands consideration. Approaching the Old Testament Epic our discussion will emphasise the Jewish elements of these films before examining both the implicit Christian content and the films' connections with contemporary genres and issues.

All the Hollywood Biblical Epics were produced for a predominantly Christian society, but one containing an influential Jewish minority audience. Obviously two of the sub-genres overtly stress Christian material, while the third (though presenting only a Christianised, 'universalised' Judaism) is the only one to present Jewish material autonomously, or, more accurately, semi-autonomously.

Our introduction combated the view that the Biblical Epic is simply Hollywood's travesty of religious meanings. Instead we emphasised Hollywood as a complex site of the tendencies and contradictions of American religious life, a unique 'local' life, but experienced as in some sense 'universal' by other ('Western') cultures where the relation of Christianity to secularism may differ in detail, but where viewers have still been able to find meaningful reflections of their own cultures' secular–religious tensions. Just as the films cannot be understood without recognising the transformative pressures of this context and Hollywood cinematic conventions on the original material, so we argue of the genre as a whole, but perhaps most strongly of the Old Testament sub-type, that it cannot be understood without a further contextualising of cultural sources. By this is not so much meant the underlyingly obvious – the film industry's place within a capitalist economy making profitability a more unmitigated factor than in subsidised film industries. So definitive is this that we take it for granted and pass on to another, the disproportionate role played by Jews at all levels of Hollywood's activities.

Jewish actors, writers and directors all played major parts throughout Hollywood's history, but this role was more than major with production personnel, and almost a gentile-less enclave as far as executive power was concerned. The title of Neal Gabler's book, *An Empire of Their Own: How the Jews Invented Hollywood* is thus not a hyperbole but to a large degree fact. The anti-Semitic paranoia often turned on Hollywood has always suspected Jews' loyalty to their country. As Gabler's account poignantly demonstrates, no accusations could have been more off-target, since the great moguls were almost all conservative Republicans enormously committed to the assimilationist ideology. Given their commitments to the centre, assertions of ethnicity were only a secondary possibility and – until the late 1960s where it began to be valued in the society as a whole – subsidiary to the assimilationist programme.

The drawback to Gabler's book is that his reliance on gaudy anecdote turns his subjects into cartoon figures and underestimates the psychic turmoil in the double allegiance they acted out. We laugh with shock at Harry Cohn's in-house anti-Semitism – 'Relief for the Jews? How about relief *from* the Jews?' – and consider ironically Mayer's cultivation of Cardinal Spellman, but an unanalytical emphasis on such extravagant material deflects the reality of their strange situation. As distinct from the 'Jewish problem' films of the late 1940s which were objects of worry and division, the Old Testament films that followed must have seemed to their producers altogether less difficult, validated as they were by gentile American pro-Israeli feeling and reparative guilt over the Holocaust. Part of the producers' psyches must have felt release from guilt, and even ethnic pride, in portraying Jews heroically. Clearly there were incentives to make these films and psychically they must have seemed less strange undertakings for even the most assimilationist of Jews than lives of Christ or triumph of Christianity films.

The contradictions of the latter sub-genres are extraordinarily complex: a 'Jewish' industry producing versions of Christianity for a dominantly Christian audience; films attempting to mitigate the accusation that the Jews killed Christ, yet often criticised by Jews for their anti-Semitism. The Old Testament films by no means escape these paradoxes, for ultimately their Jewish content is dramatised only because it has been appropriated as the prehistory of Christian meaning, not in its own terms. But for all that it ultimately bears a Christianised interpretation, it offers a much freer field as far as the expression of the Jewish-heroic is concerned. In a further complication the majority of these films were directed by artists of

Christian descent (De Mille, Vidor and King were all practising Christians), even though in two important cases (Griffith and De Mille) they had part-Jewish origins. The paradigm of a Christian director working on a Christianised Jewish text for Jewish producers aiming at a predominantly Christian audience suggests the complications involved.

Schematically simplified, the possibilities of audience readings of these films can be summarised so. (i) For everyone Old Testament films provide, as the most distanced of the sub-genres, exotic spectacle. (ii) For specifically Jewish audiences they give versions of Israel's history relatively free of Christian interpretation. (iii) For at least Reformed Jewish audiences their evolutionary thematic can be read as Judaism's development in tune with New World demands. (iv) For majority Christian audiences they act out the Judaic prehistory of Christianity, its monotheistic and democratic prefigurations, a late version of the tradition of reading the Old Testament typologically in terms of the New. (v) For the Christian audience the sub-genre, freed of the presence of Christ, can dramatise even less inhibitedly than the post-Christ film the licentious aspects of the battles of law and licence, spirit and sense. It can also approach the problem of God's miraculous interventions in history less tensely since these stories are for any but fundamentalist audiences (Christian or Jewish) semi-mythical, so that Jehovah's actions tend to be less inhibited than elsewhere and treated with the licence of mythology.

But for these possibilities to emerge certain aspects of Judaism have to vanish. Though it represents the Law, this Law must be purged of ethnic particularity and tend at all times to the universal. Thus in both of De Mille's *The Ten Commandments* all that Moses imposes on the Israelites are the ten strictures taken over by Christianity and which, in all versions (even De Bosio's later one) are de-ethnicised literally in the replacement of Hebrew script on the tablets by an invented writing. The rest of the body of the Law, the food taboos, the regulations on sacrifice and sexuality, the codes of antique quarantine and punishment and the many practices which constitute Orthodox Judaism's otherness, are expunged. Only where the drama depends on them, and where they serve a purpose intelligible to the majority audience, are they shown, as in the second *The Ten Commandments* when the Passover blood is placed on the doors of the Israelites.

Only in the Christ film are aspects of the otherness of Judaism foregrounded, usually negatively in accordance with the Grace/Law contrasts of traditional Christian thought. Here de-judaicising Judaism makes it acceptable to Christian and other 'progressive' audiences who regard Orthodox practices as unchangingly regressive. But the situation is not simply one-way. From the Jewish producers' viewpoint an assimilated

Judaism, shorn of peculiarities rendering it antiquely repressive to the majority, was a much more satisfactory image to project. Thus, rescued from otherness, ancient Judaism also becomes the prototype of the democratic state. This in turn means that any realistic treatment of the Israelites' conquest and even genocide of the Canaanite tribes is forbidden since it would compromise the clarity of the democratic ideal the films propound.

THE CHOSEN

Promised Land

The representation of Jews in American cinema has taken two basic forms: firstly, films using post-Diaspora characters and situations, usually with domestic, contemporary American settings, as in *Gentleman's Agreement* (1947) or *Humoresque* (1947), but occasionally with exotic settings, as in *Ivanhoe* (1952); secondly, films inspired by Old Testament narratives where, of course, the action happens in a very distant time and place.

For all their distinctiveness the categories are closely linked, each reflecting both the minority's and the majority's feelings about Judaism and Jewishness as cultural and ethical traditions in their own right, and as the distant origins of those of the mainstream culture. Even before the waves of Jewish immigration to the USA, following the Russian pogroms of 1881, Judaism was already deeply embedded in the American psyche. Marshall Sklare argues that Judaism's claim as one of America's three great faiths rests more on symbolic than statistical evidence, something predating significant Jewish immigration, with roots in Christian conviction that America was a new Promised Land.

In the light of this Patricia Erens's virtual exclusion of biblical films from her survey of the Jew in Hollywood cinema is unfortunate, revealing a flatly literalist approach that misses important elements of Jewish representation. While the non-biblical films address sociological or psychological questions, the biblical films both directly dramatise Christianity's roots in Judaism and reconstruct the Jew in the light of the Holocaust and the new state of Israel, with ancient conflicts between Israelites and Philistines, Egyptians and others resurrected as prototypes for the post-1948 Arab/Israeli battles.

Whereas seventeenth-century European plays based on Old Testament themes – for instance Racine's *Esther* or Tirso de Molina's *The Revenge of Tamar* – used the Old Testament, following exegetical practice, as textual prophecy of the Incarnation, Hollywood's Old Testament films not only recreate a remote historical period and signal ahead the Christian era but also dramatise a new order in post-1948 Jewish history. Even if, at one level, Old Testament Epics are variants on other popular genres (such as the Western or Swashbuckler), at another they are crucially about being Jewish in the modern world, adding further dimensions to the focus of the non-biblical films.

Non-biblical films, or the Jewish 'New Testament'

Debate is taking place at present over whether the testimony of Holocaust survivors should form a new Jewish sacred text. While Jewish history in the USA, or in Israel for that matter, cannot compete in poignancy with events under the Nazis, the great Jewish immigration to the USA opened up a new chapter in the history of the Jews, one whose experiences are reflected in the industry which Jews largely created. Hollywood films in general, but especially Hollywood films about Jews, ancient or modern, can be read as a kind of testimony of Jewish experience in America.

Films dealing with domestic, non-biblical topics fall into two closely-related groups: those with a domestic American focus, and those concerned with modern Israel. The first and much the largest reflects the history of Jewish immigration to the USA. Lester Friedman and Patricia Erens have both described the shifts of emphasis Jewish representation undergoes against the changing background of socio-historical developments in the USA. In the first great immigrations (1881–1924) Jewish characters in films tend to stereotype. Literary and vaudeville stock types – comedian, beautiful Jewish princess, Wandering Jew, but also villainous usurers, mutilators and so on – populate the screen, although very soon Jewish organisations were set up ensuring that Jewish interests were protected, in recognition of the medium's power to refuel latent anti-Semitic feeling in the gentile movie audience. The American Jewish Committee, the B'nai B'rith and the National Jewish Community Relations Advisory Council all lobbied for censorship of anti-Jewish material (with films such as *Intolerance* and *The King of Kings* undergoing changes in response to pressure).

Yet though Jews were careful to monitor negative representation, Hollywood itself was wary of dramatising Jewish questions, especially anti-Semitism. Not until the 1940s, in response to Nazi persecution, did Hollywood promote films like *Gentleman's Agreement*, *Mr Skeffington* (1944), or *Crossfire* (1947), drawing other than an idyllicised attention to Jewish ethnicity, a repression paralleled by the studios' process of anglicising the names of personnel and clearly motivated by a desire to avoid scrutiny, signal dedication to the melting-pot and distance themselves from the perceived backwardness of life in the ghettos or shtetls of eastern

Europe.

Even in the 1940s when Jewish-question films emerged, Hollywood lived in fear of House UnAmerican Activities Committee accusations of links between Jews and international communism and of loss of revenue from foreign markets if what were considered minority subjects were foregrounded. Nevertheless, with America's entry into the war, Hollywood felt able to touch on the perennial question of anti-Semitism, highly visible, for instance, in Charles Lindbergh's isolationist arguments.

In the 1940s, *Mr Skeffington* is one of a handful of films that highlight the problem. The film draws on traditional images of the Jew as financier, his wealth both despised and coveted by an aristocratic but impoverished East Coast gentile family. Claude Rains as Skeffington portrays in microcosm the history of Jewish immigration to America – 'Skeffington' is an immigration officer's garbling of 'Skavinskaya' – and of scorned yet envied Jewish wealth. The cousin of the high society girl (Bette Davis) he later marries refers to Skeffington's business as the 'Jewish Firm'. Her brother has embezzled money from the firm, and must now fall on the mercy of a man he despises. The Jew is once again cast as Shylock, but this film, made in the shadow of Nazi atrocities, and domestically taking advantage of the upward mobility of Jews into affluent suburbs and respected professions, is able to subvert the myth (the character's otherness demystified by Claude Rains) and present the Jew as self-sacrificing and socially-conscious, even as a war hero, rising to the rank of captain on active service. Many elements of *Mr Skeffington* reflect the Jewish community's growing self-confidence as well as more determined efforts by Hollywood paradoxically to foreground and desemiticise simultaneously the American Jew. These aims parallel those of the Old Testament Epics where biblical Palestine is desemiticised and Americanised through genre and star presence, making the Epics sometimes seem like heightened versions of all-American domestic narratives. For all its advances, *Mr Skeffington* remains an idealisation of American Jewish-gentile relations, failing to indicate problems of intermarriage (as seen from the Jewish side) and compromised by images of the Jew ready to place all positive qualities at the service of a de-ethnicised Americanism.

The 1940s and 1950s films tend as here to be somewhat coy in their depictions of Jewishness. Even noir films like *Crossfire* and *Gentleman's Agreement* approach it as if there were no problems about the difference of Jews or any other racial or ethnic community. But increasingly, after the rise of other ethnically self-conscious minorities (Afro-Americans especially) and the successive Israeli victories over the Arabs, more ethnically conscious portrayals found their way to the screen.

Whereas an early 1950s film like *Ivanhoe* would put the Jewish case in an almost apologetic way, stressing similarities with dominant groupings, from the late 1950s films like *Exodus*, *The Chosen*, or *No Way to Treat a Lady* expose the rougher, more semitic idiosyncrasies of Jewish life. When in *Ivanhoe* Jew and Christian discuss justice, Ivanhoe's view that the notion of justice's belonging to all is a Christian one, prompts Isaac's reply that 'strange as it may be, sir, we are taught it too.'

Such dialogue, designed to promote rapprochement, would seem out of place in *Exodus* with its raucous assertions of nationhood, in *The Chosen* with its revelry in ethnic difference, or *No Way to Treat a Lady*, a film confident enough about the status of Jews to allow itself an antic narrative structured around an oedipally traumatised Jewish psychopath. Related self-mockery, like Woody Allen's comic evocation of the Hassidic prototype in *Annie Hall*, becomes first possible then common, because in the wake of the great outburst of Jewish novel writing in the 1950s and 1960s (Bellow, Malamud, Roth, etc.) the Jew becomes so central an image to American art that self-reference is readable in all its otherness as a primary image for self-identification (Herzog, Portnoy) by the non-Jewish audience. Though protests over more recent films like *Jesus Christ Superstar*, *Once Upon a Time in America* and *The Bonfire of the Vanities* suggest unresolved problems, there is no doubt that the post-1948 Israeli factor was instrumental in sanctioning more assertive, and eventually more complex, portrayals of Jewish life, in which the reassertion of heroism both through films specifically about the new Israel (*Cast a Giant Shadow*, *Exodus*) and through the epics of ancient Israel (whatever other meanings they have) plays an important part.

The Old Testament narratives

The year 1948 also marked a watershed in the history of Old Testament narratives. While the original *Ben-Hur* certainly projects elements of Jewish heroism through Ramon Novarro, this is hardly the norm. The ancient Moses (Theodore Roberts) in the original *The Ten Commandments* (1923) is so anti-heroic that one concludes that De Mille has difficulty matching the Jewish and the heroic. In the earlier prototype Old Testament film, *Judith of Bethulia* (1914), the negative stereotypes of gentile tradition flow over into the portrayal of most of the males as spineless incompetents without the physical courage to challenge Holofernes' brutal tyranny, while, on the other hand, a desemiticised Judith is portrayed as awe-inspiring, her short-cropped hair reminiscent of the gentile heroine Joan of Arc. In taking the initiative to end her people's suffering, Judith stands out as an exceptional heroine, while the Jews in general seem a suffering, vulnerable people.

The inauguration of the state of Israel led directly (the coincidence of *Samson and Delilah* and *David and Bathsheba* appearing in 1949 and 1951 is too marked to be explained otherwise) to the promulgation of images of Jewish heroism which have their parallel and less coded apotheosis in the contemporary epic, *Exodus* (1960). Defeating incompetent Arabs in successive wars from 1948 answered traditional accusations of cowardice given their latest inflection over the failure to resist the Holocaust. In the Biblical Epics Jews are heroic: Solomon, David and Samson are placed to give the lie to the kinds of accusation hurled by Robert Ryan's Sergeant Montgomery in *Crossfire* (1947). Though we do not see Mr Skeffington on combat duty, Solomon, Samson and David, played by glamorous non-Jewish actors such as Yul Brynner, Victor Mature and Gregory Peck, are all shown in actions belying Sergeant Montgomery's vicious accusations against 'guys that played it safe during the war, scrounged around keeping themselves in civvies; got swell apartments, swell dames, you know the kind . . . some of them are named Samuels; some of them got funnier names'. The Hollywood Old Testament heroes are the General Dayans of the screen, presented as not by nature belligerent ('We are not warriors, but we would fight for what is ours', Lot tells the Sodomite Queen), yet, if provoked, capable of bravery in the field of battle.

But these Jewish heroes are also depicted as civilised, a people above all ruled by Law (however repressive in some respects that Law may be: compare David's comments in *David and Bathsheba*) and, as observed through the lens of contemporary Israeli history and American ideology, unique in the Middle East in their commitment to freedom. In post-1948 Hollywood Arabs often assume the nightmarish shapes once reserved for Nazis.

At best the Old Testament films made during the consolidation of modern Israel merely ignore the Arabs and their argument. Whereas *Exodus*, explicitly about modern Israel, has to come to terms, like it or not, with the Palestinian presence – thus allowing the characters played by John Derek (Arab) and Paul Newman (Jew) to be friends – films facing such issues through remote ancient history can afford to dehumanise the Arabs, having it both ways. On the one hand, sub-textually the films link ancient Philistines with modern Arabs; on the other, the surface meanings provided by historical distance offer an escape from accusations of anti-Arab prejudice.

In all these films there is an unshakeable belief in Jewish claims to the land. When Lot orders the Sodomites to 'get off our land', the resonances of Israeli victimisation of Palestinians in the establishing of an Eretz Israel are glossed over. But a later film, Beresford's *King David* (1985), in the light of greater world awareness of the Palestinian position, while not undermining support for Israel's territorial security, does attempt to consider the land question more evenly.

> *Philistine King*: I refer to the so-called, uh, Promised Land. Did not your God promise Moses, or was it Abraham, all the lands between Lebanon and Egypt, between the Syrian wilderness and the western sea, the land of the Hittites, the Jebusites, the Ammonites, and, uh, need I add, the Philistines? Hmm?
>
> *David*: What God chooses to give, we cannot refuse.
>
> *King*: The Law of Moses is not renowned for its impartiality towards heathens.
>
> *David*: The law of David shall deal justly with all men, heathen and Hebrew alike. I give you my solemn oath.

By the film's end the liberal David has lost out to the hardline Nathan. The prophet's over-voice complacently relates successive wars and conquests of the tribes as the Law of Moses triumphs over the law of David. Even so a Jewish (sub-textually modern Israeli) leader is shown fairly and realistically negotiating directly with the Philistines or Palestinians (the words have a convenient similarity), recognising that the strict application of theologically-sanctioned demands will inevitably fail to bring justice to the region's inhabitants. This view is expressed in a remarkably balanced and aesthetically innovative way in a film made in Israel itself, Amos Gitai's *Ester* (1986).

In a film using Jews and Arabs at all levels of production, the Arab voice is accorded equality with the Jew's. The choric songs punctuating the narrative are often sung in Arabic, and the persecution of the Jews is not recognised as becoming any more tolerable through inflictions of suffering on another people. These implications become all the more compelling as the film closes with the actors speaking autobiographically, explicitly highlighting a principle as fundamental to the Hollywood Biblical Epic prototype as to the radical Israeli offshoot, the conviction that present troubles are inextricably linked with issues that come from out of the past.

2

Questions of narrative

EFFECTS OF ANALOGY

In his biography of De Mille Charles Higham quotes a memorandum sent by the director's writer, Jeanie Macpherson, during the making of *The Ten Commandments* (1923).

> As the sins of the Pharaoh and his hordes of horsemen are avenged by the downcrashing waves of the Red Sea, which parted to let the Children of Israel, with their clear faith, pass through, so does an emotional Red Sea engulf our modern Dan McTavish who attempted to raise his puny voice against immutable laws.

She is rhapsodically describing an (ancient/modern) mode of structuring narratives that died early in the history of the American cinema, which varied from momentary inserts (for example De Mille's Babylonian flashback and Roman inserts in *Manslaughter* and *Adam's Rib*, both 1922) to the juxtaposition of separate narratives as in the original *The Ten Commandments*, where first a version of Exodus is shown, followed by a modern-day story. In *Intolerance* (1916), at once the precedent and extreme of the technique, there are not two, but four plots which are not presented in a simple a/b/c/d form but in a structure of extended 'alternate syntagama', a/b/c/a/d, etc. Curtiz's *Noah's Ark* (1928) is the last biblical film to exhibit the usual reduced double plot version of the *Intolerance* design, by now becoming unfamiliar to audiences as it is overtaken by the classical cinema's drive towards a seamless narrative consistency. In fact, though, in the Biblical Epic the older form did not absolutely disappear but left traces in the ubiquitous prologues which are positioned as the view of later time (for instance in the 1956 *The Ten Commandments* De Mille himself appears and lectures the audience).

Nevertheless, the overwhelming tendency replaced the double structure with internal allusion to the modern world running through an unbroken diegesis. For instance, in *The Last Days of Sodom and Gomorrah* (1962), when Lot's Hebrews defeat the Arab tribes by breaking the dam on their armies, allusions to Exodus combine with the modern Arab/Israeli conflict, without in any way breaking the single story's coherence. The change can be summarised as the replacement of large structures of explicit analogy by smaller structures of implicit analogy. This differs from a third possibility, radically outside Hollywood norms, demonstrated in Gitai's *Ester*. Here ancient and modern form a palimpsest, actors in ancient costume playing against the modern landscape of Tel Aviv, and, occasionally, extras in modern dress playing parts in crowd scenes. Then, at the end, the actors step out of role and talk about analogies between the narrative and the political world. In retrospect we may feel that the pressures which created the Biblical Epic's typical narrative form were in many ways conservative, and that a certain richness is lost in the abandoning of double plot structures and the refusal to embrace anything like the mode of *Ester*. At the same time we should not underestimate the complexity of conservative forms.

FIVE OLD TESTAMENT NARRATIVES

Judith of Bethulia (D. W. Griffith, 1914)

As elsewhere, Griffith presciently rehearses many characteristics of later films in this first (relatively) fully narrativised Biblical Epic. This extends to prefiguring the sub-genre's ambivalence towards its Jewish subject-matter. So in the scene-setting opening, two ghetto-like Jews walk by communicating in grotesquely alien gestures before the narrative moves to Judith and the largely de-ethnicised heroic. The title sequence also points to emerging patterns of the sub-genre, noting a combination of ancient sources and modern reworking, the Apocrypha interpreted through Thomas Bailey Aldrich's play. A second title allays audience anxiety at too scholarly a mode of reconstruction with the reassurance that the 'drama' of the subject will be highlighted.

As this suggests, the film centres on the dramatic, announcing the sub-genre's predilection for sieges and battles, colourful 'antiquarian' reconstruction and the foregrounding of sexual desire and sadism – the first in fantasies of oriental sexuality (the 'bacchanalian festivities' of Holofernes' dancing girls), the second in Holofernes' outrageous actions (having captives crucified, personally assaulting prisoners awaiting execution).

These are part of an action which, however apparently aberrant in centring on a heroine rather than a hero (a variant only recovered in the late films *Esther and the King* and *The Story of Ruth*), prefigures the future by its intensely sexualised treatment of an already sexualised source, in which Judith uses her beauty to destroy Holofernes. But whereas in the source Judith, rendering the all-powerful male vulnerable, is herself singlemindedly invulnerable, in the film, like later male protagonists, she (Blanche Sweet) is torn between duty and desire. 'The dread bull of Assur', Holofernes (Henry B. Walthall), presents an extraordinary spectacle of unalloyed super-masculinity, vast, ogre-like, with ringleted black hair, as extreme a representation of the phallic male as those later hyper-females, Delilah, Sheba and Bathsheba, are of the sub-genre's vaginal feminine.

The film does little to motivate Judith's attraction to Holofernes in personal terms. As she repeatedly hesitates to kill him we seem in the presence of symbolic sex and gender forces relating beyond the individual. Judith's own stern presence, virile and defeminised despite her female trappings of seduction, demands a historicised reading as the representative of militant moral feminism and suffragettism posed against, and destroying by a mixture of female guile and appropriated male sternness, the principle of ultra-male aggression that Holofernes represents, but forced to repress her own sexual nature in order to do it. Triumphant at the end of the film, hailed by a grateful populace, her act has been too castratory for the young widow to be placed back within sexual structures. This seems to necessitate the presence of a minor, compensatory relationship between Naomi and Nathan, like the relationship between Joshua and Lilia in the second *The Ten Commandments*, as some kind of compensation for Moses' renunciation. In her extreme renunciation Judith is closest to Moses of all the heroes of the sub-genre who follow her and encounter the temptations Holofernes embodies, but split into the sexual (feminine) and aggressive (masculine).

The Ten Commandments (Cecil B. De Mille, 1923)

Here the prefatory title addresses a world in which religion seems to have wavered under the assaults of science and psychology. 'Our modern world defined God as a "religious complex" and laughed at the Ten Commandments as OLD FASHIONED.' But in turn this rational secularism and jazz age hedonism are shaken by recent horrors. 'Then through the laughter came the shattering thunder of the World War.'

The film's dual narrative is less sophisticated than *Intolerance*'s, consisting not of alternating sequences but of the Exodus narrative followed by a contemporary melodrama echoing biblical events. Though many moments in its Exodus story prefigure the massive developments of the remake, the demi-narrative is basically a pageant of moral moments, as if one were moving through the story illustrated by Doré: the Israelites slaving with rigour; the Pharaoh's procession over a trapped worker; an ancient Moses (Theodore Roberts) appearing before Rameses, whose little son whips him; Rameses mourning his dead child; his armies pursuing the Israelites; the Red Sea miracle; Moses sculpting the Law on the tablets at the direction of God, intercut with the apostasy of the golden calf; and finally the destruction of the erring Israelites. A long dissolve at this moment of divine punishment bridges the narratives, retrospectively placing the ancient within the modern as it is revealed that Mrs McTavish (Edythe Chapman) has been reading to her two sons, John (Richard Dix) thoughtfully puffing on his pipe, and Dan (Rod La Rocque), bored and ironic.

The moment of the dissolve is revealing, for the mother later says to Dan with her dying words: 'Whatever you've done is all my fault. I taught you to *fear* God, instead of to love him – and LOVE is all that counts!' Mrs McTavish's minatory conception of God, the ultimate source of Dan's scepticism, leads to the family's break-up. Dan begins his amoral drive for 'SUCCESS', while John, having lost his beautiful flapper love, Mary Leigh (Leatrice Joy), to his brother, stays at home virtuously plying his trade of carpenter. In a double descent Dan builds a church with substandard concrete and becomes erotically entangled with a Eurasian vamp, Sally Lung (Nita Naldi), who has smuggled herself into America from a leper colony by means of one of the illegal sacks of jute Dan receives from Calcutta. The church collapses, killing his mother, and, hounded by debt and scandal magazines, he shoots his lover when she tells him about the 'leprosy' with which she has infected both himself and Mary. In the finale, Dan, after confessing to Mary, dies trying to escape to Mexico in a speedboat named *Defiance*, while Mary is rescued from suicidal despair by John: 'Mary, there is only one man who can help you – a Man you have forgotten!' As he reads to her from the same Bible the mother constantly clasped – but now the *New* Testament – Christ miraculously cures a leprous young woman, a cure doubled by Mary's as the film ends.

Jeanie Macpherson's governing structure is ingeniously pursued throughout the contemporary melodrama, not so much in straightforward parallelisms as in a plurality of analogies – for example Dan's parody (golden calf) worship of the $5 Golden Eagle; Dan and Mary dancing to 'I've Got Those Sunday Blues' (the Israelites' orgy); the mother's breaking of the dance record on the huge Bible she constantly carries (paralleling less than straightforwardly Moses' destruction of the original tablets); the collapse of the church wall on Mrs McTavish (visually echoing the Red Sea deluge).

The film also differs from later ones in its extremely overt placement of Christianity over Judaism. This accounts for the strange detail – doubly odd beside De Mille's literalism in hiring Orthodox Jews as Israelite extras – of the writing on Moses' tablets so obviously being not in Hebrew but in an invented system, the logic presumably being that God's universal language pre- and post-dates the language of Israel. Possibly, too, various feelings about Jewish/Christian interpenetration are acted out in the desire/ revulsion of the miscegenetic erotic scenario. At the end the mother's too masculine upholding of a puritanical law is transcended by Christ healing both the leprous woman who appears before him and Mary (contrasting with Moses' refusal to forgive the repentant female orgiast who begs him for mercy), a replacement of the phallic mother by a feminising Christ who moves the film at its close out of the Old Testament's orbit.

The Ten Commandments (Cecil B. De Mille, 1956)

The remake, dropping the dual narrative and vastly expanding the Exodus section, has De Mille himself address the audience in a prologue functioning partly as apologia for the reconstruction of the lost years of Moses' life unaccounted for in Exodus. An extra solemnity attached to the subject of the actual giving of the Law separates this narrative from ones like *Samson and Delilah* where no defence of narrative inventions seems required. Here De Mille gestures to ancient writers like Josephus, but manages also to suggest by a reference to the Dead Sea Scrolls his awareness of modern research in his development of that memorable 'family romance' in which Moses, the son of the Levites Amram and Jochabel, is brought up by Bithia, the Pharaoh's sister, a situation reaching its highest melodramatic pitch in the associated oedipal and sexual conflicts as he discovers his Israelite origins when the Egyptian throne is within his grasp.

De Mille seems to suggest that he has taken into account the kind of research on the Exodus summarised by Mircea Eliade. Eliade argues there is no evidence for denying the existence of the historical Moses, or the historicity of the Exodus, adding however that the latter cannot 'involve the Exodus of the whole people, but only a group . . . Other groups had already begun their more or less peaceful entrance into Canaan'.

In fact it becomes clear that De Mille's narrative resists even relatively conservative deconstruction. The point is clarified through speculation on what a deconstructive Exodus narrative might be like, a putative film based on Freud's 'historical novel' *Moses and Monotheism* (1939). There Freud claims that underneath the mythical surface a latent residue of historicity is discoverable, a narrative in which Moses, an Egyptian, perpetuates the solar monotheism of the Pharaoh Aton after his overthrow, imposing it on the Israelites whom he then leads out of Egypt. This scenario, shockingly denying Israel the invention of monotheism, proceeds to split its greatest individual into two, the original Egyptian Moses and a later Israelite Moses who are combined into one individual at the time that memories of the earlier Moses (murdered by his followers) and the primitive volcano god, Jahweh, of the later Israelites are fused. The difference from De Mille's epic infrangibilities could hardly be greater. The later De Bosio *Moses* provides interesting comparisons with its epic figure subject to partial decon- struction, his actions affirmed only in so far as they are the founding actions of the culture, in no sense immune from the criticisms that the later culture turns against the ferocity of its beginnings. When Moses (Burt Lancaster) institutes and savagely carries out the rigours of the Law, it is a Law we never witness delivered by God. And although Moses declares that the punishments are God's not his, the film insists on demonstrating the human instrumentality involved. Moses' death sentence on the man who breaks the Sabbath is the act of a ruler who, by holding a lamb in his arms as he does so, figures the later fanaticisms of Christianity as well as Judaism. Contrast- ingly, in De Mille's punishment scene everything combines to suggest inhuman agency (fire, lightning, earthquakes and the commentary above the action 'And the Lord's anger was kindled against Israel') and unquestionably divine intervention.

Solomon and Sheba (King Vidor, 1959)

Solomon and Sheba embodies the sub-genre's typical expansion of fragmentary narrative sources, a process perhaps most extreme in *The Prodigal* (1954) where, apart from the ending, almost every plot detail is invented. The biblical story (1 Kings, 10; repeated in Chronicles) has the exotic Queen arrive to ask Solomon riddles and be impressed with his answers, and ends with her praise of the King, and the exchange of gifts. The changes in Vidor's film are built around the sexualisation of the relationship between the King (Yul Brynner) and the Queen (Gina Loll- obrigida), following the inventions of Judaic, Islamic and Christian lore (for instance the Abyssinian Church's claim that Solomon and Sheba's son was the ancestor of Haile Selassie).

This prehistory encourages a more meaningful view of the film's narrative processes. The sexualisation at their centre pays tribute to the influence of the erotic, but the 'sex interest' does not automatically expel other kinds of meaning. Rather, within highly defined limits it actively propagates meanings around such oppositions/relationships as male/ female; masculine: Israel; feminine: Sheba, etc. Such polarities often tend, moreover, not to hold their simplest shape but move towards more complex forms that modify the original differences substantially.

In developing its source, the film characteristically combines invention with respect for biblical sources. For instance, when Solomon tolerates Sheba's celebration of Ragon's rites on Israelite soil, material is adapted from 1 Kings, 11, relating Solomon's love of 'many strange women' and how in his old age 'his wives turned away his heart after other gods'. The source's multiplicity and diffuseness are dispensed with so that the sexual plot takes on the classic form of monogamous romantic love, even where the love is adulterous. So Solomon's wives are never mentioned and there is only one fragmentary sequence showing the harem, economy and clarity combining with the ideology of romantic love.

Attached is a political plot centred on Adonijah's attempts to dethrone Solomon. Again the material has biblical origins, in this case 1 Kings, 2, where Adonijah asks Bathsheba for Abishag, to which Solomon's reaction is to have Adonijah killed. Typically again the source's emphasis on the ruthless demands of realpolitik, even in a figure celebrated for peace and wisdom like Solomon, is deleted to heighten the contrast between Solomon and his brother. This is a simplification, but neither motiveless nor meaningless, since it constitutes one of the major oppositions of the film. Similarly, Abishag's biblical role as the dying David's concubine undergoes complete repression as she becomes the wholly good daughter. The censorship acts to preserve David from taint and to avoid compromising Abishag, but it also has a structural function in allowing her to fulfil the role (cf. Ruth in contrast to the Priestess Samarra in *The Prodigal*) of the untransgressive woman, 'the living symbol of Israel', whom the hero admires without desiring, and whose sacrifice of herself intercedes for him.

The Story of Ruth (Henry Koster, 1960)

Like *Esther and the King*, *The Story of Ruth* returns to the heroine-centred precedent of *Judith of Bethulia*. A late desire for variation from the sub-genre's hero-dominated narratives leads to an intertextual relationship with the woman's film genre. This is especially felt where *The Story of Ruth* places its heroine (Elena Eden) in relationship with females who act as reflections of her own self, past and future; the girl Tabra whom, as Priestess of Kemosh, she trains for sacrifice, and Naomi, her mother-in-law, to whom she bonds herself after the death of her first husband. Thus beyond its focus on female bondings the narrative constructs a composite heroine (girl, maiden, widow and older matriarch in one), a multi-faceted portrait of womanhood encountering a social world that victimises women even more than men. This is emphasised in the Moabite religious rites' sacrifice of young girls (not boys) to a male god served mainly by priestesses whose 'brainwashing' in Kemoshite ideology we witness as they chant the praise of their deity – a moment which crosses the familiar portrayal of totalitarianism with a hinted critique of the female's social construction.

But, at a time different from the 'first phase' feminism which *Judith* equivocally articulates, the film reconciles change with tradition, presenting its heroine as self-determining yet ultimately domesticated (compare the impossibility of remarriage for Judith in Griffith's film) as she marries *twice*, on both occasions coming under the influence of a good mother figure in Naomi (as distinct from Viveca Lindfors's bad mother, the Chief Priestess of Kemosh).

The film celebrates, though not perhaps in a way to appeal to future radical elements, the female within a softened patriarchal context in which the various bad patriarchs (Ruth's literal father who sells her to the Priest of Kemosh; the grotesque deity Kemosh himself; the Priest of Kemosh and the King of Moab, and Tob, Boaz's rival for Ruth, who is willing to abuse the Levirate Law, in order to possess her against her will) are defeated – allowing the heroine to be paired with virtuous ones, first Mahlon and then Boaz (Stuart Whitman). The film's romanticisation of the biblical tale makes romantic love a source of ultimate knowledge. Being told by Mahlon that she is beautiful leads Ruth to look at the child Tabra outside of Kemoshite ideology, an act which leads to her eventual conversion. This emphasis is very different from the source's where marriage is connected with wealth, land law, inheritance and the need for descendants. Such realities are not banished from the film, for Boaz's wealth and protection are the solution to Ruth and Naomi's poverty, but inequality is softened by 'true love' and by the influence Ruth has (the influence woman has to reform patriarchy) on Boaz who when we first meet him is condemning the Moabite terrorist without trial or witnesses.

The film's narrative inventions move in two directions. Firstly, Ruth's outsider status (as Moabitess) is heightened by her position in the cult of the bloody Moabite god, the absolute antithesis to the worship of 'the Invisible God', presented without any reference to animal sacrifice in order to make the distinction absolute. Once in Bethlehem, Ruth suffers persecutions from the inhabitants, being blamed for the drought and falsely accused of harbouring idols. Secondly, what in the source is very much Naomi's pragmatic trick to secure Boaz as guarantor of the family, is mitigated by its being a device to secure the romantic love plot and allow the women to defeat Tob's attempt to enforce his desire for Ruth by the Law. (In the original narrative Tob is the anonymous kinsman who gives up his right to Ruth.) A last invented character, the Holy Man who meets Naomi at the well and informs her of Ruth's destiny as the direct ancestor of David, appears chorically against the landscape at the film's opening and close – some of the few moments that, in a very domestic film, have an epic feel. He inflects the film towards Christianity by adding to what is already in the source (the Bethlehem setting and the prophecy of the birth of David) the further promise, through Jesse and David, of the Messiah Jesus, by connotation a realm where the patriarchal is creatively feminised.

THEMES AND VARIATIONS

Culture heroes: culture villains

> One stands in awe and reverence before these tremendous remnants of what man once was . . . Nietzsche, *Beyond Good and Evil*

Since history in the genre is 'monumental' Old Testament epics are typically built around the titanic encounters of great individuals. These are not the 'mediocre' individuals Lukács finds in the novels of Scott, intersecting the decisive movements of history accidentally like the protagonists of the Roman/Christian films, but the primary historical–mythic agents themselves, embodying the clashing forces of good and evil, religion and superstition, liberty and autocracy, law and licence. The protagonists of the films are almost unwaveringly Israel's patriarchs, Moses, David, Solomon, Samson, and so on. At the same time the titles of three of the most central films signal the importance of the feminine by including the woman's name, announcing her as something like co-protagonist – Samson *and Delilah*, Solomon *and Sheba*, David *and Bathsheba*.

Though the female protagonists of the two late films (*The Story of Ruth* and *Esther and the King*) remind us that the first major Old Testament film, Griffith's *Judith of Bethulia*, centres on a heroine and that the most patriarchal of the sub-genres has its tendencies to feminisation, the sub-genre's protagonists tend to be male figures of the Law, caught up in the double action of its denial and defence. The pattern of those central films where the heroine shares the title is in the most obvious sense temptation by 'female' forces, surrender, the renunciation of temptation and the restoration of patriarchal Law. Here, out of the 'female' swamplands from which in the modern myths of Freud and Bachofen patriarchal order arose, female principles re-emerge to seduce the heroes back to tellurian origins. The most extreme instance of this polarisation is *Solomon and Sheba*, where

Sheba comes from a matriarchal state immemorially ruled by queens. In the only scene in the Land of Sheba, the Queen herself (Gina Lollobrigida) reclines the length of the screen in a garden oasis, a maid painting her toenails while Sheba teases a parrot with the reiterated invitation 'Come . . . Come'. The Land of Sheba in the often contradictory signification of the film is the land of polytheism and autocracy, but first of all it is a more decorous version of Henry Miller's 'Land of Cunt', the 'other' against which patriarchal Israel defines itself.

Inasmuch as the culture heroes are heroes of the sublimation upon ❦ which culture depends, the 'female', in the films' simplest movement, has to be defeated. So in the second· *Ten Commandments*, having transferred his desire from Nefertiri to the Hebrews, Moses resists the blandishments of Jethro's six younger daughters to marry the oldest and most ethical, Zephorah. But, as his wife says when confronted by Nefertiri, 'He has forgotten both of us. You lost him when he went to seek his God. I lost him when he found his God.' In the farewell scene, when the aged Zephorah tells him that she loves him, he is so far beyond human love that his face doesn't flicker even in minimal response. By the film's second half Moses' sacrifice of the instinctual–erotic shows in his change from heroic bare-chestedness to a figure of vatic form, clearly modelled on Michelangelo's statue, aged unnaturalistically while other characters remain youthful.

Moses' extreme is not followed straightforwardly by the other heroes, for elsewhere the feminine is allowed to signify more than the chaotically seductive. In all three of *Solomon and Sheba*, *Samson and Delilah* and *David and Bathsheba*, even where the female is in part defeated, she is also in some way rehabiliated, as even Lana Turner's Priestess of Astarte is in *The Prodigal*. Samson precedes the dedication of his death to Jehovah with a statement of love for Delilah who is allowed to choose to die in the Theatre of Dagon rather than abandon him, so that within its swooning rhetoric the film manages a last, almost equal assertion of the principles clustered around the maleness and femaleness of the characters; while *Solomon and Sheba*, though its ending separates the couple for ever, and through their son promises the end of Sheban matriarchy, en route suggests a more equal interpenetration of principles.

The culture hero faces temptations from the 'feminine'. He is also pitted against figures of unchecked 'masculine' power, embodied in the cultural villain. In both *King David* (1985) and *David and Bathsheba* these are the representatives of the Law itself, Samuel and Nathan. More usually, though, they are the Israelites' enemies, Rameses (Yul Brynner) in *The Ten Commandments* and the two characters played by George Sanders, Adonijah in *Solomon and Sheba* and the Saran in *Samson and Delilah*. In these Sanders leaves an indelible imprint on conceptions of Old Testament tyranny, though not for obvious macho strength – for even where Adonijah is very much the warrior, such attributes seem formal rather than essential, as in the curious battle close-ups where he languidly parries the blows of an unseen opponent as insouciantly as if marking a billiard cue.

Sanders's connotations are of an aristocratic unbeliever's cynicism, an effortless superiority conveying ennui-filled disdain for the vices that sustain him, even for Hedy Lamarr whom he addresses in lines over-ripely, parodically alliterative – 'Even a ruby loses lustre beside your lips.' When he makes no real move to stop Delilah going to Samson in the Theatre, he is more moved by fear of the banality of jealousy than loss of her. In the ancient world, he is still Rebecca's beyond-the-pale patrician lover, Jack Flavell, and the King of the New York Philistines, *All About Eve's* sneering critic, Addison De Witt. Sanders's projection of detachment, of ultimately not giving a damn, is fascinating to Americans of more puritan upbringing, and the films barely pause to sketch in obvious brutalities. In *Samson and Delilah* Sanders in one scene contemplates his pet ants, dispensing divine favours of manna-syrup from a spoon as the little citizens scurry about the Lilliputian city he has built them to make their symbolism clear. 'The Babylonians call them Zebaba. The Danites call them Memlach. We call them ants. See how these master ants collect food from their slaves. You might call them tax collectors.' The Sanders characters and others fulfilling the same role embody a chain of negative characteristics – authoritarianism, brutality, witty sadism, and a disdain for the piety of relationships and ritual. But Sanders's forte is the representation of detached rationalistic intelligence, sceptical of all sentiment. The role is complex and fascinating, nowhere better demonstrated than in the Theatre of Dagon where he is in many ways the audience's surrogate, the urbane, detached, amused Olympian spectator, whose intelligence we both admire and rebuke.

Such a figure demands a double description. Overtly his vices are challenged, exposed and defeated; covertly they are the repository of the audience's sceptical and cynical feelings. Sanders, though, is hardly an heroic figure. For that we must turn to Yul Brynner's Rameses in the second *The Ten Commandments*. Whereas we cannot imagine Sanders playing the epic hero, Brynner does in *Solomon and Sheba*, pointing to the duality of the charismatic–barbaric connotations of a star most famously and exotically the King in *The King and I*. Brynner's mysteriously Asiatic features and powerfully graceful body, more sensuously naked because of that burnished shaven head, make him a sign of materiality as he stands widefooted, arms arrogantly on hips, glaring and uttering the Pharaonic words that parody the Mosaic decrees: 'So let it be written. So let it be done.'

Of course every element of Rameses's charisma is enclosed with moral opprobrium: his defiance of Jehovah is pride; his aristocratic command is that of the slavedriver; likewise his erotic force (telling Nefertiri that he will own her like his dog or horse); his rationalism ends in prayers to the 'Lord of the Underworld' and eventually his admission that Moses' God '*is* God'. But Rameses also represents powerfully much of the audience's stake in the world of human emotion. And, as the Nietzschean anti-hero, he also represents a defence of the aristocratic as the source of the good, thereby assaulting the ideology of the classless and the democratic. Yet in that America is the mass society that acclaims the figure who transcends the masses, the democracy that celebrates the superman, it is hard not to see Brynner's force and the way the film conspires to celebrate its perverse magnificence even while condemning it, as a sign of the society's fascination with a type at once its enemy and its second self.

Patterns of contemporary allusion

Hollywood history constantly finds analogies with the present. While many are consciously structured, others are best explained as the unconscious product of a certain view of history and the forms and conventions of a particular kind of film. Of these conventions the one that most signifies the present in the past is the star system, which explains why almost the first 'reality effect' that an unconventional biblical film (such as Pasolini's *Matthew*) seeks is to find unknown actors. For not only do stars bring 'star-texts' of meanings from previous films, but most of these are inescapably contemporary.

However, our immediate interest is in the way the films develop specific sets of allusions. Some of these are constant enough to form patterns over the sub-genre, others belong to a single context. In the latter case, for instance, future viewers may be puzzled why Eve (Ulla Bergryd) in Huston's *The Bible* is Scandinavian, and may need to be informed of the 1960s and 1970s myth of a sexually guilt-free Scandinavian society, fused here with the traditional Paradise. In the same film Huston's folktale Noah echoes the beginnings of contemporary environmentalism. Rather than asserting anthropomorphic mastery over the animals, he acts out a 'green' role, leading them into the ark like the ultimate conservationist. Further, in a precise subversion of Leviticus, 11, Noah instructs his sons: 'Shem, in your care I put those animals which divideth the hoof and cheweth the cud. Ham shall tend the camels, hares, the swine and giraffes. Japheth the tigers, the lions, the cats of all kinds.' While these categorisations begin as if following Leviticus, as Noah goes on they swerve away from their source, refusing the divisions of clean and unclean so that the Levitican categories which anthropomorphically impose pure and impure on the natural world are turned into neutral taxonomies in no way based on the animal as object of exploitation (food or sacrifice).

As these examples indicate, the range of such allusions over many texts is too various to systematise, but there are two sets of consistent contemporary parallels. Firstly there is the doubleness by which the enemies of the Israelites (and Christians, both of course equated with America) are imaged in the forms of totalitarianism. By the 1950s the parallel is always with communist regimes, though such images accrete the more typically fascistic traits of the brutal aestheticisation of politics. De Mille's prologues to *Samson and Delilah* and *The Ten Commandments* clearly articulate the allegory of America: Democracy; Russia: Slavery, for all that the enemy is never named. This, the most constant motif across the genre, disappears only in the 1980s where its polarities have begun to feel simplistic.

The Cold War motif spreads across the whole genre. Central, however, to the Old Testament sub-genre is the second parallelism, between ancient and modern Israels, though again largely in de-ethnicised terms, with questions of Jewishness secondary to the idea of the small quasi-Western democratic state surrounded by aggressive Arab absolutism. Just as the De Mille prologues invoke the Cold War, so *Solomon and Sheba*'s prologue voice reminds us that 'This is the borderland that lies between the countries of Egypt and Israel. As it is today, so it was a thousand years before the birth of Jesus of Nazareth. Even then these boundaries were kept ablaze with the fires of hatred and conflict.' Here not only does Sheba make alliances with Egypt but the Moabite King boasts that 'We will drive them into the sea', and Solomon extols his country to Sheba in words echoing Israeli propaganda: 'Can you believe that only four years ago all this was a barren desert? It is a joy to make the desert bloom by bringing water from the far mountains.' In *Sodom and Gomorrah* (1962) the Israelites are attacked by Arabs after their tribes conduct military exercises, enacting the fear of a united Arab assault on Israel. However, in the battle superior Israeli technology wins the day against greater numbers.

In *The Ten Commandments*, released in the year of Suez, the Egypt/Israel conflict cannot but insinuate meanings into the narrative. Conscious, though, of his internationalist role, De Mille avoids specific allusions to this area, preferring to invoke the grander clash of political–ethical systems. The only moment foregrounding Arabness is where Jethro, the Priest of Midian, explains to Moses that he is a Bedouin who through his descent from Ishmael worships the same God as the Hebrews. Marrying one of Jethro's daughters, Moses makes a treaty before the fact between the nations of the book, a mutuality to set alongside the Israeli(te)/Egyptian conflict. By contrast the larger thematic of the great competing systems is massively given throughout the narrative. The presence of blacks in the film (for instance the King of Ethiopia; Bithia's Nubians), while alluding to racial questions in America, also signifies America's concern about the Third World beginning to fall under Soviet influence. In the Statue of Liberty allusion at the end of the film where Moses stands holding the torch of freedom, his rhetoric looks forward to the triumph of democracy, expressed not so much in the maternal, intaking words on the original statue ('Give me your tired, your poor . . .' etc.) as in the expansionist direction of 'Proclaim Liberty throughout all the lands! Unto all the inhabitants thereof.'

American matters: slavery and pastoral

Among the sub-genre's ancient/modern parallelisms two further sets predominate, idealistically linking Israel with America as in King David's federalistic, melting-pot deathbed speech in *Solomon and Sheba* where the King insists on a 'union' of the tribes 'welded together in an indestructible oneness'. The first equivalence sees two God-inspired democratic nations fighting to free the world from slavery. The second parallels two 'chosen' people formed out of the frontier, both loking nostalgically back to those origins from present urban corruptions. *the chain gang, moses (Andy?)*

The motif of slavery reappears obsessively through the 1950s, only dying away in the Beresford and De Bosio films of the 1980s where it begins to feel irrelevant. Although it cannot but form part of the subject matter of *Moses*, a non-Hollywood film but locating many of its meanings in relation to Hollywood, there is a moment where traditional meanings threaten to break down.

> *Moses*: You cannot maintain order on . . . on slavery.
> *Pharaoh*: What slavery? *Any* slavery? Or the slavery of your people? Will you not have your highest and your lowest when you shape your dream Kingdom? Will you not build your own pyramids?
> *Moses*: We will build a covenant, a bond freely embraced between man and man.

This exchange ends with Moses' affirmation temporarily stemming the critique, but the polar oppositions are being dismantled as the Cold War draws on to an end. The Cold War is the key to the motif's intense recycling into the 1960s, with 'slavery' shorthand for the whole nexus of autocracy, atheism, state control and social programming seen as the communist alternative to American democracy. In reality there are two complicating factors, the first unacknowledged, the second given cryptic recognition. The first is that while it is symbolically necessary to present Israel as a slaveless society, in fact the law in Exodus legislates on slaves. However, since this would be known to few watchers, the opposite is constantly asserted. The second is not just that America itself had a history of slavery, though it could point with pride to its abolition as well, but that from the mid-1950s on there was widespread consciousness of black unrest and increasing liberal guilt at the existence of a black underclass.

Whereas foreign rulers are associated with slavery, even the kings of Israel are paradoxically identified with democracy. So when Sheba's lieutenant, Baltar, tells her of the threat that Solomon poses with his idea of 'one God that teaches that all men are equal and none are slaves', Sheba at first says 'What a foolish idea', but then muses 'And yet if that idea were to take hold of the people, the Queen of Sheba would soon come crashing down from my throne', to which her aide adds grimly, 'As would all other absolute monarchs! In *Sodom and Gomorrah* the narrative hinges on questions of slavery from the beginning where Lot is shocked by the Queen's body slave's defence of her bondage, which in Sodom seems not just an external tyranny but an internalised psychic desire, involving, beyond the owner's sadism, the slave's masochism. Thereafter the narrative dilemma is what the democratic Israelites in Sodom will do as regards the Sodomite slaves, with Lot, growing more conservative, arguing that they cannot encourage revolt, while Ishmael claims it is their duty. Here, even in an international co-production, specifically American themes are still readable, reflecting dilemmas attached to America's exporting of democracy to the Third World, particularly the compromises imposed by two realities, the need to make alliances with unpopular anti-democratic governments in the longer strategic interest (Lot's hope that the Hebrews will convert the Sodomites by example), and the bewildering fact that many of the Sodomites do not want to be freed (the unpalatable reality of anti-Americanism in the underdeveloped world).

The dilemma of Lot and the Israelites also brings into view a heightened instance of the second motif. The Hebrews, a virtuous agrarian people, have to take refuge in the corrupt world of Sodom. This movement refracts the Israelite and American experience of pastoral origins, of the fall into urban civilisation, and then a complex nostalgia for the lost pastoral. When Lot enters the city, he justifies it with an optimistic (Bedford Falls) vision of innocent smalltown capitalism: 'We'll open up shop. Give honest weight. Fair measure. The Sodomite tyranny is ended.' But once inside the city (Pottersville) even Lot becomes corrupted, refusing to listen to his people because he is dining, surrounded by luxury, in his Assyrian art deco showpiece house. *Sodom and Gomorrah*, a late film in the sub-genre, creates an unstable tone the nearest thing to the 1960s and 1970s parody elements in many other genres. One element on the brink of over-definition is the conceit of the Hebrews' weaponry which almost completely consists of staves, other agricultural implements and shepherds' crooks, one of the latter being the weapon with which Lot duels to the death with the Queen's brother.

In De Mille's second *The Ten Commandments* both themes are fore-grounded. In Moses' conversion to Israel's God the politics of freedom versus slavery always predominate, a priority De Mille himself establishes in his prologue by defining the film's subject as 'the birth of Freedom, the birth of Moses' (in that order). His journey to belief is presented through his identification with the enslaved proto-democrats, not vice versa. And as they flood out of Egypt in the Exodus sequence, the Israelites are shown in images underlined by the commentary as virtuous free-enterprisers: 'And there went forth among them planters of vineyards and sowers of seed, each hoping to sit under his own vine and fig tree.' If the shade of what is enacted in *Sodom and Gomorrah* always troubles the celebration of pastoral, perhaps this is why the narrative ends before Moses' death and the entry into Canaan. Because of this the Israelites are never seen progressing/regressing back into the corruptions of urbanisation. Connotatively, if not literally, they remain at the end of the film in the uncorrupted (yet to be corrupted) desert pastoral.

The battle of the gods

His God? We have a hundred Gods! — Sheba in *Solomon and Sheba*

Throughout the sub-genre Jehovah's superiority over the Gods of Israel's enemies is absolute. If cruel and arbitrary, he is at least monotheistic and not an animal, and embryonically the God of the New Testament. Though hardly a democrat himself, he is, paradoxically, identified with demo-cracy, for the eternal lesson of history seems to be that without him men fall into superstition, totalitarianism and slavery.

Just as the true God speaks at key moments of the films, so there are scenes where the false Gods are shown – the Egyptian deities in *The Ten Commandments*, the veiled Astarte and Baal in *The Prodigal*, the Sheban gods in *Solomon and Sheba*, the Philistines' Dagon in *Samson and Delilah*, and the golden calf in the versions of the Exodus. But whereas Jehovah is 'invisible' (the pure word predominating over the impure image), they are objectified in statues that manifest lower forms and perverse principles. Thus Dagon bestrides his theatre in a shape that combines the Assyrian despot with the horrors of Moloch, and Ragon is a gross figure whose face, exuding sexuality, seems interstitially composed of man, monkey and goat. Where in *Sodom and Gomorrah* gods rival Jehovah in immateriality, they are the perverse counter-principles of *Thanatos* and (Sadean) Pleasure.

For Freud in *Moses and Monotheism* the idea of the immaterial God is a great human intellectual advance: 'For it meant that a sensory perception was given second place to what may be called an abstract ideal – a triumph of intellectuality over sensuality or, strictly speaking, an instinctual renunciation, with all of its necessary psychological consequences.' On the other hand, like the Israelites themselves in the various golden calf scenes, the films dramatise protests at the instinctual losses such gains entail. Sheba mocks the idea of an invisible God as she arrives in Jerusalem ('All this for a God they cannot even see!') And in another form she expresses the loss in her address to the concrete divinities of Nature, 'Kol, God of the Sun and Stars! . . . Rama, who sends the rain!'

Though the two later, quasi-deconstructive films, *Moses* and *King David*, criticise aspects of the affirmed God, like earlier films they stop short of presenting other religions as systems capable of explaining the world and of elevating their believers. The second *The Ten Commandments* is typical when Rameses and Nefertiri denounce the god who cannot revive their son as just a stone figure with a bird's head. Yet a convincing explanation for the animal aspect of Egyptian deities is that unvarying animal forms represented changelessness to the Egyptian mind. And there is absolutely no suggestion here or anywhere of the sophisticated cosmogony of a great religion where every morning 'the solar God repels the serpent Apophis without being able to destroy him', and in which the Osiris resurrection myth enters the same general terrain as the Judaeo-Christian. These simplifications are transparently purposive, for to present religious or political systems as in any way relative would be to dismantle the film's governing oppositions.

Patterns of scepticism

I think your Moses shall have been a fool. — The King in *The King and I*

Nevertheless patterns of scepticism cross the genre, varied in each sub-type (for example lower-keyed, for obvious reasons, in the Christ film). Two kinds may be distinguished: (i) narrativised resistance by sceptical characters to the 'truths' asserted in the narratives, typically rebuked as when Rameses in *The Ten Commandments* (1956) admits that '*His* God *is* God'); (ii) uncontradicted subversive material existing as an (unconscious) expression of doubt within affirmation. Two other moments from *The Ten Commandments* illustrate this. Firstly, the film never resolves the problem of the Egyptian magicians' ability to duplicate Moses' miracle of turning his staff into a snake. Though Jehovah's powers are demonstrated when Moses' serpent devours the others, the question still remains. Secondly, amidst all the affirmations of the divine there are repeated traces, both aural (reference to Mount Horeb's groanings) and visual (Mount Sinai's fiery expressionist redness) of the sceptical reduction of Jehovah's origins to a volcano god.

Scepticism in the Old Testament Epic presents less of a problem than in the other sub-types. Firstly, because the Old Testament divinity will not be wholly identified with Christianity's God, so that his sometimes terrible actions can be interpreted as the 'through a glass darkly' vision of a primitive stage of religious consciousnesses. Secondly, because much Old Testament 'history' can be interpreted mythically by any but absolute fundamentalists (Christian or Jewish). Consequently sceptical sub-texts can exist more freely in the Old Testament epic. We might, for instance, feel that Huston's *The Bible* is a myths-of-origins film addressed as much to the non-believer as to the believer, if not more, but that the critical, potentially anti-religious force of George C. Scott's 'psychopathic' portrait of Abraham can be relatively easily deflected by believers, for the reasons given above.

Nevertheless, where scepticism is attached to a character, almost without exception it is bound in with undesirable traits which give it a negative moral rather than purely intellectual meaning. Thus the Queen (Anouk Aimée) in *Sodom and Gomorrah* makes disturbingly subversive remarks, but they come from a sadistic lesbian whose rationalistic interpretations of God's wrath prove wholly mistaken. The old Pharaoh (Sir Cedric Hardwicke) in *The Ten Commandments* (1956), that rare exception, a humanely likeable atheist, calls a priest an 'old windbag' on his deathbed, but his comments can be interpreted as truthful about the Egyptian gods, inapplicable to Jehovah. Lot's wife (Pier Angeli) in *Sodom and Gomorrah* is the most complex of these characters, tragically torn between Sodom (the empire of the senses) and the Hebrews (of the superego). Her metamorphosis into the pillar of salt is the consequence of her inability psychically to leave Sodom, interpretable morally as disobedience, but psychically as a response to the pull of the instinctual, albeit an instinctual where the perverse reigns.

It is only in the late films *Moses* and *King David* that patterns of critique outside of the depraved utterer/depraved utterance syndrome exist (though *David and Bathsheba* (1951) prefigures this in interesting ways). The urbane Philistine King's critique of the madness of religion in *King David* (1985) is an example of this, and Dathan's attacks on Moses' theocracy in *Moses* are much more coherent than the earlier's wholly self-interested complaints. Even more significantly, scepticism is no longer wholly externalised on to an 'other' but becomes internalised, part of a more introspective culture hero's psyche. Thus in the late David film (again prefigured in *David and Bathsheba*) the King's search for a more tolerant religion derives from scepticism about his own religious institutions, while in *Moses* the negative consequences of Moses' innovations (savage punishments, the enforcing of ideological correctness even in a children's puppet show) eventually impinge on the hero's tortured consciousness. In De Mille, as in Exodus itself, Moses' doubts are only of his abilities. But in De Bosio Moses is conceived in the light of *Civilization and its Discontents*. But even here, where scepticism is deeply marked, it stops short of ultimate deconstruction. This is clear in the miracles, some presented as purely natural occurrences (the newsreel film of natural disasters), some as happy accidents (the manna, the quail) and some as unresolved ambiguities (the staff becoming a snake and Moses' hand turning leprous being shown only from Moses' point of view). On the other hand there are elements within the turning of the Nile to blood and the crossing of the Red Sea that retain inexplicable, supernatural qualities.

Within both of De Mille's versions of *The Ten Commandments* few such ambiguities attend the miracles. As we would expect, scepticism and rationalism are attached to wicked oppositional figures, Rameses and Nefertiri, and the minor figures of Barak and Dathan. The effects are less predictable where with Nefertiri and Rameses they are attached to characters whose wickedness stirs both conscious and unconscious admiration.

SPECTACLE

> Boy, that movie is four hours long!
> — Teri Garr (on *The Ten Commandments*) in *Close Encounters of the Third Kind*

Lost horizons

For most contemporary viewers the true dimensions of biblical epics are lost, since their experience of the films will have been not through the overpowering formats for which they were designed but through the miniaturised framings of television. Spielberg's housewife, thirty-something in 1977, would have experienced the film on the big screen as a teenager, but for her children the small screen reality is the only one. Here the cycloramic splendours with their accompanying sound systems shrink to pigmy scale, aurally as well as visually (*Samson and Delilah* claimed the first use of a magnetically recorded soundtrack, sonically enhancing moments like the destruction of the Theatre of Dagon). Relayed on television, such films may not even retain a miniaturised replica of their original shape, since an image too large for the small screen requires 'scanning'. But short of catching a theatrical revival of the second *The Ten Commandments* or *Ben-Hur*, we are stuck with the miniaturised second best. Releases of 'letter-box' videos may become more common along with big screen television and video projectors, but the image will still be drastically shrunken. However, once the liabilities that spectacle labours under in these conditions are noted, it is pointless to prolong the mourning. Audiences can view the films only in the formats available to them, and if the life of the film is then a diminished one, it is still a life.

Nabonidus's brick: epic realism/epic expressionism

At one point in the Babylonian section of *Intolerance* (1916), Belshazzar's ancient father, Nabonidus, appears at court to announce good news. The intertitle reads: 'Belshazzar's father has a red-letter day. He excavates a foundation brick of the Temple of Naram-Sin, builded 2,300 years before.' This can be read as a statement of the burgeoning ancient world epic's archaeological interests, its powerful (if limited) commitment to (at least external) historical authenticity, with the royal amateur first watched by a film audience whose knowledge of the ancient world was primarily constituted through the way those categories of history analysed by Nietzsche, the 'monumental', the 'antiquarian' and the 'ethical', interpreted the great mid-century archaeological discoveries at Nineveh, Mycenae, Nimrud, etc. Michael R. Booth, discussing Victorian stage spectacle, has pointed to the grandeur of Victorian public buildings as another factor bound in with contemporary aesthetic taste for spectacle. With specific regard to early cinema epics, that quintessentially American contribution to urban architecture, the skyscraper, may also be linked to the celebration of the spectacular. One shot in *Intolerance*, where Belshazzar and the Princess Beloved look down from the palace-top over Babylon, presents a view analogous to vistas now possible in American cities from buildings like New

York's Woolworth Tower, completed two years before *Intolerance*.

The drive to documentary accuracy highlighted at moments in *The Birth of a Nation* (1915) may, when dealing with the minutely recorded data of modern history, apply itself to the mundane, as suggested by the intertitle pointing to the site of Lincoln's assassination: 'An historical facsimile of Ford's Theatre on that night, exact in size and detail, with the recorded incident after Nicolay and Hay in "Lincoln, A History" .' But the combination of lack of documentation, and the desire to see ancient history as a Salammbô-esque realm of the extravagant, leads to a quite different emphasis, as in a typical intertitle from *Intolerance*: 'Replica of Babylon's encircling walls, 300 ft in height and broad enough for the passing of a chariot.' Here the documentary drive is wholly turned towards spectacle, used to justify a historical fantasy in the claim made by another intertitle that 'In this last act the events portrayed in Babylon are according to the recently excavated cylinders of Nabonidus and Cyrus, that relate Babylon's betrayal by the priests'. This, which in reality consists of nothing but Cyrus's historical but entirely unsubstantiated claim that the priests welcomed him, becomes the basis for the film's extraordinary invention of the rivalry between the priests of Bel-Marduk and Ishtar (representatives of a competing 'masculine' and 'feminine' unalloyed by any ethical term). But it is an invention few would wish to lose, so vital is it to the narrative's most intense concerns. That what might be called the Nabonidus Impulse is felt to be vitally important in the Biblical Epic is illustrated by De Mille's licensing Henry S. Noerdlinger's book based on research done for the 1956 *The Ten Commandments*, and by publicity for *The Last Temptation of Christ* drawing attention to the film's utilisation of recent knowledge about methods of crucifixion. But this epic realism is always twinned with another mode based on artistic models, often themselves deriving from archaeological reconstructions but transcending them in their epic expressionism's insistence that to resurrect archaeology is the necessary but not sufficient cause of the genre.

Exodus and Red Sea

A comparison of two sequences in the second *The Ten Commandments* illustrates this double principle. The Exodus itself (the 'cast of thousands' opportunity par excellence) is shaped by the mode of epic realism with the camera staying close to the seething mass of Israelites, without ever suggesting unstructured chaos. Though the commentator (De Mille himself) suggests an initial disorder when he asserts 'it is Joshua who brings order out of chaos', this strategic rhetoric is deceptive, the whole sequence being controlled not just by the triumphal commentary and music but by the ordering pattern of camera movements enacting the sequence's vital ideological design. As it picks out, follows and returns to individuals from the mass, we seem to witness the superiority of the typically conflated Judaeo-Christian and American democratic revolutions over other revolutions, a political-ethical superiority enacted in its refusal to abstract a concept of 'the people' outside of the individuals who constitute them – the little girl who has lost her doll, the blind grandfather refusing the spoils of the miniature golden calf, the dying old man whose fig tree Bithia tells him will be planted in the new land, even the obdurate donkey who will not move on the days of days, and the roguish camel chewing an irate Hebrew's grapes. Even the herds of the Hebrews are made up of individuals as anti-authoritarian as their masters, whose dual sanction is their status as simple entrepreneurs of idyllic, uncorrupted capitalism and as the children of God.

Avoiding any sense of disorder by its organisation at every level, so that the movement is not to be confused with later, more chaotic, less providential movements of the masses, one of the sequence's structuring oppositions is the antithesis between the vast Egyptian architecture of state constantly present in the background and the human masses oppressed by it. The initial hierarchy is immediately overturned at the sequence's beginning when Joshua and other Hebrews clamber over this architecture to trumpet the release. The sequence equally avoids the temptation of imposing numerous abstracting shots of the masses' movements. Only once does De Mille allow a huge aerial shot presenting the progress down the Avenue of the Sphinxes as the geometry of history, a restraint that suggests he links such rhetoric with the authoritarian rather than the democratic–monumental.

On the other hand, the Red Sea sequence belongs predominantly to the mode of epic expressionism. If we can get behind the fetish of the famous 'special effect' to matters of affect, the sequence is the culmination of a process gathering force from Moses' return to Egypt halfway through the film, in particular the way that, as the plagues strike, the colours in Rameses's palace become increasingly expressionistic, dominated by blacks and brooding reds, blues and purples, making the dissolve from that scene to the fauvist reds and greens of the studio-created Mount Sinai part of a more than mimetic logic. The green smear in the night sky, turning into a kind of talon, and then into the mist stalking the city's firstborn, attacks Rameses's followers in a rooftop tableau that De Mille quotes from a favourite painter, John Martin (*The Plague of Egypt*) whose *The Destruction of the Egyptians* is also inscribed in the Red Sea sequence in the way Moses and the Hebrews are positioned on a promontory jutting over the sea as they face the Egyptians. The sequence's climax, the towering of the waters above the Hebrews crossing the seabed, is also conceived within a visionary-painterly mode in which the obvious back projection is less a failure of realism than a marker of artifice. As such the scene passes beyond the realm where special effects are made obsolete by newer technologies, precisely because its effects are mediated through images of images: for instance Heston's Michelangelo-derived Moses outlined against the hyper-baroque of the swirling stormclouds. Such attention to visual sources collapses any rigid opposition between the monumental realism of the first and the art-inspired expressionism of the second, since though the visual art origins of the first are less dramatically obvious, they are none the less powerful, much of the early section of the film owing to a painting like Sir Edward John Poynter's *Israel in Egypt* (1867), which has been properly seen as a source of the Hollywood epic's pictorial style.

Both scenes are 'spectacles' in the most obvious sense, involving large masses of characters and huge events. But Deleuze directs attention to a diffusion of spectacle throughout epics when he notes a simultaneous expansion and contraction into 'the means of action and intimate custom, vast tapestries, clothes, finery, weapons or tools, private objects'. Specifically he draws attention to scenes in which 'The fabrics become a fundamental element of the historical film, especially with the colour image, as in *Samson and Delilah* where the display of cloth by the merchants and Samson's theft of the thirty tunics constitute the two peaks of colour'. Of course similar display is a constituent of other genres, but without the complex duality of celebration of the past's barbaric richness and the contrary severity of a moral perspective that always haunts the display: an implication caught in the moment in *Cleopatra* (1963) where the dazzling arrival of Antony's and Cleopatra's fleets at Tarsus is briefly surveyed by sternfaced Israelite patriarchs.

The roughest taxonomy of the sub-genre's dissemination of spectacle must include the following, many of them with slightly differently inflected parallels in the Roman sub-genre, though fewer in the Christ film where spectacle is more restrained and dominated by pathos:

(i) The spectacle of *architecture*, usually bearing negative moral connotations, for example the Theatre of Dagon in *Samson and Delilah*, or the slaves lining the stairway of the Tower of Babel in *The Bible*

(ii) *Geographic* and *cosmic* spectacle, for instance the Creation in *The Bible*, the vast deserts in *The Ten Commandments* and *Solomon and Sheba*

(iii) The spectacle of *the body*, often in the sub-genre taking on what are seen as more primitive, less culturally assuaged forms of absolute maleness and femaleness, culminating in

(iv) the spectacle of *the orgy* (see below)

(v) the spectacle of *presentations, ceremonies, gift-givings*, invoking the unstinting wealth of the ancient world, for instance the gifts of Ethiopia in the second *The Ten Commandments*

(vi) the spectacle of *costumes, fabrics, jewels, ornaments*

(vii) more darkly, the spectacle of *Forbidden gods, rituals and religions*, for instance Ragon in *Solomon and Sheba*, Kemosh in *Ruth*

(viii) the spectacle of *ancient warfare*

(ix) the ubiquitous spectacle of *slavery*

(x) the associated spectacles of *sadism, masochism, torture, punishment*, for instance the Theatre of Dagon sequence in *Samson and Delilah*, the sadistic entertainments of *Sodom and Gomorrah*; and

(xi) the spectacle of *the act of God*, that is, manifestations both aural and visual of God himself, for instance the Burning Bush in De Mille's second *The Ten Commandments*; the presentation of miracle, less constrained than in the other sub-types as is the punitive, destructive act, the fantasy of the defence of righteousness and the destruction of one's enemies, such as the collapsing of the Theatre of Dagon or the blasting of Sodom. That unconstrained amateur theorist of the Biblical Epic, Alex in *A Clockwork Orange*, sums up the difference of Old Testament spectacle in his words: 'I liked the parts where these old Yehudis tolchock each other and drink their Hebrew vino and getting onto their beds with their wives' hand maidens.'

Law and orgy

> Dances with movements of the breasts, excessive bodily movements while the feet remain stationary, the so-called 'belly dance' – these dances are immoral, obscene and hence altogether wrong. — *Motion Picture Production Code of 1930*

PAGAN LOVE SONGS

> 'I'll be calling you . . . ooo . . . ooo . . . ooo. — *Rose Marie* (1936, 1954)

Biblical film orgies offer Hollywood semi-respectable opportunities for flesh exposure in scenes justified historically and morally as images of decadence and corruption of the civilised law. Sometimes though, as in *Solomon and Sheba*, where the Sheban god of love Ragon's feast is sacrilegiously honoured, such scenes intuitively acknowledge the more profound features of orgy as sacred ritual.

Writing about orgy Mircea Eliade points to seven essential features:

(i) the paralleling through sexual release of the divine couples' mating

(ii) the dismantling of barriers between humans, society, nature and the divine

(iii) the restoration of wholeness

(iv) the regeneration of nature through rain, reflected in the fertilisation of the female by the male

(v) the affirmation of community

(vi) the renewal of self and the fusion of emotions, a state in which 'neither form nor law is observed', and

(vii) the re-entry into a primeval state of chaos.

As defined by Eliade, orgies often form an integral part of the structures of myth and ritual in primitive societies. But even if in Western industrialised cultures the life-affirming dimensions of orgy· are lost beneath condemnation of uncivilised modes of behaviour, or conversely an emphasis on nothing but sexuality, in the orgy scenes of all but the most trivial films there is potentially a momentum that disrupts such attitudes. In Buñuel's *Viridiana*, for instance, the orgy scene becomes a subversive explosion, a grotesque 'return of the repressed' as the beggars' take-over of their masters' dining room develops into a frenzy of outrage, culminating in the parody of the Last Supper. Made suddenly aware of the material luxuries denied them, the beggars rebel against both their earthly masters and the Christianity that has denied them even the random pleasures of the flesh. As they commit sacrilege against the Eucharist, dark instincts are unleashed to overthrow, however temporarily, what the film sees as the repressive values of the Christian order.

Less radical images of rebellion against the Judaeo-Christian law appear in other films using paler versions of orgy as temporary release before eventual safe return to the certainties of mainstream religion and morality. Here (with Joan Collins in *The Stud* for instance) orgy means little more than exploitation. But, more interestingly, even the film versions of *Rose Marie* (1936; 1954) capture some of the ritual significances defined by Eliade.

While it is the second version of *Rose Marie* (1954)with its craggy outdoor setting and flimsily-clad female dancer in the 'Totem Tom Tom' number that seems more directly to inspire the orgiastic mise-en-scène and choreography of *Solomon and Sheba*, it is in the first that other dimensions of orgiastic meaning are made plain. Thus there is the explanatory dialogue between Rose Marie and the Mountie waiting to see the natives go into their frenzied dance.

> *Mountie*: . . . Their Corn Festival.
> To show their appreciation for a good crop.

Rose Marie: Oh, like our Thanksgiving.
Mountie: Yes, but we thank only one God. They thank everybody
. . . the corn, the sun, the rain, the birds, their ancestors.

The religious dimension and its connection with sexuality, fertility and agricultural cycles is much in evidence. As the Indians begin their dervish-like ballet, the outdoor space is walled in by huge phallic totems, reaching stiffly up into the sky, connecting heaven and earth, sacred and profane. In the Old Testament Epics, ruled by a law of denial, orgies are less affirmations of the community's religion than a means of rebelling through other more orgiastic deities against the strict moral and social laws of Judaism. In *Sodom and Gomorrah*, for instance, the opening scenes challenge the norms of accepted sexual practice by highlighting the lesbianism that rather coyly stands in the film as a synecdoche for all homosexuality; and in *The Ten Commandments* the Jews construct a gilded calf in defiance of their law. *Solomon and Sheba*, like these and other films, includes a *de rigueur* orgy scene.

SOLOMON AND SHEBA PATRIARCHS AND MATRIARCHS

The scene of the great orgy of Ragon works in two ways: firstly, as affirmation of a culture contrasted with the more rhetorically approved Hebrew world; secondly, as an elaborate metaphor for the unconscious. Although the objections of the ascetic Hebrews make Solomon's permission for the feast seem reasonable, ultimately, as in other instances, the Hebrew world triumphs – the indulgences of repressed instinct legitimised only through recognition of their ultimate domination by chaos. Nevertheless the force of the orgy scene undermines confidence in the uncompromising restoration of the old order from which Solomon has been in flight.

The affront to Judaism in *Solomon and Sheba* is all the greater through the appropriation of the sacred ground on which, as embodiment of the patriarchal law, Solomon himself – until succumbing to Sheba's beauty – had struck up a covenant with Jehovah. Wherever she moves Sheba colonises her space, dominating her interlocutors, for instance in the pastoral scene with Solomon, where her positioning in the frame often prioritises her spatially. Equally, the sacred mise-en-scène becomes the ritualised space of the profane, the rocks transformed from Judaic icons of spiritual austerity into projections of sexual excess as the setting is invaded by a troupe of minimally-clothed athletic dancers, raising their arms to Ragon, prostrating themselves before Sheba, lifting her above their heads in sexual affirmation. At one point Sheba intones, 'Hear us, oh Ragon, God of Love, giver of life. Let thy spirit enter our bodies, endow our men with strength and vitality, and our women with endless fruitfulness.'

Eliade's scholarly categories are rephrased here in Sheba's act of worship: fusion between mortals and divinities, collective affirmation, unbounded sexual energy as prelude to natural renewal, regeneration and agricultural fruitfulness are all invoked here verbally before her dance. As the music begins, Sheba strips off a silver cloak to reveal a voluptuous body covered only by red pantaloons, gold brassière with each cup a mons veneris, gold belt fastened well down the abdomen to show off a bare midriff and naked navel, an eroticism further stressed through alluring styles of coiffure and cosmetic jewellery, especially her dangling ear-rings with their circular patterns suggesting orifices of desire.

Gina Lollobrigida's olive-complexioned, faintly gypsyish look of raven hair, almond-shaped dark eyes, slightly contemptuous retroussé nose and parted, swollen ruby lips are the perfect foil for the virginal, Law-approved Abishag (Marisa Pavan) in competing for Solomon's affections. Before being magnetically pulled into Sheba's space, Solomon remains in his palace, his will gradually eroded by the insistent rhythms of the orgiastic music. Unfailingly dressed in Hebrew homespun, her baleful looks the expression of sexual innocence, Abishag approaches Solomon in a doomed effort to make him resist Sheba's call to his buried self. Her unearthly form of womanhood fails to spark in Solomon the desires fuelled by her rival. As the virginal girl, cradled into her father's chest, stares up at him like a besotted infant, her attraction to him is unlibidinal, only to his embodiment of the Law. As she speaks, Solomon's eyes are fixed beyond the constraints of the frame and the Judaic law, on the imagined scenes of Sheba's orgy on the altar of Ragon. The pagan love song, or Indian love call of other films, with their displaced orgiastic meanings, here becomes a demand the King cannot resist.

The focus is double. Yielding to chaotic, self-destructive instincts, transgressing the laws of which he is the supreme representative, Solomon, like other heroes such as David and Samson, is a flawed individual who must undergo an ordeal that, in the triumph of spirit over desire, will act out the Old Testament hero's prefiguration of Christian standards of behaviour. For the patriarchal audience, American as well as Judaic, Sheba's rule and self-assertion is an anathema deserving exposure and humiliation.

However, for others less constrained, Solomon's seduction by Sheba portrays what might be called a pre-oedipal, pre-social set of (at least partly) recuperable possibilities. As Robert Lang notes, 'Sheban sexuality is necessary to lighten the dour face of Judaic law', So the orgy, ultimately symbolic of the female, of the return of the repressed, functions to accuse the

① Renounces "normal" heterosexuality
② Denies the "perverse" possibility of homosexuality.

69

sacrifices demanded by the ultra-patriarchal Law. Scenes of carnal excess, as here, open up an alternative, unconscious realm that is both an affront and a pre-civilised memory challenging the established order. In Slavslark via Andy's wife

Although both Sheba and Solomon ultimately suffer retribution, their transgression questions accepted modes. Ruled by a female principle, the embodied by the Queen herself (a queen, however, who worships a male sisters deity), Sheban culture is a pre-oedipal recalling of an at least partially pre-phallic law. Myths of matriarchy and Amazonism, as invoked by see feminists through writers like Bachofen and Briffault, illuminate the film as it explores the dialectic of mother-right associations with body and earth, and father-right identifications with the mind. Ultimately father-right, the phallus as patriarchal law, triumphs, for just as the Sheban male god Ragon signifies enduring masculine power, so the victory of Mosaic Law at the film's closure ensures that continuity of the status quo. But along the way, Solomon finds not only the woman who arouses his repressed sexuality in the austere moral confinements of Hebrew law but also a figurehead who goes halfway towards questioning the validity of the patriarchal law, asserting as far as possible a pre-oedipal, feminine principle. The film, as usual, has it both ways, satisfying the audience's desire for their union while simultaneously upholding the Law.

Solomon's law is a fusion of both the pre- and the post-Christian order. Sheba's orgiastic presence not only places it in often negative perspective but also addresses obliquely contemporary American sexual/political preoccupations concerning, especially, the access to women of various forms of power in the hotting-up battles on sexuality. Sheba repents, converts to Judaism, returns home to destroy matriarchy for the sake of patriarchy. But even if the closure is conservative, the film's middle, especially its spectacular orgy scene, suggests at the very least the opening-up of a repressed world of desire in which, as Eliade puts it, transgressions against form and law in a fusion of emotions lead to greater harmony between creature and creator, self and community, nature and nurture.

homosexual desire is 'brutalized' rapture in the film but has to be symbolically dealt with in a 'codified' way.

3

Henry King's *David and Bathsheba* (1951)

Moving from underlying structures to a detailed examination of a major example of the sub-genre, our choice of *David and Bathsheba* is determined by many considerations (for example the association of its director, Henry King, with religious themes; its use of Gregory Peck's aura of Protestant integrity), but chief among them its concentration on a figure almost as central to the Old Testament as Jesus is to the New.

No Old Testament epic lacks fascination, but *David and Bathsheba* more than most approaches its subject with a rare elegance, subduing spectacle to psychology. Even an extended analysis cannot hope to be comprehensive, but in concentrating both on wider, extrinsic contexts (what the director and stars bring to the film; the film's relations with non-biblical genres) and on narrower, intrinsic ones (the film's narrative structure, its thematics of Protestantism, adultery, etc.), we aim to explore the complexity of a thoughtful, unusually restrained, somewhat unclassically classic 1950s epic.

DIRECTED BY HENRY KING

The combination of a Methodist upbringing and a growing attraction to Catholicism left its mark on many areas of King's work. While some films, like *The Song of Bernadette*, tackle religion directly, others indirectly establish parallels between Old or New Testament texts and more contemporary issues and settings (for example David's mother in *Tol'able David* reading about David and Goliath to her son). Alternatively they may include religious characters, like Father Bartolomé in *Captain from Castile*, to trouble the conscience of the more worldly characters, or else adopt general standards of Judaeo-Christian values, even if sometimes their tensions and contradictions demand scrutiny and exposure. Signalling his concerns, King's films are liberally sprinkled, too, with biblically named characters, for example Esther and David in *Tol'able David*, Jesse in *Jesse James*, Jake in *The Sun also Rises*.

Both the religious or biblical films and those indirectly concerned with religion exhibit strikingly melodramatic features related to three areas of constant preoccupation: nationhood, family and identity.

Although several King films have exotic settings, they resemble others directly addressing questions about American nationhood where exoticism serves multiple purposes. The past is often in films like *Tol'able David* or *Wilson* a source of nostalgia, and, in certain circumstances, paralleling *David and Bathsheba*, of regeneration inspired by the sufferings of maturity. Yet, negatively, the past is often also a source of tyrannies. The films suggest that the inspired forms of American nationhood are forged out of the crucible of Old World corruption. As the greater excesses of the old Judaic Law in *David and Bathsheba* are highlighted partly to look ahead to the humane reforms of the New Testament, so among more secular films *Captain from Castile* epitomises the clash between Old World barbarities and more civilised New World alternatives.

Yet even in this film, religious themes predominate. Old World Christianity is corrupted by privilege and the administration of an order distanced from Christ's teachings, creating 'a kingdom within a kingdom'. The Inquisition exercises a stranglehold on ordinary people, who find release only in exile and the search for virgin territories in which to practise the teaching of the Gospels.

In films dealing specifically with North American history, the sense of good triumphing over evil in the land of opportunity continues to make itself felt, even if the New World seems to have found no way of keeping out some of the corruptions of the Old. Sometimes the triumph of the new order, as in *Margie*, resounds more emphatically, as America's blessings force themselves more consistently into view, yet at the darker end of the spectrum American values often fail citizens chasing after the Dream's goals only to find disaster their reward. So in *The Sun also Rises*, *The Snows of Kilimanjaro*, *Jesse James*, *The Gunfighter* and *Love is a Many-Splendoured Thing*, the main characters are compromised or even killed in ways suggesting sociological as well as psychological reason for failure.

Nevertheless, even in the darker films, a sense of endurance or understanding is rarely eclipsed by the poignancy of tragedy. In *Carousel*, Billy dies, but remains part of the family; in *Snows*, Harry may have lost Cynthia, but he has a nurturing Helen. Though these endings are not without their ironies, 'Christian' acceptance and calm understanding tend to prevail. We are not overwhelmed by a sense of waste, as at the end of some melodramas by King's great contemporaries. This pattern is clearly evident, too, in *David and Bathsheba*, where the estrangement from God and community, leading potentially to tragedy, is avoided through repentance.

The point is equally prominent in 'American' and 'non-American' films.

As Wilson celebrates the new's triumph over the old, establishing a political ideal, or 'covenant' (as he significantly puts it), so *David and Bathsheba* looks ahead to Christ's new order, David's reconciliation with God and community arising from the bending of the Mosaic Law which, in its application of mercy to the adulterous pair, at once recognises and seeks to eradicate barbarous idiosyncrasies. Wilson formulates sentiments implicit in *David and Bathsheba*:

> I believe . . . that democracy with all its faults and failures if properly guided and interpreted holds the future of the world. My great dream is that as the years go on the world will turn to America more and more for those moral inspirations which lie at the basis of all freedom . . . and that her flag is not only the flag of the many but the flag of humanity.

Films like *Wilson* eulogise American achievement, while others like *David and Bathsheba* use their exotic historical focus to highlight enduring difficulties. Naturally there is no democracy in *David and Bathsheba*, but the flag of courage, leadership and, above all, of humanity, as Lamar Trotti's *Wilson* script has it, is flown as an example to other traditions.

Like *David and Bathsheba*, *Wilson* balances its heroics of government leadership with melodramatic preoccupations with the vicissitudes of family life. King's families measure themselves either explicitly or implicitly against the standards of the Christian prototype, the Holy Family itself. Early in *The Song of Bernadette* Father Peyramale distributes pictures of the Holy Family, his gesture reinforcing a Christian ideal. But although King's fathers retain their patriarchal status, his films are too disturbed by the greater tyrannies of the Law not to allocate an equally significant role for mothers. As if inspired by Christianity's more concentrated efforts to feminise self and society, even films not directly concerned with religion seem inspired by the example of the Holy Family. Often the narrative prominence reserved for women characters, especially mothers, overshadows their imposed ideological conformism, such as when in *Wilson* female intervention in male lives is taken as a crucial element of their rescue from the grosser excesses of masculinity. In *The Song of Bernadette* the spiritual inspiration of the mother of Christ who appears to Bernadette in the grotto parallels and validates the resilience used to keep the family together by 'Maman'.

But elsewhere tensions between the drives of masculinity and the overprotective instincts of mothers for their sons surface, and nowhere more vividly than in *Tol'able David*, readable as a flashback film to the youth of the David character, seen largely in maturity and in a time-zone switch from the David and Bathsheba Old Testament narrative, at a moment when his manhood is held back by the mother. Moving in a contrary direction, *David and Bathsheba* exposes the ambivalent virtues of masculinity and the neuroses suffered by the male's traumatisation by the absent mother.

David and Bathsheba shows that maturity, the attainment of masculinity, has its drawbacks, that the patriarchal ideology David espouses as King of Israel is severely deficient in the checks and balances of the female voice. David's attraction to Bathsheba represents in part an attempt to recapture his lost childhood in his search for the mother.

But if King's women consistently provide civilising examples to the men, negatively, as in the case of Tol'able David's mother, this can lead to oedipal trauma and the stunting of normal emotional development in the male, or to the wife/mother's own self-sacrifice to her husband/son's career. At one level these films fail to challenge tradition by positioning them as women content to define themselves, beyond a flourish or two in the direction of self-fulfilment, through relationships with men. As Cyn – the pun in her name reaffirming the femme fatale aura of her roles in films like *The Killers* – Ava Gardner in *The Snows of Kilimanjaro* joins the International Brigade only in a desperate gesture to obliterate the memory of a love she had hoped would become the prelude to matrimonial conformity. Like Bathsheba, Cyn craves wifehood, while Gregory Peck's Harry, like so many other King heroes, is tortured by contradictory tendencies towards settling down and soul-searching independence. The Gunfighter, Harry, Pedro de Vargas, Jesse James, Stanley all belong to a 'lost generation': writers, hunters, tough guys, all restless, questing, even marginalised secular pilgrims, torn between a desire for romantic love leading to marriage and family normality and an unshakeable wander-lust, the desire (as *Tol'able David* makes particularly clear) to avoid any further retardment through domesticity of the liberating drives of the male.

This conflict lies at the heart of most King films. In *The Snows of Kilimanjaro* it takes the form of a riddle to be solved by the hero: what was a leopard, now a frozen corpse, seeking on the snowy slops of Kilimanjaro? The answer is always ambiguous, though from conventional male perspectives the life of solitude and danger has its own justifications.

Almost invariably in these films the male protagonist, realising he may have been pursuing the wrong quarry, returns to the wilderness, the edenic origins of his formation as a man, to work off the fat not only of the body but also of the soul. Even if, as in *Snows*, a hyena laughs by way of ironic commentary on Harry's desire to start again, the audience knows that the desire of the male to redirect himself is a worthy enough ideal, whatever its likely disappointments.

'I'm Harry Street and I'm lost' could stand, substituting his name for

Harry's, as a summary of David's state of mind in *David and Bathsheba*. The glories of heroic rulership have become tarnished as he attempts through Bathsheba to reclaim his finer instincts and past. In the world of matadors, boxers, gunslingers, newspapermen and epic rulers, killing often becomes second nature. In an extreme case, Jake's impotence in *The Sun also Rises*, King seemingly endorses the implication of Hemingway's novel that for other tendencies and instincts to find expression in the male an aggressive sexuality must sometimes be sacrificed. Yet, of course, for all but the most unregenerate manhaters impotence is not really the answer. Even so, at least its accidental occurrence – as a result of a First World War wound – gives Brett and Jake the chance to discover other aspects of their personalities, liberated from the overbearing urgency of sexual desire. In *David and Bathsheba* David's means of self-renewal dispenses with such drastic remedies, the accidental sighting of Bathsheba leading him away from the embattled, ultra-phallic self he had gradually become to a more authentic identity, restoring him, perhaps only temporarily, to his own community, destiny and God.

CRISS-CROSS: GENERIC INTERACTION IN AN OLD TESTAMENT NARRATIVE

The Biblical Epic's frequent allusions to other Hollywood genres generate both positive and negative effects. Positively, not only are the films deepened by such references but various modern parallelisms can be established. Negatively, sometimes these films are in danger of losing their historical and cultural distinctiveness, becoming just another species of exotic adventure story.

In fact *David and Bathsheba* is guided by sober considerations in its echoes of other genres which, in a film tracing the reflection of the modern world in the ancient are, while not flamboyant, often inventive and significant. The traces of three genres are visible: Film Noir, 1940s Melodrama (particularly the romantic 'Woman's Picture'), and the Western pastoral.

Echoes of film noir, especially films built around a crime caused by fatal sexual attraction, like *The Postman Always Rings Twice*, infiltrate as a fateful moral counterpoint to the narrative's struggle to soften its crime, as when Uriah is made crudely anti-feminist, and practically demands a suicide squad mission in battle, reminding us that the story is still a murder story with only the authority of the Bible allowing the lovers to live on in defiance of cinematic codes of morality, though not altogether happily (their firstborn dies, family dissension will continue). In *Postman* Cora and her unborn child die in the car crash, and Frank is executed.

In its process of dramatising their crime and then negotiating forgiveness for the lovers, *David and Bathsheba* enters the world of Film Noir not only in its plot (the husband's murder) but also through two specific allusions. The first concerns the couple's bitter quarrel before their wedding. The Bible simply notes that Bathsheba mourned her dead husband and was then sent for by David who made her his wife. In the film David brutally avoids telling Bathsheba they must temporarily part by making Abishai deliver the message. The couple only meet again when she is being dressed for the wedding, and the scene echoes the central trap of *Double Indemnity*, what Cain defines in the Preface to his source-novel as the 'love-rack', the binding together of the sexual criminals that ends in hate.

In the biblical film the guilty lovers' reunion lacks *Double Indemnity*'s excess, but their brief plummet to disillusionment is desolate before passing into reconciliation. Complaining of abandonment, she sarcastically calls him 'my lover' and he finds himself grimly arguing that they cannot abandon their marriage since their crimes have committed them to it. If the scene here both enacts and allows escape from internalised punishment, David's action at the end of apparently condemning himself to death by laying his unsanctified hands on the Ark invokes external justice, a kind of judicial self-execution, mirroring the state's justice in the crime film, above all of 'the Chair' in the lightning flashes that accompany what seems to be his last-second reliving of the early events of his life and the sudden momentary irruption of darkness (compare the sudden dimming of the prison lights as the switch is thrown as *Beyond a Reasonable Doubt* begins).

Allusions to the world of melodrama also infiltrate. Deletion of David's other wives from the narrative turns the film into a classic 1950s nuclear family romance, a situation in which the spurned wife and the more powerful of the sons defy their husband/father. But, additionally, crossed by traces of males-in-crisis melodramas, this film takes on the forms of the 'Woman's Picture'. This fragmentary heroine-centred sub-film – enough to make the title *David* and *Bathsheba* not merely formal – evokes intricately several constituents of the 'Woman's Picture'. Susan Hayward herself (Bathsheba) was later quoted as having asked why the film was not called *Bathsheba and David*. If at one level the question seems misguided, since Bathsheba appears only fleetingly in the greater saga of David to which the film frequently alludes, at another it does have a point: King's Bathsheba is complex enough to have prompted the remark.

The film's allusions to the 'Woman's Picture' include the woman's dream of acquiring power through marriage to a powerful male (father) figure also possessing refined 'female-world' qualities of sensitivity and aestheticism – David is a poet and musician as well as soldier; the threat of being relegated to secondariness (compare *Back Street*), avoided by Bathsheba on one level, but unavoidable on another – for example watching and hearing David reliving his tragic past on Mount Gilboa, his love for Jonathan inevitably overshadows her; escape from the world of patriarchal punishment, achieved when God lifts his curse at the end, but under which she has suffered in the death of her child (compare Mildred's daughter's death in *Mildred Pierce*).

Pastoral settings (Western and non-Western) are also common in King's films. Here Mount Gilboa's sparsely populated ruggedness and simplicity, open spaces, flowering cherries, characters like the oldtimer shepherd and youthful helper, all take positive meanings from analogy with the Western. As the site of David's youth it is the place of Israel's and America's youth as well. Around this time, though, when the myths of Hemingway and his heroes are especially potent, some films, moving to the harsher pastoral world of Africa, have heroes who no longer solve their problems in the vanishing American pastoral, confronting the meanings of their lives instead in the Kenyan or Tanganyikan wilds, in motions similar to David's return to Hebron.

Finally, *David and Bathsheba* echoes other elements of two of these films, both starring Gregory Peck, one directed by King, made just before and after *David and Bathsheba*. In *The Macomber Affair* Peck has an affair with Joan Bennett who accidentally shoots her boorish husband. Or was it an accident? At the unresolved ending Bennett like Bathsheba admits she may have wished her husband's death. Like *Macomber* and the penultimate sequence of the biblical film, *The Snows of Kilimanjaro* is a flashback film from the hero's perspective as, injured on safari, he revisits in fantasy the ruins of his life. More optimistically perhaps than in the source narrative, the plane's arrival at the end of the film suggests release as well as the hero's acceptance of his imperfect relationship with Margaret (again Susan Hayward), just as in *David* the rains signal forgiveness for the kingdom and a future for the lovers.

'TELL THE DOCTOR': GREGORY PECK AND KING DAVID

Of all the great Hollywood male stars Gregory Peck seems most to combine beauty and moral uprightness. His beauty is undisputed, but within it the sense of the overridingly ethical is deeply ingrained, so that for all his handsomeness there is little directly erotic about Peck. Except in the antic dance of his role in *Duel in the Sun*, one feels easy sex would be anathema to him. This sense of cautious principle often extends to a slowness about all intimacies. Even in a relaxed part, the newspaperman in *Roman Holiday*, his joking command to Audrey Hepburn, 'Make a wish. Tell the Doctor', playfully refers to the aura of bed-side-manner responsibility surrounding him.

Such connotations constantly point a moral through physique and physiognomy. Peck's tallness and leanness relate him to a pioneer ranginess declaring the absence of urban self-indulgence in a usually city-dwelling character. In *The Big Country*, though a Westerner, he retains his Easterner's uniform, the equivalent of his grey flannel city suits. Though 1950s films liked exposing the 'beefcake' torsos of their male stars, the Peck character resists such exhibitionism. So in *The Big Country* neither he nor Charlton Heston strips to the waist for their fist fight. This reticence produces an unlikely situation in the Riviera sequence of *The Snows of Kilimanjaro* where Hildegarde Neff swims around him in a skimpy bathing suit, while he lies implausibly fully clothed on the raft in the middle of the sea.

Peck's Lincolnesque face inspires political analogies. In *The Paradine Case* there are moments where the frame holds both Peck and Louis Jourdan in profile. The contrast with Jourdan's delicate features and air of sulky amorality underlines how stolidly ethical is Peck's handsomeness: luxuriant but ultra-controlled hair, eyebrows twin banks of rigour, cheekbones high and firm like an Aztec's, long and massive head. Here, his facial semiotics, softening occasionally (compare *Roman Holiday*), making him not impossible as a lover, only difficult to reach, are generally muted. Again, the connotations of such restraint are positive, the minimal lip-movement of his smiles, minor frowns, head bows and downward tugs at the corner of his mouth to denote crisis, suggesting a reassuring control and modesty. The scene in *The Paradine Case* where his wife informs him she knows he loves a client, and Peck is consequently in considerable but underplayed moral torment, is as good a display-case for these traits as any. The look is counterpointed by his vocal characteristics of deep bass voice inscribed with reticent authority and slightly fatherly, slightly pedantic enunciation. The extreme of these implications is that he should play a priest, as in *The Keys of the Kingdom*.

All these meanings inform the casting of Gregory Peck as King David. Handsome and heroic, considered a star projecting seriousness, he is also democratic, responsible and undemonstrative, qualities in accord with the David of King's film. If he is seldom really felt to be wholly eroticised, though the film hinges on his adultery, there are two necessary glosses on this. Firstly, King's film is more thoughtful than sensuous, anxious to relate David's desire for Bathsheba to further issues rather than glorify it in itself. Secondly, although an extreme case of playing against type, Peck's part as Lewt (Lewd?) McCanles in *Duel in the Sun*, with his cries of 'Yay-Bo!' and his singing refrain 'Gotta get me somebody to love', is, for all its unrepresentativeness, necessarily a heightening of sexuality latent in the image.

Less obvious are what David Thomson describes as those roles 'displaying subliminal hints of erosion on the face of Mount Rushmore', a subtext of dissonant strain contributing to the cross-filmic possibilities of his persona. If the total reversal of the usual characteristics for his role as Dr Mengele in *The Boys from Brazil* seems more a sport than anything else, a more significant late role is his American Ambassador in *The Omen*, caught up in a horror plot forcing him into actions parodying his benevolent paternalism, making him an unremitting Abraham set to sacrifice his anti-Isaac of a son, and being destroyed by him. Considering this role reminds one that Peck played Ahab in *Moby Dick*, a casting heightening into paranoia characteristics usually presented in positive terms: hints of rigour, authority, smouldering will to recititude, a catalogue of puritan virtues ossified into Ahab's Manichaean mania for domination and destruction. The process becomes sinisterly parodic in *Cape Fear* (1991) in his role as grotesquely black-eyebrowed and moustachioed, lily-white-haired evangelical lawyer.

These late extremes remind us that however much the narrative of *David and Bathsheba* attempts to soften the circumstances of the killing of Uriah, David is still a murderer as well as an adulterer, and that his portrayal must suggest the capacity to commit such an act. Hitchcock's use of Peck highlights the sense of difficulties and strains within decency, the incipient breakdown in a slightly more than conformist idealism, compromising his lawyer's calm and fidelity to his wife in *The Paradine Case*, making him in *Spellbound* a doctor of the mind himself an amnesiac, his unconscious haunted by repressed memories of his part in the death of his brother.

But Hitchcock's treatment is symptomatic rather than exceptional. In *The Great Sinner* the speed with which the Peck character surrenders so completely to the seductions of gambling cannot but be disturbing. In *The Macomber Affair*, though suspected (wrongly) of murdering Joan Bennett's husband, he has committed adultery. Here his image is subjected to enough degradation for the short story's constant epithet of (alcoholically) 'red faced' to be applied to him throughout. No such impropriety attends the journalist of *Gentleman's Agreement* who sets out to expose anti-Semitism by pretending that he, a WASP, is a Jew. But what becomes disturbing in his exposing of the covert prejudice in the ironically named New Canaan is its degradation of the hero's composure, a parallel revelation of his own, not prejudice, but propensity to disorder and even masochism. Here Peck's abbreviated facial kinesics are accompanied by a tendency to blink almost hyperactively to indicate neurotic turmoil. This is a mannerism reserved for modern roles, not carried over into period films like *David and Bathsheba* where, though, in one of several films made at this time by Peck in which his role concentrates on heroism past its prime (often seeming older than his 35 or so years), many of the modern motifs of his worried heroes find an ancient parallel.

THE DAVID NARRATIVE: SEARCHING FOR THE SELF

I still feel kind of temporary about myself. — Willy in *Death of a Salesman*

As Gabriel Josipovici argues, there is no single character, other than Jesus, to whom the Bible devotes as much space as David. And, as Robert Alter insists, the David of 1 and 2 Samuel is an extraordinarily various figure:

> David ... is first a provincial ingenu and public charmer, then a shrewd political manipulator and a tough guerilla leader, later a helpless father ... then a doddering old man bamboozled or at least dominated by Bathsheba and Nathan, and, in still another surprise on his very death bed, an implacable seeker of vengeance against the same Shimei whom he had forgiven after the defeat of Absolom's insurrection.

To which one might add so many other dimensions as to underline the seriousness of the joke in Joseph Heller's *God Knows*, of presenting David as a universal Everyman figure criticising Shakespeare, Michelangelo and Freud. So there is the male friend of Jonathan; the poet of the psalms; the inspirer of personal loyalty in an alien like Hai the Gittite; the complex lover and husband of Bathsheba and other women, and much more.

Any adaptation of the David character and his narrative has to pursue two divergent paths. On the one hand, the Books of Samuel narrative presents, unlike most other Old Testament sources, such an excess of incident that any modern version is forced to select and contract radically. On the other hand, since the incidents themselves are so abrupt, so committed to an extreme of contracted implication, any treatment centring on individual incidents demands expansion. *David and Bathsheba*, scripted by Philip Dunne, concentrates on the events signalled by its title, but through its end-of-narrative flashbacks, as well as through earlier allusions, provides a wider focus by referring to events lying outside the narrative frame. For all its focus on a single episode, the King/Dunne strategy is as far removed as possible in attitude from Dan Jacobson's, also treating a single incident in his novel *The Rape of Tamar*. For whereas the latter relentlessly marginalises and demythicises David, Dunne and King, like Beresford and his writers on *King David*, and like Heller, place him firmly at the centre, retaining along with that centrality many aspects of the heroic, although the films' stra-tegies are more conservative than Heller's comic conceit of placing David's voice outside of as well as inside history.

Nevertheless, though more implicitly, working within conventional narrative strategies, the film moves between historical and contemporary meanings. *David and Bathsheba*, relatively low-key, all but neglecting the expected spectacle of the genre, lays far less stress than usual on the exotica of the epic, making relationships with the present all the more prominent, creating a more pronounced feeling of doubleness even than usual. Here the historical David serves also as heightened metaphor for corporate executive man with his minor empires and conquests, anxieties and neuroses, as the spectre of non-authenticity begins to haunt the art of the time, with growing intellectual critique of an increasingly conformist late 1940s/1950s society, characterised by the decay of deep-seated religious belief and erosion of the ideals of solidarity and community of wartime existence.

Seen like this, the opening sequences of the film display a character whose almost every action suggests internal crisis. So, for instance, in the quarrel between David and his estranged wife Michal, her thrusts at the precarious political legitimacy of David's kingship turn into a deeper assault on David's self-image when Michal, after David has agreed her father 'was every inch a king', replies 'And his successor every inch a fraud'. Significantly, rather than disputing what she says, David agrees with her, his self-condemnation laden with a weighty introverted seriousness.

David's isolation not just from women but from other men in the all-male world in which he lives is noticeable. There are suggestive analogies between the executive's womanless world of male relationships wholly based on role, patronage and hierarchy, and the King's. In the palace only Abishai (James Robertson Justice) seems wholly trusted by him, but Abishai's role is always that of the faithful servant rather than friend, significantly transformed from the original narrative's younger nephew into – contrasting with Nathan, Saul and Jehovah – a powerless father-figure.

Read in relation to such questions, David's very first actions in the film become double-focused. His sortie with Uriah behind the Philistine lines is not presented solely in terms of military or reconnaissance value; rather, much of its meaning seems to reside in the significance David gives it when, noticing a slight wound, he remarks: 'It's a long time since I've shed any blood. It's good.' In other words, his rash commitment to the dangers of the skirmish is an attempt to restore lost vitality. The film's presentation of David's psychology derives much of its sense from the youthful contest with Goliath (whose mythic accretions he treats jokingly in the pastoral holiday with Bathsheba), the moment that returns to him in flashback at the end of the film. The only overt judgement made on David's brief active service by a character other than David himself is when Joab makes a sneeringly hierarchical remark about the King's 'crawling on his belly like a common soldier'. This – along with David's remark to Bathsheba that he refused the throne till all the Israelite princes had begged him – secures the idea of the autocrat as democrat, providing another of the bridges between past and present. In this way David's actions, consistent with his character, may simultaneously suggest a peacetime nostalgia for the meaningful action of war and corporate man's hankering after what he believes is the superior life of the frontier.

David is beset by failure and a sense of lost authenticity. Michal chastises him for his narcissism, playing on the etymology of his name when she accuses him with 'David meaning beloved. David the beloved of David'. But this is only part of the truth. The overactive conscience that makes him describe himself as having destroyed Jonathan may take forms where self is paramount (with Jonathan becoming less a person than alter ego, symbol of David's lost self), but the King's failures reach out to become Everyman's, as he searches for lost meanings, youth, desire, fathers, mothers, pastorals, all cohering in the master image of the search for the lost God of his youth.

A PROTESTANT'S PROGRESS

> We have contrasted the Church with the Soul. In the soul then let redemption
> be sought. — Emerson, *The Divinity School Address*

David's progress in *David and Bathsheba* is ultimately – irrespective of Henry King's own drift towards Catholicism – a Protestant progress in a sense transcending sectarian divisions, reflecting tendencies operating on the whole spectrum of American Judaeo-Christianity. The shape of American religious belief and practice, which cannot but be influenced by the ideology of individualism and self-assertion, irrespective of particular beliefs and practices, tends to the Protestant rather than the institutional pole. Among the paradoxes that this exhibits are a Catholicism or Reform Judaism that are 'Protestant' because displaying characteristics given pronounced form in the Protestant revolutions. An accompanying paradox is that this individualist Protestantism may be, in practice, deeply conformist.

David's struggle to recapture his boyhood's image of God and withstand the fanatical will of the prophet Nathan (Raymond Massey) is readable in several ways. Some of the minority Jewish audience might see it as a quest for a more enlightened vision of Judaism. Because, unlike the other subgenres, there is no overt Christian presence, this is possible. On the other hand, the film would be read by the Christian majority as David's assumption of a prefiguratively Christian function, his desire for change pointing forward to Jesus's transcending of the Law. This becomes most sharply focused when the guilty couple see the woman stoned to death for adultery. Here the Christian implication is that David's descendant will in the same situation intervene and create the revolution in morals. A further reading might lay less emphasis on David's search for a God defined as more personal and merciful, and more on David's scepticism about Nathan's reading the action of God into everything that happens, his attribution of Uzzah's collapse to natural causes, his statement 'We have had droughts before, Nathan', and sceptical remark 'we have no Joshuas among us to make the walls fall down'. David, more 1950s man than Israelite, seems to be trying to reconcile religion with science by making out different spheres for the operation of scientific laws and for God. The project is successful in its conceptualising a God not responsible for arbitrary tyrannies like Uzzah's death when he attempts to stop the sacred Ark falling, or decrees demanding death for adultery. But it cannot avoid inconsistency, for David seems to accept that he is being punished in the death of his child and the drought afflicting Israel, which a merciful God lifts at the end. The somewhat confused implication is that some acts belong to the world of cause and effect and that some are divinely-ordained, and that in the latter sphere harshness and mercy co-exist. Sometimes it almost seems that David has moved God, by his superior perception of him, to a phase of higher activity, a feeling that hovers between literal and metaphorical concepts of the deity. Though the 'Protestant' bias affects all forms of religion, this attempt to make an accommodation with science is very much more typical of mainstream Protestantism than mainstream Catholicism in the late 1940s and 1950s, with Pius XII's conservative papacy and its dogmas of papal infallibility and the assumption of the Virgin Mary.

For David to have this role, culminating in his refusal to obey Nathan over Bathsheba's trial, instead speaking to God at the Ark rather than his intermediary, it is necessary for one aspect of traditional interpretation of Judaism to be inverted. In Christian readings the Jewish prophetic tradition is highly valued as a kind of proto-Christian criticism of the legalism and orientation towards outward observance seen to characterise Rabbinic Judaism, a disturber of the 'routinisation of charisma' into which religion is overwhelmingly likely to descend. But in *David and Bathsheba* Nathan is the repository of a tradition viewed twice negatively as a combination of the legal-institutional and the militantly intolerant, both of which concepts of religion, as well as its absolute patriarchalism, David is presented as struggling to escape.

ADULTERY

The Old Testament's attitude to adultery as a transgressive act against natural, social and divine law is clearly expressed in Deuteronomy, 22. There are two cases of adultery in *David and Bathsheba*: in the first an unnamed woman character is stoned to death, the first stone cast by the betrayed wife, something witnessed by David and Bathsheba; in the second, the adultery committed by David and Bathsheba, once again the betrayed wife, but also in this case a son (Absalom), are willing to testify against the adulterers. In the first case there is no sign of the adulterer, while in the second he is prevented as God's anointed by the prophet Nathan from suffering his traditional fate. Whatever the justifications for the exclusion in this instance of the male from a barbaric form of justice, clearly a double standard operates, so that the women (emblems of male honour) are punished more than men. In *David and Bathsheba* adultery is not treated in isolation. Although of primary importance, it also allows, through the story of sexual desire, for exploration of the imbalances of social laws and their institutionalised structures.

Both parties are guilty, for we later learn that Bathsheba was aware of David's gazes at her, delighting in her specularisation by the male, though also herself appropriating the look and spying back at David. When we learn something of Uriah's attitude towards her and women generally, we realise why. Once Uriah's views are expressed, it is clear that the film will minimise moralistic condemnation of adultery, exploring instead some of its implications, the power structures of sexual relations and the lengths to which adulterers are prepared to go in risking their own lives.

The film's stress falls on the meanings of transgression, in a mode free of the more moralising tendencies of scripture, the sexual codes of which even in conservative 1950s American society no longer justify demands for retribution. The random impulses of sexual desire as a means of accounting for male attraction to attractive women are not ignored here, for the male protagonist has a historic reputation for sexual insatiability. But, given that Gregory Peck plays him, an interest purely in male libido pales beside a commitment to examining sexual desire and transgression. More than usually in films of this type, *David and Bathsheba* attempts to offer a double focus on such questions, looking through female as well as male per-spectives. Once again in a King film a hero's traumas are, implicitly, partially attributable to maternal loss or absence. For all his defences of the Law ('with our people the law is everything. It's in their bones', he reminds Absalom) David seems in this respect deprived, suffocated by an excess of maleness. His most faithful retainer is Abishai, his conscience and scourge God's prophet Nathan, his daily companions male attendants at court or soldiers, like Uriah, in the field of battle.

This all-male seclusion is stressed further in the film's altered emphasis from the opening description of the David and Bathsheba narrative in 2 Samuel, 11. There, David has not accompanied his men at the time when 'kings go forth to battle'. Instead, he is on the palace roof spying on Bathsheba. But in the film he is first seen heroically leading an expedi-tionary force in a skirmish with the enemy. This shift makes two important points. Firstly, David, his star of Israel proudly worn on the chest of his every garment, and no longer now the sign of shame of European ghettos and concentration camps, emerges as a heroic leader of Israel. Secondly, in keeping with the film's partially dehistoricised focus on marital and extra-marital relations, his first appearance, in a military rather than a sexual context, accentuates the feeling that his confinement to all-male activities is connected with his malaise and eventually his advances on Bathsheba. The narrative's partial dehistoricisation, traced with elements of an implicit rehistoricisation touching 1940s and 1950s realities in America, is achieved through the removal of all but Michal (Jayne Meadows) of David's wives and paramours, which makes her seem more like a single betrayed spouse than a chief wife among many. Equally, David's disaffected wife's relish in damaging him through the enforcement of a primitive law is re-readable for 1950s audiences as the modern woman's strict application of the retributive law not of stoning but of alimony.

David's motives in seducing Bathsheba cannot be to appropriate the status and attributes of the cuckolded husband. Since Uriah (Kieron Moore) is clearly inferior to David, the latter's interest in Bathsheba contradicts the patterns of homosocial bonding detected by writers who

have theorised adultery through the loyalties and rivalries of competing
males in the complex triangles of emotional involvement. For David,
Bathsheba represents desire, transgression and lost motherhood, not an
opportunity for bonding with Uriah. Susan Hayward's Bathsheba represents above all female beauty inflected by sexual experience, something that
works on David to compound a more comprehensive protest against the
Law that Nathan so pitilessly embodies. Viewing her from David's
voyeuristic perspective, Susan Hayward, nothing like Rembrandt's demure
nude, seems knowing, in her measured glances and controlled movements
projecting an image of self-conscious eroticism, aware of her effect on the
male. In the first shot of her inside David's private chamber, she is framed
with a bowl of fruit, a composition emphasising her identification with
appetite.

Twentieth Century Fox accentuated all the narcissistic decadence of
the Hayward persona in publicity for the film, special photo sessions
maximising the voyeuristic impact of the bath scene. Even though in the
film itself it lasts only a minute or so (and in long shot, with none of the
close-up exposure of the stills used for *Life*) the distant scene manages to
convey an ambience of voluptuousness, as Bathsheba languidly stretches
out her naked arms, and plays self-consciously with her tousled red hair.

In her transgression Bathsheba seems too self-absorbed to be troubled
by thoughts of potential retribution. De Rougemont has compellingly
argued that a Freudian death-wish lies at the heart of the motivation of
literary adulterers as, from Tristan and Iseult to Anna Karenina, they have
been prepared to sacrifice all for love. In this film, while Bathsheba is
prepared to risk stoning, David would go into exile with her to Egypt, the
equivalent in 1950s Old Testament films of Stalinist Siberia, asserting that
nothing would prevent him trying to save Bathsheba from the barbarity of
the Jewish law against adulterers. On this reading, acceptance of the
hazards and destructive transgressions of adultery amounts to acceptance of
self-annihilation, even of cravings for death. The lovers are clearly drawn to
each other sexually, but both are in conflict as much with the Law as with
their marital partners, both governed by a death-wish that is largely a social
protest, a desire to transgress against laws and individuals by whom they
have seemingly been deserted.

In the scene where he plays the harp for Bathsheba, reciting the 23rd
Psalm, attempting to recapture the memory of his closeness to God as a
shepherd boy living in harmony with nature, David acknowledges his
remoteness from God. If Nathan's moralistic inflexibility truly reflects
divine decree, and not some private or institutionalised neurosis, we hardly
wonder that David and God have drifted so far apart, David finding it

difficult to find God in the city, symbol of civilisation and, within the rhetoric of this film, both of secular duties (arbitration over ambitious wives or squabbling sons) and of an excessively demanding religion. But in the country, religion and natural laws seem to find a less difficult harmony. Although David discovers Bathsheba in the city, she represents his hope for a route back into the past, into a more primitive, more fulfilling relationship with God. In the palace his frustrations are given verbal expression in the characteristic rhetoric of the unhappily married man's definition of a wife's failure of understanding: 'I am only a man, Bathsheba. I need someone to understand that. I need the kind of understanding that only one human being can given to another. Having someone to share my heart.' The scene on the roof provides not only an opportunity for erotic gratification but also release from the suffocations of the palace. Like the rain symbolically purging the lovers of their sin at the end of the film, the cool night air temporarily soothes the cares of office, anticipating the more fulfilling embrace of nature in the pastoral scene of the lovers' idyll.

The country literally represents David's past: partly childlike and innocent (emphasised by the presence of the shepherd boy) it is also identified with experience, in that it is the setting both for the death of his beloved Jonathan, as well as of his surrogate father Saul himself, and a childhood apparently wholly bereft (since flashbacks to childhood show us Saul, Jesse and Jonathan, never his mother), of maternal influence. These issues raise two questions with wider relevance to the discussion of sexuality in most Hollywood films of the period: male friendships verging sometimes on homosexuality, and oedipal trauma.

The love that 'was wonderful, passing the love of woman' seems to be denied, on this occasion at least, especially since David is played by Gregory Peck, an actor never compromised by questions about wavering sexual orientation. Although the theme of David's friendship with Jonathan is important, its representation, though intense, is fragmentary (in the aurally remembered battle scene, one direct mention by David, and a sighting of him as a child in the Goliath flashback). Have difficult marital relations (if those with Michal are anything to go by) led to a perpetually doomed search for the kind of intimacy so highly prized in his friendship with Jonathan? And, in the wider context of the film's reflection of contemporary attitudes, are 1950s men – brought up either too close to women, whom they therefore flee, or too distanced, so that they view them with fear or awe – simply failing to see the 'otherness' of the women they marry through imposition upon them of familiar behavioural patterns characteristic of men? If *David and Bathsheba* only hints at such matters, it probes much more deeply into the oedipal causes of transgressive male behaviour.

Even if his claims to moral superiority over the kings of Egypt (that exiled sybarite, King Farouk of Egypt, was much featured in the yellow press of the early 1950s), in his refusal to impose his will on unwilling victims of his libido, seem plausible, David's attraction to Bathsheba includes both oedipal and neurotic tendencies in the complex mixture of responses triggered off by her beauty. Their relationship, especially in view of David's desire for the shepherd boy to watch their lovemaking, demands attention in the light of Freud's remarks about mother/whore fixations in the essay on a 'Special Type of Object Choice made by Men'. Here Freud considers the lover whose attraction to an object of desire entails injury to a third party. The objects of desire must be of ill repute, of dubious fidelity or reliability, someone to be rescued from adverse circumstances – usually an unhappy marriage – all feelings originating, according to Freud, in 'infantile fixation of tender feelings on the mother' which 'represent one of the consequences of that fixation'. The transference by the adult would-be lover of oedipal neuroses on to the desired woman and her husband results in the reactivation of longings for the mother, and of punishment of the father. On this reading David is, as well as universal/Protestant Everyman, the neurotic Jewish son, the 'nachas'-troubled little boy eternally attempting to please his parents (biological or divine), but endlessly also trying to destroy them to achieve liberation and independence. Estrangement from God therefore may also include besides theological disaffection transferred psychological rebellion, even if we see nothing of David's relations with Jesse, against his real father.

Both of the conditions described by Freud are met by Susan Hayward's Bathsheba. Firstly, an aura of debasement is suggested by her knowing sexual self-consciousness; secondly, she desires release from marital entrapment to a man epitomising the inflexibility of the law of the father, not literally David's father Jesse but the symbolic father, the bearer of the phallus. In hurting Uriah, David strikes at the embodiment of a law he has begun to find too severe and inhuman. 'Is that manhood?' he asks when in discussing Uriah with Bathsheba he remarks contemptuously that the former has found only six days in seven months for his wife. In Bathsheba David seems to be looking for a feminine, maternal principle buried beneath the patriarchal realities of Israel. Bathsheba herself acts complicitly towards this end.

In the scene where they escape to the country, she asks David to describe his boyhood. As the solicited memories transport him back into childhood, making the man become the child again, she herself, not paralleling his inner journey by regression to her own childhood, becomes a mother surrogate. The lost lamb looking for its trapped mother that both

David and Bathsheba watch acts as a symbolic focus for David's transference of oedipal fixations on to Bathsheba.

Bathsheba is also in flight from the restrictive constraints of the law of
the father, in this case from marriage to a man to whom women's feelings
are unimportant. Even before David becomes aware of Bathsheba's beauty,
Uriah is close to the King, through such contact identifying himself with
authority and tradition, epitomising the dehumanised inflexibility of the
zealot: 'You will serve me better if you live, Uriah.' That comment predates
David's infatuation with Bathsheba, but it prepares the ground for a view of
Uriah as a highly principled man, upright to the point of mechanisation,
blind to the realities of human needs. There is no hint here of Uriah's
possible awareness of Bathsheba's adultery with the King. His refusal to
visit his wife's bed is motivated by his manly code of purity and solidarity
with his fellow soldiers, not sexual fastidiousness in relation to sleeping with
an adulterous wife. Nor is there any suggestion that Uriah is prompted by
homosexual desire. His incapacity for love, revealed in conversation with
David, is partly responsible for driving his wife into another man's arms:

> *Uriah*: My wife is nothing beside my duty.
> *David*: They say she's very beautiful.
> *Uriah*: As women go.
> *David*: Have you ever tried to think of things from her point of view?
> *Uriah*: No, sire.
> *David*: But supposing her wishes and yours come into conflict?
> *Uriah*: A woman's wishes cannot conflict with a husband's, sire. That is the law
> *David*: The law? The law can only control what we do, not what we think.
>   What does your wife think, Uriah?
> *Uriah*: I do not know, sire.
> *David*: Is it possible that you believe that she does not think or feel? A woman is
>   flesh and blood, Uriah, like us. Perhaps even more so, because we give her so
>   little to think of but matters of the flesh. In all our history only a handful of
>   women have been permitted to write their names beside the men: Miriam,
>   Deborah, Jael, perhaps one or two more. A woman's occupation is her
>   husband and her life is her love, but if her husband rejects her love, she puts
>   another before him.

The extraordinariness of Philip Dunne's script is not Uriah's denial of a
wife's needs but her sensitive defence by another man. Judged by extreme
feminist positions, in which no male ever adequately represents female
desire, David's representation of Bathsheba's feelings and condemnation of
Uriah might be considered a perpetuation of male false-formulations of
female needs. Yet this film forcefully acknowledges male responsibility for
revising social systems endorsing male power structures. While Uriah talks

of duty and the law, boasting ignorance of his wife's thoughts and feelings, David stresses the need for recognition of the woman's perspective. When he says 'the law can only control what we do, not what we think', the focus shifts from the historical context of a less sceptical Old Testament world to a contemporary American setting where, even taking into account the framework of King's own religious interests and widespread American adherence to Judaeo-Christian moral codes, the principles sustaining such codes could be more easily questioned.

As David argues, some women are lucky enough to find liberation from stereotype or subjugation through involvement in public affairs, but for the majority like Bathsheba a likelier means of counteracting the effect of private frustrations appears to lie in the exchange of one sexual partnership for another.

Bathsheba's exchange of Uriah for David highlights questions raised by more general patterns of female desire. Her remark that the man not his status attracted her is disingenuous: how is it possible to divorce David's public status from her perception of his private self? Clearly, a side of her, like the 1950s executive mistress/wife, seeks the powerful man.

In seeking David the man as well as the king, she expresses a desire for human warmth, compatibility and love. But just as Bathsheba represents for David oedipality as well as sexual desire and companionship, a woman who arouses negative as well as positive, unconscious as well as conscious impulses, so David is attractive to Bathsheba not only because he seems the antithesis of the values embodied in Uriah but also, paradoxically, because in other ways he is their perfect formulation. For if at one level David seeks a mother in Bathsheba, at others Bathsheba seeks not only a son but also a father in David.

So Freud's view that in the oedipal phase the female child turns from mother to father as a means of appropriating her missing phallus, recognising that power resides in the father, and not in the mother, seems relevant to Bathsheba's involvement with David in this film, attracted to a man perceived to have the power of the phallus, through whom vicariously she experiences agency rather than the passivity to which she is often confined. In offering herself for display Bathsheba seems to be accepting her role as love-object, endorsing an image of herself reflected in the mirror of male desire, taking pleasure in being desired rather than in actively seeking to satisfy her own desire, reliving childhood patterns of turning towards the father, and by displacing on to David, a father figure, such feelings as prelude to the receipt of the phallus.

To the question posed by David 'What do you want?', Bathsheba replies, 'To please you'. At one level this means that in a relationship's give and take she wants to gratify her lover; at another, it means that in view of social and cultural constraints she accepts her destiny passively to gratify the desires of the male, thus becoming through receipt of the phallus the object of desire of the father. Not a Deborah, Bathsheba gives expression to her desires in a predominantly sexual form.

The narrative is predicated on the principle of the absent mother, absent to a large extent both in Judaism, in terms of her status in the Mosaic Law, and to a certain extent too in 1940s and 1950s American ideology. Undervaluation of the maternal has led to a desire for its recuperation. Bathsheba's father-fixations, first through Uriah and then through David, lead to the text's recognition of cultural overvaluation of the law of the father, the power of the phallus, and the failure to allow equal status to the maternal/feminine. This Bathsheba attempts to reclaim power by transgressing through adultery against the law of Moses ('If the Law of Moses is to be broken David, let us break it in full understanding of what we want from each other'), even if in the act of transgression she submits through marriage to the power of the chief bearer of the phallus.

Part two

THE CHRIST FILM

10 The great storyteller: Cecil B. De Mille unabashedly fills in for a notable absentee, surrounded by the twelve apostles, in this publicity shot for *The King of Kings*

11 The five ages of feminised man: H. B. Warner's Jesus with John, Mark, Peter and perhaps Joseph in the background

12 Jeffrey Hunter, Ray's beautiful rebel with a cause in *King of Kings*

13 Female presences in the Christ Film: Jesus's women on the Via Crucis in De Mille's *The King of Kings*

14 'The shadow of the Galilean': subdued scepticism at the close of Ray's *King of Kings*

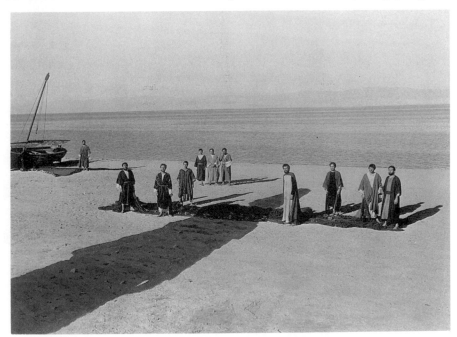

15 On the road: Max Von Sydow's other-worldly Jesus framed by Stevens's cross-generic Western and biblical mise-en-scène in *The Greatest Story Ever Told*

16 Graduate school for alternative values: Jesus holding a seminar at the house of Lazarus in *The Greatest Story Ever Told*

17 De-iconisation in *The Last Temptation of Christ*: Jesus, the Magdalene, Judas and Jesus's mother caught in their separate interiorities

18 Willem Dafoe's introspective, troubled Jesus exposes the hypocrisy of the Law-obsessed accusers of the Magdalene (Barbara Hershey)

4

The lives of Christ: the greatest story ever screened

RETELLINGS AND REVISUALISATIONS

He will not be a Jesus Christ to whom the religion of the present can ascribe, according to its long-cherished custom, its own thoughts and ideas, as it did with the Jesus of its own making. — Albert Schweitzer, *The Quest of the Historical Jesus*

The Hollywood Life of Christ is characterised by an absolute directness of presentation. If in nothing else, it is Miltonic in its head-on approach, avoiding the symbolic obliqueness of so many Hollywood films where secular heroes attain Christ-like status, suffer analogues of the Passion or die in cruciform pose. It also differs from a film like *Jesus of Montreal* (Denys Arcand, 1989), where, acting Christ in an updated passion play that infects his ordinary life, the hero confronts a post-Christian society with the force of an enduringly challenging spirituality. Such allusiveness has the enviable freedom of witty analogue over literal representation, as for instance when the television studio bust-up parallels the cleansing of the Temple, or when the dead hero's transplanted organs survive him in the only post-modernist Resurrection available. In contrast, the four Christ narratives of the Hollywood cinema – *The King of Kings* (De Mille, 1927) *King of Kings* (Nicholas Ray, 1961) *The Greatest Story Ever Told* (George Stevens, 1965), and *The Last Temptation of Christ* (Martin Scorsese, 1988) – share an unambiguous directness. Even when *The Last Temptation*"s epigraph warns of its prioritisation of Kazantzakis's novelistic fantasy over scripture, it resembles the others in presenting the Jesus narrative straight on, avoiding the circuitous strategies of literary versions (other than Kazantzakis's), where the story may be told by a narrator long after the event (Agabus in Robert Graves's *King Jesus* (1946), by a contemporary who never actually meets Jesus (Gerd Theissen's *The Shadow of the Galilean)*, or through the eyes of a lesser figure (as in George Moore's *The Brook Kerith* (1916), where much of the story is told by Joseph of Arimathea).

Equally, although all four films develop parallels with the present they never become analogues so sustained as to transform the Christ story into the vehicle rather than the tenor of the narrative's interests, as in, say, Bulgakov's *The Master and Margarita*. The Hollywood cinema may often present Christ in ways complicit with rather than challenging secular cultural values (though, for Schweitzer, modern Christian culture in general shares that guilt) but the complexity of the films – whose makers, De Mille, Ray, Stevens and Scorsese, form as central a quartet as the American cinema provides – requires an approach adequate to the sub-genre's boldness as well as to its timidities.

This full-frontal boldness is compromised by highly elaborate ideological and aesthetic constraints. Ultimately, the Hollywood version derives from eighteenth- and nineteenth-century lives of Christ, most easily consulted in Schweitzer's *The Quest of the Historical Jesus*, that scep-tical monument to modern Western man's desire to 'know Christ after the flesh', to reconstruct out of Gospel accounts giving 'no hint of the character of his self-consciousness' the historical reality of Christ. Inevitably, in the popular cinema of a culture, where since the mid nineteenth century a huge gap has existed between advanced theology and mass belief, the devotional and consolatory rather than the critical traditions of such lives have exerted the greatest influence: Renan's *Vie de Jésus* over D. F. Strauss and Nietzsche.

However, merely to evoke Renan raises complex questions, for his work combines the devotional–consolatory in its most picturesque form with a scepticism so muted that the reader is hardly aware of Christ's descent from supernature to first place in the humanist pantheon. This softened version, without the rigorous critical analysis of Strauss's work, or the demolitions of Nietzsche's, provides the shadowy second outline of the primary narration, faintly registering secularism's progress, leaving scepticism as a secondary, optional consideration. For the greatest constraint on the Hollywood Christ narrative is its requirement at least formally to accept Christ's divinity. The way in which it does so changes, from an earlier rule of actively expressing belief (within which sceptical counter-texts may operate) to the rule of not actively expressing disbelief (however much scepticism may be expressed). In either case the film must mean most things to most men: literal belief for the believer, a metaphor of human aspiration for the unbeliever. What these films never enact are specific deconstructive readings of the Gospels – to take the most excessive, for instance, Karl Kautsky's Christ as proto-communist, or Hugh J. Schonfield's Jesus of *The Passover Plot*, a leader who stages his own death, or John M. Allegro's Christ as screen for cults involving hallucinogenic mushrooms.

It is simplistic to see the director as detached from these tendencies, being forced to use them in ways that bow to the attitudes of the largely believing mass audience, despite potential conflict with his own private scepticism. De Mille, for instance, was a practising if contradictory Protestant, while Scorsese's attitude to his early Catholicism is obviously complex. In other words, American film makers lean, at the least, towards a reverent agnosticism in which the lines between literal and metaphorical belief overlap.

The Hollywood Christ film is also marked by formal conservatism. Its visual origins are in Renaissance iconography, heavily moderated by Victorian sacred art traditions. These have en enduring influence only comprehensively challenged in *The Last Temptation of Christ*, via the crucial impact of Pasolini's *Gospel According to Matthew* (1964). In ways that may ultimately be inappropriate, through generic affinity with the Old Testament and Roman/Christian films, it is also bound into a spectacular epic format, the greatest story ever told demanding the greatest resources ever tilled. Again the Scorsese film, through the examples of Pasolini (and Rossellini), is the first to liberate itself from these demands. The Hollywood Christ film is also bound into many specific conventions (some of them parodied in *The Life of Brian*), of music, casting, acting styles, language, etc. It is also governed by the rules of 'classical' cinema – cause and effect, linearity, closure, seamlessness, redundancy, goal-orientation and so on – that tend to narrow the scope of the subject-matter's treatment.

To take a single example, Dreyer's unfilmed script *Jesus from Nazareth* gives uncharacteristic prominence to Jesus's telling of the parables. But it is not just that the parables are told. In a way reminiscent of late Buñuel, Dreyer creates semi-independent sub-narratives by moving directly into the world of the parables after Jesus begins to narrate them, following a new set of characters, and rejoining the main narrative only at the end of the brief story. Dreyer's narrative inventiveness highlights certain blandly conservative tendencies of the American genre. On the other hand, an emphasis on Hollywood's constraints should not blind us to their strengths, or to the fact that within them there are almost infinite choices of procedure.

Whereas in the Old Testament film the narrative sources tend to be so concise as to require major projects of expansion to produce film narratives, the Gospel sources offer an excess of material so that major choices have to be made: which actions to be shown? which discourses spoken? which miracles enacted? to begin at the beginning or middle? And so on. Equally, as regards character, certain immediate problems demand solution. Which disciples will be highlighted? which of the women? Though invention of major characters is usually avoided, minor characters may be introduced, often bearing a representative force (for example old Aaron, in *The Greatest Story*). Or the role of peripheral characters may be enhanced (Hollywood here following traditions as old as the Acts of Pilate or the Gospel of Mary Magdalene) as in the case of Pilate's wife in Ray's *King of Kings*. These examples suggest only a few of the multitude of significant options facing the film maker.

Since the directness of the Hollywood Christ film projects Christ as actual rather than implied narrative centre, the question of his physical representation is primary. Although the mechanisms of censorship have controlled many aspects of religious films, the American situation had no parallel with the absolute prohibition on the depiction of Christ inherited by British film censorship from the nineteenth-century theatre, requiring as late as 1928 the granting of a special licence for the London screening of *The King of Kings*. However, this freedom to portray Christ clearly aroused mixed responses. *The New York Times* review of *Intolerance* describes it as 'always a questionable procedure if the feelings of many are to be respected', while a decade later (the unwritten law on avoiding close-ups of Christ having lapsed) the same paper's review of *The King of Kings* claims that 'the presence of Jesus creates a feeling akin to resentment, largely because Mr De Mille has insisted on having his camera too close to the player'.

Such inhibitions did not extend to pictorial representation in itself, for the late nineteenth century was notable for the art of Biblical Illustration, two of the most significant exponents of which, Doré and Tissot, profoundly influenced film representations of Christ. It is presumably the extreme realism of film, far surpassing the realism of theatre, let alone the most realistic painting, that causes problems, as well as the actual impersonation of Christ by an actor, which is seen as qualitatively different from a painted ideal. In the Hollywood Christ film, given the demands of the star system, the Christ-impersonator will not have the decorous anonymity of an unknown actor – such as used by Pasolini in *The Gospel According to Matthew* – but the aura of a star from the Hollywood system. Many stars were too secular ever to have been considered for the part, but those considered spiritual enough to play him bring with them secular sub-texts from their other films. The stories of De Mille's attempts to shroud the making of *The King of Kings* in piety and to enforce high moral standards on his actors can be seen as illustrating a generally felt tension about the secular industry's handling of the most sacred of subjects.

Other factors compound the difficulties. The imputed vulgarity of Hollywood's treatment of the subject can lead to the mockery of Jeffrey

Hunter's physically beautiful Christ (in Ray's *King of Kings*) in the joke title 'I was a Teenage Jesus', though one wonders what the scorners would make of the effeminately beautiful Christs of, say, Botticelli or Raphael. On the other hand, when a contemporary reviewer criticised De Mille's Jesus, H. B. Warner, more general problems were highlighted: 'Mr Warner's expression is a little severe, and his smile, despite his obvious earnestness and sincerity, is more mundane than spiritual; it is not the smile of sympathy or piety.' It would be hard to imagine a more pious Christ than Warner's. Yet, in its broader implications, the statement reads as an example of the difficulty of negotiation between subjective individual fantasy and the highly defined screen image.

The problem is hardly new. In *Painting and Experience in Fifteenth Century Italy*, Michael Baxandall discusses the relationship between subjective spectatorial vision (specifically, visualisation of events from the Gospel) and what he claims are representations, in paintings like Masaccio's *Tribute Money* or Bellini's *Transfiguration*, of 'persons and places . . . generalised and yet massively concrete', which do not compete with personalised vision but complement it by providing the 'concrete and the patterned'.

There are huge differences between paintings produced in the fifteenth century for connoisseurs and films made in the twentieth for mass audiences, but the negotiation between individual and generalised images of Christ is still necessary. Arguably a similar paradoxical concrete generality is demanded of the film Christ, an image providing a powerful outline to which individual fantasies can relate. These latter will perhaps be more difficult to satisfy than Quattrocento ones, not only because of scepticism but also because of the proliferation of Christ images: a Victorian patriarchal Christ, a youthful, beautiful Christ, a Byzantine Christ, to take the most obvious aspects of the Christs portrayed by Warner, Hunter and Von Sydow. Where a Christ is portrayed outside accepted traditions, as in *The Last Temptation of Christ*, the shock – pleasurable or not – is extreme.

ANCIENT AND MODERN

The historical location of these films may be around 30 AD and their content timeless ('Lo, I am with you always'), but each has its own precise contemporary location, through which the Christ narrative touches current concerns. For instance, among the images of Roman oppression in the historical prologue to Ray's *King of Kings*, a soldier throws the corpse of a Jew towards a bonfire laden with bodies. Given the film's emphasis on the

Jewish context of Christ's life, this cannot fail to evoke the Holocaust. In *The Last Temptation* the casting of a youth-culture star, David Bowie, as Pilate gives the pairing of Jesus and Pilate a symbiotic quality in which Pilate subtly takes on connotations of the yuppie executive, while Jesus speaks of anti-materialism. The twinned nature of their relationship, two timeless types of humanity, fleetingly concretised in suggestions of a particular recent succession of radical by conservative, is stressed when Pilate familiarly lectures him on the dangers he represents to the status quo.

There are four crucial areas of historical dual focus in all the films. Two of them register the stresses of theology as refracted in the texts: the portrayal of the miracles and the Resurrection. Both are areas where the treatment is intimately bound up with questions of belief or disbelief. The other two relate to the way major contemporary social interests are relayed through the portrayal of the ancient world, in those secondary but necessary figures of the Jews and women. We shall look at these in turn.

The miracles

The miracles are crucial because whatever is done with them characterises attitudes to the divine in a world under pressure from the attritions of modern science. Significantly, in spite of aesthetic and other temptations to 'specially effect' the miracles, the Christ films are remarkably sparing in their use of them. Ultimately this is explicable by those processes of criticism most memorably expressed in Strauss's *Life of Jesus* (1835), with its detailed deconstructions of the miracles, from which only those readable as psychosomatic healings survive as other than 'myth'. Dreyer's script openly describes them in these terms, as in this commentary to a scene:

> Jesus' purpose in sending away the relatives is to create a positive atmosphere of faith, hope and confidence by eliminating the negative influences of mourning and every tendency toward doubt and disbelief . . . Jesus always impressed upon the people he helped the importance of not speaking to anybody of their miraculous healing. For a person who has been healed by the power of suggestion often meets with doubt and disbelief which undermines his faith, so that the psychological causes of the disease return.

This is the ground to which the Hollywood films move, even surprisingly De Mille's *The King of Kings*, for of all of them it might be expected to be unregenerately supernaturalist. Yet it shows only three miracles: the healing of the blind girl, the Magdalene's exorcism and the raising of Lazarus. Ray's version has only a short generalised sequence where the narrator announces 'It was the time of miracles', the only openly staged incident being the curing of the demoniac. The more traditional *Greatest Story* has only the healing of the cripple in the synagogue, the woman healed by touching Jesus's robe, the unblinding of old Aaron, and the raising of Lazarus, again, as in De Mille, with only Lazarus falling outside the healing pattern. *The Last Temptation*, too, contains only four: the healing of the demoniacs, the changing of the water into wine, the healing of the servant's ear and, again, the raising of Lazarus. Here, surprisingly, three of the four seem to belong to the category of the inexplicable. However, both the Cana and ear miracles reflect the instabilities of the film, so that whereas the Lazarus miracle is presented in deadly earnest, the other two seem, in the first case, provocatively playful (Christ apparently enjoying the joke), and in the second, like an episode from a naively staged miracle pageant (the restoration of the ear being notably unrealistic).

Stevens and Ray share similar strategies in dealing with the non-healing miracles, not representing them on screen but referring to them verbally. In *The Greatest Story* first the priests discuss reports of water being turned into wine and five thousand being fed, then when a soldier informs Pilate that Christ is said to have walked on water, Pilate bellows 'Get out!' Similarly, in Ray's film, the Roman centurion Lucius, caught between scepticism and belief, reports accounts of such miracles to an unbelieving Pilate and his more receptive wife. The strategy here is plainly a way of asserting the more unlikely miracles, but in a modified form not involving their dramatisation, and in a way taking refuge in the scepticism which on the surface is condemned (affirmation and disavowal in the same movement).

Thus the only indubitably inexplicable miracle common to all the films, except Ray's, is the raising of Lazarus, which somewhat contradictorily even Dreyer includes in his script as the greatest of Christ's healings. Its exclusion from Ray's film is further proof of that film's more sceptical approach.

So the films tend to remove with one hand what they give with the other, to downplay the miraculous elements severely while simultaneously staging the most miraculous of all. Zeffirelli's television *Jesus of Nazareth*, in a way perhaps more naive than in the Hollywood films, simply gives a bravura treatment to miracles like the loaves and fishes episodes. The culturally specific path open to Pasolini in *The Gospel According to Matthew*, where he is able to stage the miracles (the cured leper, Jesus's walking on the water) without reservation, because his film announces itself as the recitation of shared cultural history but not belief in it, is something denied the Hollywood cinema.

The Resurrection

If the presentations of the miracles are highly symptomatic in their attempts to satisfy belief and scepticism, supernature and nature, so is the culminating episode of the Resurrection. Of the four films, only *The Last Temptation* fails to dramatise the discovery of the empty tomb and Christ's subsequent appearances. In De Mille and Stevens, at least outwardly, things are unproblematic. De Mille's Resurrection is presented in the sacred opera of the Magdalene at the tomb, the movement into colour and the hymn 'Jesus Christ is Risen Today'. Neither does Stevens cultivate doubt. On the other hand, Ray's version, bearing in mind the convention (only broken by *The Last Temptation*) that the Resurrection has to be shown, may make us feel that it is not ultimately committed to a metaphysical Christ, though such doubts can only be expressed in the context of exterior certainties. The risen Christ certainly appears to Mary Magdalene at the tomb, but in the film's last moments, as the apostles receive his words, the framing denies us any sight of him and, after they have departed, his lengthening shadow intersects their abandoned fishing nets to form the shape of a cross. The moment is readable orthodoxly, but the emphasis elsewhere is so much on Jesus as a principle of peace rather than divinity that the image is also open to interpretation as one of the 'shadow of the Galilean', his influence rather than metaphysical ascent. Again, the unambivalent notation in Dreyer's script would not have been possible, even if desired. There, the crosses of the thieves disappear, leaving only the lengthening shadow of Christ's reaching out of the frame, and the narrator's commentary: 'Jesus dies, but in death he accomplished what he had begun in life. His body was killed, but his spirit lived. His immortal sayings brought to humanity all over the world the good tidings of love and charity foretold by the Jewish prophets of old.'

The Last Temptation is the only one of these films which ends without the Resurrection. When Jesus dies saying 'It is accomplished', the screen is filled with an intense blue unstably punctuated by bursts of colour and fleeting images of film stock. Here there is an ambiguous void readable as absolutely the end, or – from a Christian point of view – as a modest silence, from the perspective of human ignorance, before whatever is experienced in death.

The Jews

The consequences of the Judaic origins of Christianity are a permanent complication for both traditions and for any work of art which brings them into contact, something largely avoidable in the Old Testament and

Roman/Christian films but not in the Christ films where the material is immitigably present, demanding constant choices as to its method of representation. Again Dreyer's project, outside even the European art film mainstream and of course never actualised, presents the most radical treatment of Jewish material. The emphasis in his sub-title, *Jesus the Jew*, points to a desire to combat Christian anti-Semitism, underlined in the three essays appended to the script which draw analogies between the Nazi occupation of Denmark and the Roman occupation of Judaea, defend as nationalistically understandable Caiaphas's actions against Jesus, and attack the tradition of a non-Semitic Jesus. In his script Dreyer also accompanies the Last Supper with Passover detail, actually intercutting the scene with an Orthodox ceremony and takes great care to make the antagonism between the Pharisees and Jesus only gradual in development, putting the Pharisees' case.

Lacking Dreyer's commitment to rescue the Jewish elements of Christianity, the Hollywood cinema's more ambivalent position is conditioned by numerous factors over and above Christianity's unavoidable claim to be the fulfilment of Judaism, for instance traditional emphases on Christian/Jewish differences rather than similarities, latent American anti-Semitism, and the activities of Jewish groups pressing for the removal of anti-Semitic material. Altogether, the Hollywood cinema approaches the material more spasmodically than systematically, not so much exploring the real relations between Christ and his surrounding culture, but where forced to recognise inescapable Jewishness, improvising ambivalently, though in the later films with increasing 'liberalism'.

Stevens's film is full of such examples. A voice preaches against animal sacrifices, and we are led through a huge overhead shot above the wilderness until we find the source of the speech not in Christ but ecumenically in John the Baptist. Equally, Jesus replies to a hellfire-preaching rabbi, 'Ours is a God of salvation, not of revenge', the 'Ours' stressing relation rather than difference, both moments portraying Jesus as the culmination of tradition rather than its destroyer. In Stevens, as in De Mille and Ray, the Jewish priesthood is shown as under the control of the Romans, something which diminishes imputed Jewish guilt, and Jewish leaders hostile to Christ are carefully balanced with others sympathetic to him, though, as we shall see in the De Mille, latent anti-Semitism may coexist with its opposite.

In certain ways these examples from Stevens have a more representative force than parallel moments in Ray, untypically stressing Jewish interests, not just in Judas's wavering between secular and religious Messiahs, but in the historical prologue, and in the portrayal of Caiaphas as a patriotic pragmatist acting against Jesus on Jewish/nationalistic grounds. In *The Last*

Temptation, made over twenty years later, the representation of Jewishness is, as ever, complex and uneven, as it can hardly fail to be, given the conflicting impulses and vexed history that makes any representation contentious. At times the Judaic elements are underlined, as in the politicisation of Judaea and the Passover elements surrounding the Last Supper. At others, they disappear into the exotic orientalism of the background. While the dominant attitude of the film to Judaism is that Christianity rescues from it concepts of monotheism expressed in parochial forms, the film also redeems the grossly caricatured Caiaphas of the novel, presenting him as a figure of fierce dignity. And even more than any of the other films *The Last Temptation* avoids the fraught matter of Jesus's trials, dramatising only Jesus's interrogation by Pilate. Overdetermined by complex conflicting pressures in all the films, the representation of the Judaic in *The Last Temptation* is too volatile to summarise easily, but two underlying factors may be noted. Firstly, since *The Last Temptation* differs from all the other films in presenting a riven Jesus, the film is able to carry its mixture of criticism and affirmation of Judaism more easily than the others; freer in its treatment of Christianity, it is arguably less neurotic in its treatment of Judaism. Secondly, a context of at least marginal improvement in Jewish/Christian theological relations (the conciliatory Vatican II 'Nostra Aetate' and the more far-reaching statements of various American Protestant Churches from the late 1960s to the 1980s on the anti-Semitic consequences of the 'teaching of contempt') might be felt to allow more freedom to the makers. There is also the irony that part of the fundamentalist crusade against the film reversed the usual pattern, so that instead of Jewish pressure groups objecting to representations of Jews, Christians accused Universal Studios of a Semitic plot against Christianity.

The women

The development of feminist perspectives in theology as elsewhere opens up even sacred texts to new questions and readings. No longer are the women in the Gospels taken for granted. Feminist theology may at the same time maintain a commitment to the Gospels while criticising patriarchal modes of transmission and interpretation, and claim in early institutional Christianity a retreat from the revolutionary egalitarianism of Christ's teachings.

Viewed so, the Hollywood Christ film is as unlikely to be revealed as a radical text in this sphere as in any other. But it would be reductive to argue that the end result can be calculated in advance as a double negative, a closed patriarchal reworking of a patriarchal source. These films are complex negotiations between the original texts and later cultural moments marked by female demands for autonomy and by an instability in the meanings of masculinity and femininity. Even where the films carry the heaviest stereotyping, there may be sub-texts of a less absolute kind. This can be shown by briefly meditating on the two primary female figures of the films, the two Marys, Madonna and Magdalene, mother and sacred prostitute.

Nowhere is the conservative thrust of the films more evident than in the reiterated depiction of the iconic Mother, an absolute of asexual purity and self-sacrifice. Nun-like, wimpled, in De Mille she sits at the loom, surrounded by doves; in Stevens she holds a loom; in Ray a huge close-up concentrates on her basket of coloured yarns. Only in Pasolini's and Scorsese's late iconoclasm does realism deconventionalise stasis. In Pasolini she moves from the adolescent girl of the film's beginning to the aged peasant women of its end. In Scorsese she is touchingly ordinary: middle-aged, plain. However, the point is not simply that realism can subvert stereotypes but that the stereotypes themselves may operate to produce more exploratory patterns. In Ray, for example, the Mother's piety is given through the Irishry of Siobhan McKenna so extreme a register that it becomes part of a calculating dissonance created by tensions established between the demands of realism and myth.

The treatment of Mary the Mother in all four films follows one narrative option, an acceptance of her background place. On the other hand, the treatment of Mary Magdalene in two of the four films, De Mille's and Scorsese's, opts for the possibility of narrative expansion. The reduced, idealised sexuality of the Virgin contrasts markedly with Mary Magdalene's traditionally heightened eroticism. This singling-out of the Magdalene, except for the brief incursions of Salome and Herodias in Ray and Stevens, to bear the whole burden of sexuality plainly carries strong ideological meanings. Only *The Last Temptation*, by shockingly emphasising Christ's active sexuality, redresses the balance, though very ambivalently. Nevertheless, even De Mille's film, which employs to the full the most massive stereotypes of whorishness and purity, works more intricate gradations in its explorations of femininity through the thesis–antithesis of the two women. And, of course, the three films which include the material of the Resurrection are obliged to follow the Gospels' fleeting moments of primacy for Magdalene at the tomb. Indeed both 1960s films take tentative steps towards redefinition. When at the end of *King of Kings* the apostles receive the command to go forth and preach the Gospels, there are close-ups of the Magdalene among the male group. And in *The Greatest Story*, as Jesus converses with the disciples in a pastoral setting, Mary is present sitting, relaxed, with the men.

The Scorsese Magdalene is much the most developed version, her complexity lying not in an attempt to counter the stereotype of Eve's daughter but in exploring it in ways more wide-ranging and intense. Often foregrounded, and played by an actress (Barbara Hershey) who brings not only intense sexuality but also a vivid, pained seriousness to the role, the character cannot be reduced to the sum of stereotypes. Equally, it must be stated that all three artists, Kazantzakis, Schrader and Scorsese, pursuing their visions of spiritual odyssey, find it difficult to move outside traditional conceptions of women, even though the film contains moments playing powerfully against these: for instance, the unprecedented appearance of the three Marys and Martha at the Last Supper, and the unresolved contradiction of Jesus's agitated movements between the patriarchal and the matriarchal. The view of women implicit in the striking person of the film's Magdalene is perceived almost wholly from a particularly male angle of vision. Woman as the earthly other to spiritual man embodies sexuality and domesticity. *The Last Temptation*'s insistence on the human ordinariness of Mary the Mother debars her from religious development, but when she is portrayed in the other films in her most iconic form she is somehow still not presented as spiritually self-contained. De Mille, Ray and Stevens, in staging the pathos of the mother–son farewells, all insist on the mother's primary biological–emotional relationship to the son.

5

'Abide with Me': Cecil B. De Mille's *The King of Kings* (1927)

CHILDREN

Fear not little flock . . . — Luke, 12: 32

The first shots of Jesus in the Christ Film are always moments of great intensity, surrounded by suspense, since this is, even in post-Christian culture, the representation of representations, 'Behold the Man'. In *The King of Kings* De Mille heightens convention as the story first of all concentrates on the Magdalene. But even when it moves to the house where Jesus is staying, it insistently refuses to disclose him when the camera moves inside and shows us, though we know he is there, only the various disciples. Even after this, only through following the quest of the little blind girl aided by Mark do we finally arrive at out first long-withheld view of H. B. Warner's Jesus.

When these shots eventually come, they are suitably extraordinary: fully subjective point-of-view shots from the perspective of not just a child but (doubly loaded) a *female* child, and further, stressing innocence and helplessness even more, a *blind* female child, whose first sight of the world this is. As Jesus 'speaks' the words 'I am come a light into the world, that whosoever believeth in me shall not abide in darkness', the audience's position becomes unified with the girl's as she/we first see only blankness, then a radiance, then a fuzzily clarifying outline, and finally, filling the screen in close-up, the Saviour's paternal face looking down from the position of a father gently addressing a child.

In arguing the significance of this first view of Jesus for the film, it should be stressed that this is no isolated effect, for the motif of the child has already been recently doubled in the moments leading up to Christ's appearance by the presence of the youthful Mark (Mickey Moore). Aged about 10, Mark must be an orphan, for no family is ever referred to, and he is quickly adopted by Peter (Ernest Torrance) and Mary the Mother (Dorothy Cumming), who assume a quasi-parental role towards him.

Introduced before the blind girl, he has himself (in a scene implied but not shown) been miraculously cured. Spotting the little girl lost, he leads her through the crowd, gently preventing her from pricking her hand on a cactus, through the window of the house and into the presence of Mary the Mother. Just as the child motif is doubled here, so also is the parental – especially patriarchal – one, for, moments before discovering the girl, Mark has high-spiritedly tossed away his crutch, which hits one of Caiaphas's spies, who then threatens the child. Peter – characterised as 'the Giant Disciple, a fisherman quick of temper but soft of heart' – intervenes to help him, threatening the hypocritical aggressor with a gesture in which he holds the crutch aloft like a hammer. But this male ferocity is followed by moments of intense 'feminisation', as he bestows on Mark melting looks, his eyes brimming with tears which indicate, as does his reluctant turning away, a world of gentle paternal love for the boy.

The surrogate parent–child relationship between Mark and Peter is given a less obvious variation in the film's play with the mythology of the so-called Petrine source of St Mark's Gospel. This is the claim which stems from Papias's recounting in the second century that Mark 'though he had neither heard the Lord nor been his personal follower', later followed Peter and included Peter's teachings in his account. So when the title describes 'Young Mark . . . healed by the great physician, and destined to become one of the FOUR to write the immortal Gospels', the intent is surely to create yet another personalised paternal/filial relationship (Christ/Mark; Peter/Mark; Peter's discourse/Mark's discourse), establishing a doubly personalised origin for the Gospel in the child's eye-witness memories, supported by the most authoritative of the disciples' authority. This emotionally underwritten transmission is extremely significant in its reassurance at a time when the ravages of 'Higher', 'Form' and 'Tendency' criticism were breaking down the transparent integrity of the Gospels into the impersonality of traditions and sources about which it was becoming difficult to hold ideas of absolutely certain derivation. De Mille's backward-looking strategy here may be interestingly compared with Kazantzakis's methods in his novel *The Last Temptation*. There, although borrowing the comforting, out-of-date fiction that the Matthew who wrote the Gospel was the eye-witnessing apostle, Kazantzakis uses the simplification to very complex effect by giving Matthew proto-Straussian characteristics as he composes his account with a consciousness of its status as myth beyond fact.

The film's early emphasis on children is continued in the sequence immediately following the woman taken in adultery. Here a bridging title reads, 'And it came to pass, that He went throughout every city and village, preaching and showing the good tidings of the Kingdom of God.' From this the viewer expects a section devoted to Jesus's teaching, but instead Jesus and the disciples walk through an orchard where children clamber in fruit-laden trees. As he passes, Jesus playfully pulls the leg of a tree-climbing ragamuffin, and accepts the fruit he is offered. As the children flock to Jesus, Judas (Joseph Schildkraut) rather officiously tries to prevent them bothering the Master. This moment, the film's invention, a pejorative reallocation of what is a generalised action in the Gospel narratives (e.g. Matthew 19: 13–15, 'the disciples rebuked them. But Jesus said, Suffer little children, and forbid them not, to come unto me: for such is the kingdom of heaven'), significantly brands Judas alone as blind to the value of children. After Judas departs, having been gently reprimanded by Jesus for his insensitivity, Jesus, in one of the film's few comic moments, continues with the children. A dark-haired moppet, again a female child, asks Jesus to mend her broken doll: 'Mark saith thou canst mend broken legs.' In the film's most playful passage 'the great physician' displays an impractical bachelor's inexpertise, looking slightly embarrassed and fiddling inef-fectively with the doll while two of the older disciples look on amused. Then, like any suburban father, he improvises a new joint and is embraced by the child whom he happily swings off her feet, an echo of his embrace of the blind girl in the earlier healing scene of which this is a tender pastiche, the main function of which seems to be less to convey doubt about the real miracles than to invest the patriarchality of Christ with a domestic warmth.

The news of Lazarus's death ends this sequence of incidents built around children, but, as with the meanings that surround the female figures, a chain of recurrences keeps such questions in mind. These are centred on Mark who is present throughout: at the Magdalene's exorcism; in the sequence with the adulterous woman where one of the disciples seems to be worried about his youthful exposure to violence; leading the crowd to Jesus when the secular crown is offered; appearing at the tomb when Lazarus is raised; and prominent in the post-Ressurection appearance in the closed room. In all these instances, sometimes in close-up, he is found in some situation, making some gesture that impinges on the viewer's attention, an obvious instance being when, on the way of the cross, angrily choking back tears, he accosts Simon of Cyrene with 'If I was as big a man as thou art, I would carry His cross for Him'. Mark's role in the final moments of the film is especially interesting. Just before Thomas the Doubter enters the room, Christ is standing with one hand being kissed by John, the other around Peter. The camera cuts to Thomas entering, then back to Jesus's group, but now John has receded to screen left, and the boy has taken his place, clinging to Jesus.

This shot, in which Mark has suddenly replaced John, is symptomatic, for it crystallises, in a situation centred on the disciple known for pragmatic scepticism (and thus representative of modern man), the need for childlike faith. To return from this moment near the close to the little girl's point of view at the beginning is to grasp the significance of the original shot as its meanings have increased throughout the narrative. The coincidence of the little girl's and the audience's first view of Jesus places the audience in a child's perceptions as the proper place to be, a subject-positioning sustained by a complex of strategies throughout the rest of the film, so that although the child's literal subjectivity is never restored it continues to govern all the other viewpoints.

The various child-centred texts in the Gospels are so paradoxically forceful that it is hard to think of a Christ film not highlighting them in some way but only in De Mille do they take on governing centrality. So it is no accident that in the Last Supper sequence Jesus's words from John's account are chosen: 'Little children, yet a while I am with you.' In *The Greatest Story*, a sympathetic member of the Sanhedrin, hearing the miracles dismissed as children's stories, resolves to investigate, saying that he likes children's stories. The point depends on a set of resonances deeply important in Western Christian culture (the child as innocent eye, as seer). The other side of the equation is the child's naivety and malleability, its possible deception by the children's stories adults tell (something St Paul recognised in Corinthians, 13). How the balance between positive and negative is produced in De Mille's film, which in its dominant trope has announced itself as the child's story, seen with the child's eye, is an important question.

AND WOMEN FIRST

> Jesus saith unto her, Mary. She turned herself, and saith unto him, Rabboni; which is to say, Master. — John, 20: 16–17

De Mille's most startling invention is his focus on Mary Magdalene (Jacqueline Logan) which brings her under Jesus's influence when she confronts him over her lover Judas's defection from her to him. It is a sequence that accords with De Mille's reputation for indulging the erotic under cover of the pietistic. But to agree that De Mille is the master of such contradictory effects – the pleasures of the Magdalene's haughty libido, gleaming flesh and daringly fetishistic costumes, followed by her submission to the patriarchal gaze of Christ – is not to exhaust the interest of what is so uninhibitedly given.

Recent reassessments of De Mille's early career, arguing his representative centrality in signifying major early twentieth-century American cultural shifts, invite responses less crude than denigration or camp celebration of the old vulgarian's magnificent obsessions. Rather, we might see them as popular art's uninhibited expression of tensions central to the culture and even to culture in general, for, vulgar in some respects as it may be, De Mille's immediate blatant foregrounding of the sexual does nothing less than act out unrestrainedly various relations of the greatest importance between culture, religion and sexuality. As Weber in *The Sociology of Religion* notes:

> Indeed the power of the sphere of eroticism enters into particular tensions with religions of salvation. This is particularly true of one of the most powerful components of eroticism, namely sexual love. For sexual love, along with the 'true' or economic interest, and the social drive toward power and prestige, is among the most universal and fundamental components of the actual course of interpersonal behaviour.

Seen so, De Mille's excesses become more interesting, since the conflict represented is repressed in all the other Christ films except Scorsese's. In *Intolerance* Griffith's drive, half-erotic, half-ethical, parallels De Mille's in many ways (and in his religious films de Mille is profoundly influenced by Griffith), but he manages to avoid or solve the problem through a multiple narrative which creates, in counterpoint to the ethical ancient world of the Christ narrative, the erotic Babylonian ambience of the carnal lovers, Prince Belshazzar and the Princess Beloved, something presented as both highly desirable and hopelessly decadent, contrasting with the Christ world but not entering it. De Mille has the two worlds clash immediately, so that his film is, surprisingly, in this sense, closest to Scorsese's. In the clash we may read both the general conflict between sexuality and the religion of salvation and, in its particular features, the cultivation of certain kinds of eroticism, female display, assertion and then purifying control of female sexuality, more particularly relating to early twentieth-century American sexual ideology.

Thus the film begins in the Magdalene's vast pleasure palace, where she entertains various clients at a banquet, a compendium of oriental and African orgy exotica, decorated with muscular slaves, zebras drawing her chariot and a court orchestra. Above all, there is the spectacle of Mary of Magdala herself, gleaming with flesh, jewels and metal, spread out on a chaise longue in front of the banqueters' curved table, the centre of their attention, but with eyes only for her pet leopard, symbolising her narcissistic, dangerous sexuality. When one of the elderly suitors grabs her, complaining that the beast is getting more attention, she topples him backwards with a contemptuous push. When one of the others says he knows Judas's whereabouts, she launches herself at him violently, pinning him to the table.

The film's fascination with her combination of female allure and usurped masculine power is obvious. The intertitle emphasises the double aspect of her transgressions: 'The beautiful courtesan MARY OF MAGDALA, laughed alike at God and Man.' As regards the former, the Magdalene is in many ways presented as a traditional Jezebelline figure: her luminous flesh lit to a lustre that opposes the effulgence radiating from Christ's countenance throughout the film. At one level she represents the power of animal sexuality itself, pulling the soul away from God, a power, it hardly needs underlining, defined as female. The second focus of the intertitle is less the eternal female and more the contemporary, for it is clearly not just the power of her body that allows Mary to laugh at man (read gender-specifically), but the usurpation of male power accompanying it. Here, despite the film's attempts to escape from the complexities of history to an abstract realm of the eternal, we feel the pressure of present circumstances, since what else is Mary acting out but an extreme version of the 'new' woman, more then half celebrated in De Mille's comedies but here seen dangerously as, to use the title of one of his films near in date to *The King of Kings*, *The Godless Girl* (1928). Powerful, wealthy, contemptuous of family and marriage, she is a fascinating, minatory vision of the female not just removed from the male order but exercising control over men.

Her remarkable confrontation with Jesus plays out both the general and particular meanings. Advancing in confident, angry sexuality, she demands to know the whereabouts of the carpenter who has taken Judas (Joseph Schildkraut) away from her. But, under Jesus's silent gaze, her aggressive sexuality falters. At his exhortation, 'Be thou clean', the various sins, headed by Lust and Pride, are expelled from her body in a brilliant use of double exposure and, at Jesus's command, vanish. Transformed, the Magdalene is now in a frontal shot, indicating a passive, submissive receptivity. Looking down at her body and, perceiving it to be immodestly exposed, she rearranges the dark cloak she is wearing into a nunnish robe that imitates the clothing and headdress of Mary the Mother standing nearby, and then kneels at the Saviour's feet.

Not only the Magdalene but her antithesis, 'Mary the Mother' (De Mille quoting *Intolerance*), enters the narrative before her son, the initial counterpoint of Holy Mother and Magdalene making absolutely overt the much-analysed Madonna/Whore duality in Judaeo/Christian notions of the female. As we might expect, the Mother is presented as the absolute opposite of Magdalene, settled as she is in the domestic common round at the loom. Whereas the Magdalene is half undressed, the Mother is dressed chastely, no flesh showing but face and hands. When the herald sounds the commencement of the Sabbath, she piously ceases to wave and stations herself at the window by the doves. Her gentleness and spirituality symbolised by these birds, she is immediately associated with children (in a way reminiscent of the 'Out of the Cradle endlessly rocking' leitmotif in *Intolerance*), by her welcoming in of the little blind girl and her request to her son, 'This little one hath need of thee'. The initial absolute contrast between types of womanhood is aided by the fact that, although dressed in a matronly way, Mary the Mother does not appear to be much older than the Magdalene, and certainly in realistic terms is an unlikely parent for the rather elderly Christ we are soon to meet. But here realism is hardly at issue, becoming so only when Pasolini or Scorsese create shocks by playing extreme realism against conventions of non-realism, giving us a Mary in Christ's maturity as an ageing peasant woman. The other tradition – Zeffirelli's convent-schoolgirl virgin Olivia Hussey providing the most representative example – offers various meanings here. Firstly, the contrast between the two Marys, pure and impure, would not have the same resonances if the Mother were much older; secondly, there is a clear desire to represent the Mother as an ideal of female beauty; thirdly, in a tradition of veiled eroticism, the Mother represents a desired but untouchable (desired because untouchable) sexual object; and finally, she represents a pull on the most powerful oedipal fantasies, the mother eternally young in the adult's memory of childhood.

In the moment after her exorcism, the Magdalene becomes largely assimilated to the Mother, imitating her dress and appearing in a shot where Mary (with the young Mark at her shoulder), watches and approves her transformation. Subsequently the two are often seen together; they are given equal emphasis at the crucifixion; the Magdalene is surrounded with the doves associated with the Mother when she visits the tomb; and they enter the closed room together after Thomas, to be imaged as a pair, their faces in close-up, a few moments later, and then again in a composition where Christ embraces his mother while Peter falls at his feet and the Magdalene looks on.

We should not oversimplify the effect of what might seem to be a use of female stereotypes of a wholly contrasting kind, leading to an unconditional assimilation of the dangerously undomesticated and erotic to the comforting and pure. Above all the equivalence between the Mother and the Magdalene cannot be complete since in a secular culture where sexuality is increasingly defined as the most desirable of commodities, some sort of more complex negotiation between the two poles has to be reached. Critics like May and Higashi have demonstrated the way in which De Mille's marital comedies achieved the transition from Victorianism to consumer culture, a movement which highlights the leisure and consumerist pleasures of eroticised marriage in which the female (still the prize for the successful male) has, within the limits of ideology, her own desire and autonomy recognised, with the proviso that these do not overstep the mark. The basic patterns of the biblical film tend, as Higashi notes, to older ethical stereotypes of pure and wicked femininity. Nevertheless there are ways in which Mary Magdalene evolves into a kind of third female state, less absolute than either the courtesan or the mother, though more ethically defined than in the new commodity world of the comedies.

For instance, she is prominent when enthusiastically, even if mistakenly, calling for Jesus's coronation, and later when attempting to subvert Caiaphas' agents' bribing of the crowd. She also tries desperately to stop the soldier from piercing Christ's side. All three invented incidents dramatise a passionate involvement very different from the Mother's passivity. And, significantly, though we have noted her movement towards the Mother's style of dress, there remain important differences: for instance, her arms, and beneath her head-dress her luxuriant hair, are always visible, so that in this as well as elsewhere hints of eroticism are always present. That the role of women in the early biblical film does not simply fall into polarising stereotypes (though these are the basic materials of characterisation) can be shown in the more exuberant clash of opposites in the Babylonian episode of *Intolerance*, where the audience is left to decide between the negatives and positives implied by the languorously erotic Princess Beloved and the independent tomboyish Mountain Girl. To make these points is hardly to exhaust the significance of the female roles and the meanings of the 'feminine'. Their complexity will be further clarified through the discussion that follows of the masculine centre of the film, Christ himself.

THE GOOD PATRIARCH

How often would I have gathered thy children together, as a hen doth gather her brood under her wings, and ye would not! — Luke, 13: 34

The Christ whom the little girl sees, and before whom the Magdalene repents, was played by the British Hollywood veteran H. B. Warner. Whereas Jeffrey Hunter was 35, when playing the part, Max Von Sydow 34, and Willem Dafoe 32, all young men playing a man assumed to be around 30 years old, Warner was over 50, the father, as it were, incarnated in the son, or the son in the father. Either way, in a film of powerful conceptions, his middle-aged *gravitas* is one of the most striking, and demands attention.

Various factors suggest themselves. Victorian males married later, and were thus literally older fathers to their children. Also, in 1927 De Mille was roughly the same age (46) as Warner. Saying this is not to suggest – notably egocentric from all accounts though De Mille was – that he simply identified himself with Christ; rather that De Mille, who saw himself as a patriarchal storyteller and, as Higashi notes, saw his audience as his children, produced his Christ in the image of himself in that sense, happiest with a figure reflecting his position towards the audience as he retold the Gospels. The prelude to the second *Ten Commandments* has De Mille himself delivering a little homily. Here, interestingly, his form of address is 'Ladies and Gentlemen, Young and Old', which can be seen as more than a charming allusion to the family audience, especially since the project on which he was working at his death was a life of Baden-Powell, the founder of the Boy Scout movement, who in this perspective can be seen as yet another variation on a theme, the secular father-successor to Christ, addressing his disciples as children, and to the twice-depicted Moses leading, inspiring, disciplining, punishing the children of Israel on their Exodus from the land of Egypt.

These factors intersect with a visual tradition inherited by De Mille of Victorian religious painting, an iconography of the mature Christ as the 'Man of Sorrows' epitomised in the brooding figure of Dyce's *The Woman of Samaria*, the 'pale Galilean' of Burton's *The King of Sorrows*, and above all in the slightly elderly, melancholy figure of Holman Hunt's *The Light of the World*. All, like Warner, share a world-weary melancholy attributable less to realism than to the immanence of nineteenth-century religious scepticism.

Perhaps even more influential, because enshrined in the Bibles of so many households, were the Biblical illustrations of the painter Tissot and the engraver Doré. It is from a combination of all these visual sources that Warner's Christ comes into being. Among the 276 representations of religious paintings claimed to be in the film, Renaissance models outnumber others, but the Victorian influence is the most significant since it is embodied in the image of Christ himself. In his psychic attachment to these images De Mille is at one with his audience, for it cannot be overstressed how common was acquaintance with these representations, pervasively available in the home. (The huge Bible constantly clutched by the mother in De Mille's original *The Ten Commandments* looks like an illustrated one.) Tissot and Doré are an important link with the emergent cinema, which from the beginning was attracted to religious subjects, in combining in their work elements of the archaeological (Tissot researching in the Holy Land, Doré working from contemporary photographs and museum collections) and the ethical; in other words a semi-scientific passion for geographical and archaeological precision combines with a transcendently supernatural aura, which could be said to effect a resolution of religion and science by placing the former in a world reconstructed by the latter as if there were no real conflict between them.

Though opposition to the portrayal of Christ in the cinema was obviously based in part on a fear of what a deconstructive realism might do, these fears prove as groundless as they are in Tissot or Doré. The realism of the cinema in fact gives us a Christ before whom the crowd following the adulterous woman part as in sympathetic magic as he advances, as in Doré emitting a constant light from his features, always dressed in immaculate white, repeating a consistent repertoire of transparent gestures that in immediately accessible terms mediate between the authoritative and the consolatory, the constantly pointing index finger, the characteristic con-solatory gestures of arms spread out, palms outward, eyes constantly lifting heavenwards to credit their eternal source of inspiration.

This extreme iconicity and familiarity of gesture finds its perfect expres-sion in the tableauesque style of the film, the constant stasis of compositions and poses deriving from the Victorian spectacular theatre with its tradition of creating living representations of famous paintings. The effect is com-pounded by silent film's need of intertitles, so that Christ's words are not given, as in the sound films, in the distinctive grain of the actor's voice but in written form, predetermined and authoritative, qualities underlined even more by De Mille's quoting at the bottom of the frame the Gospel sources of the titles.

All these elements cohere in various ways with Warner's elderliness. They are highly suited to his representation since familiarity and immuta-bility belong with the oedipal structures we have described at the centre of the film. Both from outside and inside Christianity, the whole cluster of associated elements may be viewed with some hostility as an expression of a passive, pejoratively childlike version of Christianity, and the urge to deconstruct is probably in proportion to the overwhelming effect of the film's emotionality and the depth of the irrational appeal of its oedipal strategies. In *La Voie lactée*, Buñuel comments on the history of artistic representations of Christ, and it is highly probable that *The King of Kings*, which must undoubtedly have left a great impression on his early work, is still being remembered here in 1967. In *La Voie lactée*, a Maitre D' is interrupted during the course of a lecture on the dual nature of Christ by an underling who remarks, 'but he could laugh and cough, couldn't he? He's always depicted as so solemn, walking slowly, with his hands held like this . . .' The next shot transports us to the ancient world where Christ actually runs into the picture, pants, pauses for breath, and then says he is hungry. Buñuel's mischief contains a profound critique in the few short scenes in which Christ appears. Extremely youthful in contrast to De Mille's Christ, he speaks extemporarily the 'hardest', most paradoxical, least consolatory of the Gospel's texts. By contrast, the texts De Mille's Christ speaks omit as relentlessly as Buñuel's includes them sayings concerned with disturbance, paradox or ambiguity. Clearly there are so many actions and speeches attributed to Christ in the Gospels that every Christ film inevitably makes choices in which omission as much as inclusion creates meaning. For example, though in itself the omission from the film of Jesus disowning his family might not be necessarily significant, taken in the context of the film's pronounced oedipality and the omission of any associated texts demoting the family in pursuit of the kingdom, its absence obviously gains in meaning.

This is especially so when we further note that the film manages to dispense with almost anything of a parabolic, ascetic or socially disruptive nature in the Gospel accounts of Christ's teachings. Where economics is a factor, it appears only as the simplest motivation for Caiaphas's (Rudolph Schildkraut) actions: 'The Roman appointee CAIAPHAS, the High Priest – who cared more for revenue than for Religion – and saw in Jesus a menace to his rich profits from the Temple.' In fact Theissen in his *The First Followers of Jesus* argues that Jesus's criticisms of the Temple were a direct threat to the Jerusalem economy, largely built around the Temple. But this kind of consideration is exactly what we do not get here, as with Caiaphas (especially when he gloatingly drops the pieces of silver in front of Judas) the complexities of the economic order and its relationship with religion are replaced by almost medieval figures of Avarice.

What Christ does give forth in the film are major texts of another kind: 'I am come a light into the world that whosoever believeth in me shall not abide in darkness'; 'My peace I give unto you. In the world ye shall have tribulations, but be of good cheer – I have overcome the world'; 'Blessed are the pure in heart – for they shall see God', and so on. It is not that these texts lack significance. Indeed they are central to Christian meaning, but they are texts that are enormously familiar, felt almost, when quoted in isolation, to be self-explanatory, self-defining. Removed from a specific context they tend to become talismanic, the source of comfort alone, with no sense about them of the discomfort of renewal and the shaking of the foundations.

There is no doubt an overdetermination of reasons for De Mille's choice of an almost neoclassically compact narrative design. But a dominant one must be that omission of all the early Gospel narrative material allows the maintenance of an unchanging image of Christ which again is in line with the child's perception of the father figure we see as underlying the film. Another curiosity, the complete omission of the drama of Peter's betrayal of Christ, may perhaps be similarly explained as the product of primitive, childlike placing of all blame on the scapegoat figures of Judas and Caiaphas, thus avoiding complicated divided motivation in the main figures. Just as Jesus appears in the film his mission already well under way, the origins of it unexplained, so – unlike other Christ films where the selection of the disciples, their first contact with Jesus's charismatic glance, is a major moment – the disciples appear always to have been present.

When we pause to consider the other side of this representation, the characters of Judas and Caiaphas, the film's archetypes of evil, related patterns emerge. In his autobiography De Mille complains about 'organized opposition of certain Jewish groups to this filmed history of the greatest Jew who ever lived', claiming that 'we went to great lengths in *The King of Kings* to show that the Jewish people of Jesus' time followed and heard him gladly, that his death came at the hands of a few unrepresentative corrupt leaders and the cowardly and callous Roman government'. De Mille's protests are both understandable and naive. His own ambivalent personal circumstances, leading him to conceal his mother's part-Jewishness, did not inhibit him from celebrating Old Testament Israel in three of his films, in which the Jews are presented as proto-American democrats. In a context where Christianity lies only in the future, Judaic monotheism can be celebrated for its universality. In *The King of Kings*, however, the situation becomes more difficult, for Christianity is no longer a distant evolutionary step towards which Judaism moves, but is in the active process of displacing it. Undeniably *The King of Kings* creates a series of ambivalent effects, especially around Caiaphas. Extreme care is taken at certain points to exculpate 'the Jews' from blame. For instance, in response to Jewish pressure, the opening title of the film was inserted, and reads: 'The events portrayed in this picture occurred in Palestine nineteen centuries ago, when the Jews were under the complete subjection of Rome – even their own High Priest being appointed by the Roman procurator.' The explicit meaning here is clearly that Caiaphas is not representative of the Jewish people.

In constructing his narrative, De Mille enlarges the character of the High Priest into a melodramatic villain dominated by materialism. The plot against Christ is seen as wholly the work of Caiaphas and his minions, and in the court scene representative Jewish figures protest at the injustice. Such care is taken to isolate Caiaphas that he alone is given a version of

Matthew's minatory words, 'And with one voice the people cried "His blood be on us, and on our children" ' (27: 26): 'If thou, Imperial Pilate, wouldst wash thy hands of this Man's death, let it be upon me – and me alone!' By taking all blame, he even achieves a perverse nobility: 'Lord God, Jehovah, vent not thy wrath on thy people Israel – I alone am guilty.' Given this, one can see that De Mille might be straightforward in his feelings that he had done everything possible to liberalise the interpretation and shift a generalised racial blame.

However, things are hardly so simple. Caiaphas, the Romans' Jew, asserted to be in no way representative of Jewry, is an anti-Semite's dream caricature of wickedness: obese, cynical, rubbing his plump fingers together in gleeful anticipation of his plots, appearing like a well-fed devil at Pilate's side to whisper 'Crucify him!' So the scapegoat who apparently frees the Jews from blame is simultaneously the living epitome of ethnic guilt. It is perhaps unlikely – given his celebration of Jewishness in other films – that De Mille was conscious of this, and it would be wrong to read it merely as a consequence of his own ambivalence towards his part-Jewishness. That factor may be important but, if so, it finds support in the often explicit anti-Semitism of America in the 1920s. Whatever its deeper causes (Freud's speculations in *Moses and Monotheism* offering the classic analysis), anti-Semitism in America was given impetus by waves of immigration, the connections of some Jews with Labour agitation in America and the part played by Jews in the Russian Revolution, the spectre of which hung over America in the 1920s. The anti-Semitism of Henry Ford and his recycling of *The Protocols of the Elders of Zion* in *The Dearbourn Independent* is an extreme example of such irrationality. But with De Mille one also suspects that there is in part another non-religious explanation that lies in tendencies towards the 'children's story' producing, in antithesis to the good father, the bad father, an ogre of traditional evil imaged (even while disclaiming it) after centuries of anti-Semitic caricature.

In drawing out the implications of H. B. Warner's version of Christ in this film it is no accident that we have highlighted Christ's involvement with women and children; a Christ of and for women and children. It may at first seem exaggerated to argue further that the film's fatherly Christ is in some important way himself 'feminised', for obviously he is in the simplest sense far less feminine than certain images of the youthful Christ (for example John Rogers Herbert's *Our Saviour subject to His Parents at Nazareth*). But in his passivity, his detachment from notions of masculine force (even in the cleansing of the Temple scene his anger is more ethically parental than forceful), this Christ, at one level so patriarchal, is at another extremely 'feminised'. In his autobiography, as we saw earlier, De Mille at first claims the opposite, but ends up being interestingly implausible: 'All my life I have wondered how many people have been turned away from Christianity by the effeminate, sanctimonious, machine-made Christ of second-rate so-called art, which used to be thought good enough for Sunday schools.' Although De Mille does remark on Warner's sensitivity, his praise of him largely takes the opposite direction: This man of Nazareth was a man with a body hard enough to stand forty days of fasting and long journeys on foot and nights of sleepless prayer.' This call on the soldier's or athlete's Christ (the Christ of the 'Good Fight' and 'Onward Christian Soldiers'), is for someone totally absent from the film, however much De Mille would like or thinks he would like, him to be there. Significantly, the passage in question is followed by an anecdote making exactly the opposite point, where meeting him many years after the film a minister is supposed to have said to Warner, 'I saw you in *The King of Kings* when I was a child and, now, every time I speak of Jesus it is your face I see.' Alongside the image of the 'Man of Sorrows' there is a marked tendency in Victorian art to view religious sensibility as female. One instance is Millais' *The Return of the Dove to the Ark* where two female children are framed with doves. Other paintings of this period (such as Charles Collins's *Convent Thoughts* and Millais' *The Vale of Rest*) exemplify what Susan P. Casteras has defined as the 'Cult of the Nun', an underlining of the idea that women embody the softer, more idealising elements of humanity. An equally interesting tendency portrays Christ as a youth both in paintings (for instance Holman Hunt's *The Finding of Our Savour in the Temple*) and in certain currents of Victorian hymns (often written by women such as Mrs C. F. Alexander), such as 'Once in Royal David's City', where the author's/congregation's assumption of the child's believing viewpoint parallels the film's.

In pinning down the more feminine of these connotations it is helpful to turn to Ann Douglas's *The Feminization of American Culture* and its analysis of ante-bellum movements in nineteenth-century American culture, with their most overt expression in the work of the sentimental women novelists of the period, centring on the idealisation of female 'influence' on the unregenerate male world. At the extreme end of this view Douglas finds not only various identifications of the female with God and Christ but also an extraordinary passage in *The Christian Examiner* where a Minister writing in 1854 on the 'women question' is not content merely to assert that the 'womanly element' predominated in Christ but also actually likens woman to the Messiah, a view which if literally scandalous has a great deal of metaphorical resonance in the period.

Turning to Warner's Christ, it is clear that the Saviour he represents is one who, while still, of course, a man, is surrounded by women and children with whom he predominantly interacts. As an older man he is also removed, like the child, as far as possible from dominant aggressive maleness. In other words, he is feminised not so much wholly in looks as in his inhabiting of a sphere more female than male, and in his distance from the male strength and power which, particularly in its proletarian aspects, is seen as committed to violence and brutality and an unregenerate world. At various points in the film, most spectacularly in the post-Resurrection appearance, the disciples – especially the ruggedly hirsute Peter – produce a cascade of gestures of softening, derigidifying vulnerability and receptivity that, transgressing gender codes, can only be described as 'feminising'.

Seeking to escape from history (both external socio-political disorder and the internal crises of Christianity in conflict with science and scepticism) into a realm of perfect faith far removed from modern complexities, *The King of Kings* re-encounters history as what seem eternal verities are revealed as historically conditioned responses to the Christian narrative. Though the problems of the modern world are apparently firmly repressed, the film's very last image brings them strikingly into view, in a version of the apotheoses with which Griffith ended both *Birth of a Nation* and *Intolerance*, where Christ floats in the ether to the music of 'Rock of Ages' and the intertitle, 'Lo, I am with you always'. But the final sight of him is above an image less optimistically pastoral than Griffith's visions of a reconstructed Elysian future: a vision of the present, an urban cityscape, part modernistic architecture, but also part grim factories belching smoke, an urban working-class environment very much perceived as the failing place of Christianity, a brute environment devoid of the softer feelings felt to reside with the feminine.

This riven industrial world, even in the economic upswing of America's late 1920s pre-crash era, exists as the antithesis of – and ultimate test for – Christianity, a dystopia of underprivilege, holding within it the potential for social upheaval and even revolution. The last image, with its intertitle 'Lo, I am with you always', may assert eternity's unchanging view, but it is the difficult present over which Christ hovers and to which we realise retrospectively the film is addressed. This apostrophe to an urban industrialisation is in some senses a desperate one, since it is able to envisage its psychic transformation only through images of the father and the child, and a feminisation which, however desirable, looks sentimental in the face of a brute industrial milieu.

Perhaps the force and rationale of the film's overwhelming nostalgia can best be summed up in a passage from Frances B. Nichol, a fundamentalist writer:

[the true believer] looks back, not on a foggy horizon, with the fog made even more dense by the dark vapours arising from the evolutionary swamps and mines. Instead he looks back to see clearly etched the majestic figure of God . . . Then he hears the footsteps of that great God in the garden in the cool of the evening, to commune with our first parents.

CODA: A LITTLE NIGHT MUSIC

Rock of Ages, cleft for me, Let me hide myself in Thee.

De Mille's *The King of Kings* is, of course, not literally a silent film. Its action is enfolded by Hugo Reisenfeld's musical score attached to reissues in the sound era which parallels the strategies dominant in the film in its evocative use of familiar hymns that at key moments well up out of the late romantic symphonic background, music with inevitable communal, and especially nostalgic childhood Church and Sunday School-attending, resonances of recollected security, momentarily converting the secular dark of the cinema into a dim simulacrum of church or chapel. Even today the emotions this music, with its intensely known lyrics, evokes are powerful for viewers brought up in hymn-singing traditions, lulling them into a mood of participation, echoing the secular singalong of the early sound cinema. The primarily nostalgic aura is heightened by comparison with the music of Charles Ives which also evokes intense nostalgia through quotations from popular hymns, but within a fragmented modernist context. In the film the contexts are straightforward. 'Lead Kindly Light', for instance, accompanies the little blind girl's regaining of her sight; 'Blessed are the Pure in Heart' the exorcism of the Magdalene; 'Jesus Christ is Risen Today' the Resurrection; 'Abide with Me' the Last Supper and Christ's appearance in the closed room; 'Nearer My God to Thee' the death of Jesus; and 'Rock of Ages' the film's final 'Lo, I am with you always' images.

Just as the film's visual images are constructed around a palimpsest of memory traces awakened in the viewer, so a musical tide of familiarity washes over the visual images, enhancing their effect. De Mille's exploitation of the emotive force of this music (and the implicit lyrics from which the music is inseparable) recalls D. H. Lawrence's celebration in his essay 'Hymns in a Man's Life' of images from childhood worship positively preserving for the adult the child's undiminished imagination, beyond 'any criticism or analysis': 'To me the word Galilee has a wonderful sound. The lake of Galilee. I don't want to know where it is. I never want to go to Palestine. Galilee is one of those lovely glamorous worlds, not places, that exists in the golden haze of a child's half-formed imagination.'

In Lawrence's memory these hymns represent a sphere beyond ideology, his perceptions warning us against the contemporary critic's drive to reduce all poetry to ideology. At the same time, though, we cannot ignore the critic's duty to deconstruct, an activity which in this case must stress the other side of things, the theology and ideology embedded in the hymns, doubly so as they are used in the context of a film looking nostalgically backwards to images of security.

Significantly, De Mille and Reisenfeld in key passages use two perennial Victorian hymns, 'Abide with Me' and 'Lead Kindly Light', both messages of hope and salvation, yet also suffused, like Arnold's *Dover Beach*, with intense Victorian melancholy arising from the conflicts of science and religion and the growth of secularism and industrialism. Both are dominated by images of darkness ('Fast falls the eventide / The Darkness deepens' . . . 'amid the encircling gloom' . . . 'The night is dark'), dispossession and abandonment ('And I am far from home'), by a passive yearning for direction ('Lead thou me on') provided by the lantern-bearing presence of Holman Hunt's Christ in *The Light of the World*. A desire for rest and stasis is inflected only slightly differently in the words of the chorus that ends the film, 'Rock of Ages, cleft for me; / Let me hide Myself in thee', which turns the crisis of evolution (rocks, geological strata, the evidence of the existence of life forms outside the scope of biblical explanation) back, even as we remember that the film was made only two years after the Dayton evolution or 'Monkey' trial of 1925, into images of comfort, solidity and refuge.

6

'Son of Man:' Nicholas Ray's
King of Kings (1961)

HOLLYWOOD AND THE HOLOCAUST

Like the narratives of Greek tragedy, the Christ narratives dramatise a familiar story, the rudiments of which we are familiar with, even if we may not be believers, perhaps even more so than with those of other biopics, a genre to which in significant ways the Christ narratives belong. These films are obviously obliged to avoid making full use of what Barthes calls the enigmatic or hermeneutic codes, since they trace over well-known territory, their primary interest focusing, as narratives, on the rhetoric and form of the narration.

Within Hollywood's constraints, *King of Kings* strays furthest from the devotional aura of the Gospels. Of all the films, too, Ray's seems most self-aware of the processes of intertextuality, reminding its audiences, at first through its allusive title then through other devices, that meaning is possible in art only through the generative processes of earlier texts. Just as Jesus and John the Baptist refer back to the prophets and find their own meanings in the traditions that preceded them, so *King of Kings* gestures back in various ways to an earlier *The King of Kings*, exemplifying Harold Bloom's notion of the anxiety of influence, as the 1960s text plays out an oedipal conflict with its 1920s progenitor.

Especially in the light of post-Holocaust Jewish history, the treatment of the Christ story varies significantly from De Mille's. For a start, it takes advantage of the consequences – in ways, interestingly, that Stevens, slightly later, avoids – both of movements towards greater secularisation at many levels of American society and of less self-effacing strategies from within the Jewish community. *King of Kings* very often gives a dual impression both of self-conscious midrash on the origins of Christianity and of universalising the Christ story in a way that upgrades humanism over divinity.

Just as there are many Gospel traditions, so there are many inflections of the Christ narrative. *King of Kings* seems acutely aware of this. Through the use of an archaic 'biblical' voice-over text, the familiar resonances of Orson Welles's theatrical voice-over, through various modes of visual composition (ranging from the garish Christmas card colours and patterns of the Nativity scene clashing markedly with other more 'realistic' elements in the film, to the Quattrocento variations of some of the Garden of Gethsemane and Crucifixion images), the film is conscious of diverse, even contradictory traditions in the treatment of the Christ story, presenting it (for all the 1950s generic elements, which actually become part of its self-consciousness) in something approaching self-consciously metafictional modes of elaborate secularising frames. This taste for selfconsciously highlighting the processes of narration draws Ray's work into the more modernist traditions of the Hollywood cinema, allowing audience speculation on questions of narrative and ideological intelligibility. Ray's earlier biopic *The True Story of Jesse James* (1957) had explored problems of historical truth and its representation in the scene where Jesse reads about himself on the train. The selfconsciousness of *King of Kings* does not originate from the character of Jesus himself – for only the Scorsese film offers a subjective Jesus, but even then does not go as far as Kazantzakis's scene where Jesus comments on his own portrayal in the Gospel Matthew is writing – but it emerges from the generic and cultural frames through which his mission is presented.

Generically, the film also falls into the patterns of self-recognition, ordeal, triumph or tragedy of the Hollywood biopic hero or heroine. The choice of Jeffrey Hunter for Jesus roots the film even further in star-system values in a way that *The Greatest Story* tries to avoid in its drive to universalise the story by importing Max Von Sydow for the role. Equally, Ray's film's obedience to generic laws means that many characters and incidents are introduced out of a desire not for fidelity to the Gospels but to the codes of 1950s and 1960s epics: thus Lucius the Roman soldier slowly moving towards conversion is an extra-biblical invention, out of films like *The Robe* and *Salome*, as he is first involved in the slaughter of the innocents, then in meeting the Holy family a few years later, then in working for Pontius Pilate where he again comes into contact with Jesus. Among other inventions are scenes involving Pilate's wife, also moving, in the contrary direction to her husband, towards conversion; Mary Magdalene's visit to the Virgin Mary; Jesus's conversation with John the Baptist and Lucius in prison; the Virgin Mary's reception of John the Baptist at home; the meeting, only just missed, between Judas, Barabbas and Jesus; and the appearance of Lucius, Pilate's wife, Judas, Barabbas and Caiaphas at the Sermon on the Mount. Additionally, too, not only through the evangelical idiolect of the voice-over ('And Herod, passing pleased . . .'), but also through Welles's own post-*Citizen Kane* status as the great self-conscious innovator, the ground is prepared for a text of multiple allusion. The effect is further stressed through the use of Christmas card imagery of stars, eastern kings and so on.

King of Kings is double-focused. On the one hand, it uses the Jesus story as a means of tuning into late 1950s American preoccupations with personal identity (this is the period of the so-called 'crisis of masculinity'), not so that Jesus is himself given, as Victor Perkins sensibly remarks, a complex personality but so that he becomes the conceptual focus for such questions. In this respect Jesus's divinity may not be a primary concern for Ray, but in so far as Christianity continued to be, at the least, a unifying cultural force, an essential element in the upbringing of the vast majority of American citizens, it could be used to measure late 1950s ethical norms against the fundamental values of Jesus's teachings. On the other hand, in the post-Holocaust period, an opportunity arose for an exploration of the relations between Jews and gentiles, Judaism and Christianity everywhere (but especially of course in the USA), above all of rescuing Jews from the pariah status of their assumed culpability for the crucifixion of Jesus. As, in *King of Kings*, we see human corpses thrown on fires, and hear the voice-over intoning 'For more than 50 years the history of Judaea could be read by the light of burning towns . . . like sheep from their own green fields the Jews went to the slaughter . . . They went from the stone quarries to build Rome's triumphal arches', memories of Jewish persecution by the Nazis (compare Dreyer) overshadow the literal meanings of the narrative. In ways more surprising, though more coded, than in the Old Testament narratives whose subject, above all, is Israel, people and state, ancient and modern, *King of Kings* focuses on the post-Suez (1956) consolidation of the Jewish state, linking Roman brutality with the Arab threat. Furthering this, the role of Barabbas (the film stressing his name *Jesus* Barabbas to make the connection between him and Christ absolutely clear), in contrast to Jesus', is identified with the call for armed struggle in contemporary Israel, something acknowledged by Ray in interview, where he draws direct parallels between the narrative and Jewish persecution by Nazis.

In some ways Jesus, Judas and Barabbas, a group easily and favourably contrasted with Caiaphas, Herod and Pilate, constitute a triumvirate of Jewish resistance to Roman tyranny. While Jesus and Barabbas (Harry Guardino) represent alternative methods of resistance, Judas (Rip Torn) is caught in the middle, turning towards one, then the other, trying but failing to bring them together. While one is, as the voice-over puts it, the 'Messiah of War', the other is the 'Messiah of Peace': Judas is presented less as betrayer than as a confused, tormented patriot, often strikingly identified with Jesus, not only in shots of him suffering as he sees Jesus being lashed and the carpenters preparing the cross, but when there are close-ups in the Last Supper scene on his eyes in ways reminiscent of the treatment of Jesus's eyes throughout the film, where Jesus's power seems to be transmitted through the mesmerising gaze of Jeffrey Hunter's aquamarine-blue, other-worldly, unsemitic eyes. As the close-ups of Jesus's and Judas's eyes follow one another in the Last Supper scene the affinity as well as the imminent parting of the two patriots is signalled.

These two related issues, of individual identity and the struggles of the nation, are given a structural emphasis through the film's lengthy historical introduction. Unlike Stevens's film, *King of Kings* does not begin with the story of Jesus's birth, nor, like Scorsese's or De Mille's, with Jesus's mission. Instead, a more epic approach is taken, before the focus concentrates on the individual life and death of the hero (and even then only one of three heroes), as the tragic history of Israel unfolds. On the surface, the film asserts orthodoxy, presenting itself as a Christ narrative, of primary interest to Christian audiences. But underneath the Christian structure it simultaneously offers a set of historical explanations – perhaps even grounds for scepticism about official Christian accounts – for the life and ministry of Jesus, viewing these through the prismatic lens of post-1948 American and Jewish history.

In fusing these elements, Ray's flair for dramatic composition is unsurpassed in the film's opening, as the cruelty of the Romans and the decadence of their Semitic puppet rulers form a composite image of the terrors and humiliations to which the Jews are subjected. With their blood-red capes, helmet plumes and scorpion-emblazoned shields, Ray's Romans form spectacular images of tyranny, especially when the legion marches up to the Temple, before Pompey, its leader, violates the inner sanctuary by riding in on horseback, dismounting only to slash the veil that guards the holy scrolls.

The narrative stresses the oppression of a people, the conquest of a land, sacred both in the more universal sense embracing believers everywhere – both Christian and Jewish – and in the narrower Zionist sense. Significantly in this film, too, Caiaphas, often elsewhere an arch-villain, is presented more cautiously. Telling Pilate unflatteringly that 'the people have little love for any men appointed by your Emperor', he attends the Sermon on the Mount to find out more about Jesus, ultimately coming out against him because he might (again compare Dreyer) 'stir the people up against the Romans', who might 'use Jesus and his followers as an excuse to massacre our people'.

Against this background two figures are seen struggling, their separate missions given meaning by the historical events in which they are fatefully caught up. At first, though, it is the seeker of justice through armed struggle, Jesus Barabbas, not Jesus Christ, who comes into focus, his Stern Gang exploits in the hills of Judaea (as, early in the film, he attacks the caravan taking Pilate and Herod to Jerusalem) given narrative priority not simply in order to appear insignificant beside the more metaphysically profound call to the Jews by Jesus but to articulate one term of a genuine dilemma (force or influence). Ultimately, of course, *King of Kings* is primarily a heavily codified Hollywood sacred biopic, but it never loses its commitment to the exploration of Jewish victimisation under the Romans, explaining figures like Barabbas, Judas and even to some degree Jesus in terms of historical contexts, nationalism and colonialism.

JEWS, ARABS AND EDOMITES

Whereas Stevens's Herod, Jose Ferrer, an actor frequently identified with complex, often sympathetic roles (such as Cyrano de Bergerac, Toulouse Lautrec), allows space for nuance, Ray's Herod, Frank Thring, a largely unknown actor, personifies an obese, parricidal, sybaritic, lisping English-accented caricature of villainy. Ignoring the realities of history (Antipas was an Idumean, or Edomite on his father's side and, on his mother's, a Samaritan), *King of Kings* adds to the usual nightmare figures of the Hollywood cinema with that more accessible symbol of otherness in the post-Suez, pro-Israel atmosphere of the late 1950s, the Arab.

The voice-over commentary actually defines his father Herod the Great (George Coulouris) as 'an Arab of the Bedouin tribe'. Frank Thring approximates as closely as possible to a negative stereotype, the other side of the romanticised Tony Curtis or Yvonne De Carlo largely pre-Suez fantasies projected by what Edward Said has called a process of 'Orientalism', that refusal to see the reality of Semitic cultures in terms other than those proposed by the Western imagination's search for difference by which to measure its own realities. Intelligibility to the early 1960s audience is therefore largely made possible here both by the usual ahistoricising norms of Hollywood villainy and also, on the contrary, precisely by the historical circumstances of a growing awareness in American society at large, fuelled by Israel-associated propaganda, of the rise of a new bogeyman threatening civilised standards. As ancient Babylon had once been ancient Israel's shorthand for decadent baseness, so the Arab states replace Germany and

Russia in the later post-war period as the new Babylon of Western consciousness. Even compared with Roman cruelty, 'Arab' savagery remains
unsurpassed: Lucius the Roman soldier-hero draws the line at atrocities his
'Arab' master orders with the slaughter of the innocents: 'I am a Roman
soldier. I do not murder children.' In this film, moreover, there are two trial
scenes involving Jesus. In the second, he is handed over to Antipas so that in
a distortion of history he can take responsibility for Jesus's fate. There
Herod, the 'Arab', is the character seen attempting to subject Jesus to
humiliation and placing a robe on him in a final act of parody before
despatching him back to Pilate.

The image of corruption heightened by Herod's presence finds its lurid
equivalents in the mise-en-scène, on the one hand of sumptuous, fussily-
decorated, butterfly-pattern stained floors to which both Herods seem
sometimes to be pinned, and on the other the ever-threatening presence of
the palace dungeons. This decadence, also associated with Salome and
Herodias, those traditional figures of desire, something relayed either
through the colourful language spoken by, say, Wilde's Salome to the
Baptist ('The roses in the garden of the queen of Arabia are not so white as
thy body') or through the frisson-charged mise-en-scène of Flaubert's
Herodias ('some cinnamon was smoking in a porphyry bowl, and powders,
salvers, filmy fabrics, and embroideries lighter than feathers were scattered
about') resurfaces here in the voluptuous shapes of Rita Gam as Herodias
and Brigid Bazlen as Salome. While the florid language ('his heart should be
ripped from his body') lacks Wildean finesse, the Sadean streak, as when
Salome feels like cutting the Baptist's flesh to see if blood flows in his veins,
and the surrounding aura of decadence in appearance and movement in the
dance sequence that ends with her striding, thighs exposed, over her
uncle/stepfather, is partly designed to arouse the disapproval of an audience
being made to conflate (Arab) tyranny with decadence and sensuality. But it
is also partly designed to gratify the *mauvaise foi* expectations of an audience, already sustained by a rich diet of Hollywood glamour, television
sybaritic spectaculars and a whole range of other channels of popular
culture celebrating the excesses denounced by the official culture, prepared
only to condemn excess when practised by unAmericans.

At least to the moral view, the Herodian world is one of moral and
spiritual imprisonment, the dungeon finding its equivalents in the bird-
cage rarely out of view in the above-ground palace scenes and the miniature
one Salome holds in the scene of Antipas's trial of Jesus. At one point
Salome is deliberately viewed through the bars of the cage at the palace. It is
to this world of various imprisonments that Jesus comes offering salvation.

Herod, Herodias, Salome and the Romans form a pattern of pagan cruelty, signs of the fallen world whose victims cry out for redemption. From a sickly, neurotic world Jesus emerges, at least in the more Christ-centred areas of the film, as its would-be physician ('The healthy have no need of a physician, but the sick do' Jesus replies to a questioner during the Sermon on the Mount scene), here appealing to the buried altruism and noblemindedness of Western-motivated ideals of adolescence.

REBEL WITH A CAUSE

King of Kings is, after all, the work of the director of *Rebel Without a Cause* (1955) and Jeffrey Hunter seems almost as young a man as James Dean, equally idealistic, often moody, but less confused and delinquent. *Rebel* shows the family's slide into decline; *King of Kings* might be seen indirectly to point the way to its restoration. While the son follows his heroic destiny, women are kept in their place, with the softly-spoken, bread-making Siobhan McKenna reinforcing a sense of tradition in the roles mothers are expected to play inside the family, becoming in the process a sign of pure motherhood, the madonna who will 'intercede' (pronounced with almost parodic Irishry), and combating the sterility of unreconstructed maleness.

But the issue is complicated because, although aspects of traditional forms of maleness are reaffirmed, the cruder variants associated with dominant American standards of masculinity in the late 1950s are discredited; symptomatically, whereas in the De Mille film Jesus takes on the role of the father, Ray's Jesus is much more son than father. Masculinity is a primary topic of Ray's films, as in that representative moment in *Rebel* where Dean asks 'What can you do when you have to be a man?' In Ray's world masculinity ideally allows for gentleness as well as power, healing as well as aggression. This is where Ray and Christianity seem to coincide, in a way objectionable to Nietzsche for whom Christianity was waging a war on the higher type of man. There is a certain prophetic logic to his conviction, borne out by the film, that Christianity is only a freer expression of Judaism, for in a film very sympathetic to the Jewish cause it is instructive to see the extent to which Judaism and Christianity are here unified. Jeffrey Hunter's looks, that unmistakable paradigm of WASP male beauty of the era, point to the projected solidarity of the great Western superpower (and not just Christianity), with its Middle Eastern ally and the Jewish traditions from which, as the film painstakingly explains, it springs.

Alongside its interest in both the Christ story and racial/ethnic issues, *King of Kings*, like Ray's other films, returns repeatedly to problems of male

identity, where characters struggle to come to terms with their gentler
natures: the brutalised cop (Robert Ryan) comes to value his tender
instincts in *On Dangerous Ground*; or, developing motifs he may have found
appealing in Christianity, Ray has Bogart in *In a Lonely Place* take the side of
the underdog, here not the prostitutes and outcasts of the Gospels but a
washed-up actor victimised by bullies. In all of these films and others there
is a moment where the male protagonist must make a decision about the
direction to be taken for the rest of his life. His own male identity rests on
that decision. In *Rebel* this moment of renewal actually takes place against an
Easter background. Though the Ray male is a product of urban life, he
frequently draws inspiration from nature in films like *Bitter Victory* (the
desert), *Wind Across the Everglades* (the Florida swamps) and *On Dangerous
Ground* (the Montana countryside). In *King of Kings*, it is in the wilderness
and the rural settings of Judea, that John the Baptist, who, as the man
crying in the wilderness, becomes almost a kind of halfway house through
which Jesus must pass. As played by Robert Ryan, the Baptist personifies
not only righteousness but also a kind of crude animality, a maleness the
Christ figure must encounter and transcend, with Ryan's characteristic
ruggedness accentuated here by a covering of animal skins and a wild
excrescence of bodily and facial hair. Additionally, the Baptist's anger,
commented on by Salome ('You frighten me, you angry man!'), prefigures
the righteous anger of Jesus. As Welles's voice-over commentary puts it,
Jesus withdraws the disciples to a pastoral environment implicitly identifying himself with country people because they are 'pure in heart' and kept
outside the corruptions of the city. His first appearance as an adult in the
film coincides with the pastoral baptism scene. Water symbolism here
recalls the hero's speech in *Wind Across the Everglades*: 'You see, they're sort
of the way the world must have looked on the first day. When it was all
water, and then the first land beginning to rise out of the sea. You feel the
life force in them in its purest, earliest form.'

In *King of Kings*, too, water is important as Jesus is constantly identified
with it ('I am fire, he is water' says Barabbas), in images obviously inspired
partly by John's Gospel ('But whosoever drinketh of the water that I shall
give him shall never thirst', 4: 14, etc.), and partly, as Ray himself acknowledges, by Jung's fire and water symbolism of the collective unconscious.
And, as Jesus begins to construct the heroic identity that will lead him to
fulfil his destiny, he recalls not only the Gospels but the theme of self-
discovery so marked in many of Ray's films. Dialogue from *Johnny Guitar*
provides a more secular dimension to the topic:

'And who are you?'
'The name's Johnny Guitar.'
'That's no name.'
'Anybody care to change it?'
. . . 'You must be the Dancin' Kid.'
'That's the name. Care to change it?'

Like Jesus in *King of Kings* (though 'King of Kings' will give way to another more interesting title), Johnny and the Dancin' Kid have names or labels that define their identity, but like the Bogart character in *In a Lonely Place*, this identity is nothing if not self-sacrificing, or, in the positive sense of the term, selfless.

Ray's restructured hero, someone, as Perkins argues, often in confusion, retains the energy and willpower of the traditional male, reactivates adolescent idealism, rebels against the decadence and materialism of a corrupt society, finding a self – usually tragically – through a sense of mission embracing fellow feeling at the expense of aggression, philanthropy at the expense of self-centredness. In *King of Kings* these issues cluster around the key moment – the Sermon on the Mount – when Jesus refers to himself, in a way paralleling the name and identity exploring scenes involving Johnny Guitar and the Dancin' Kid, as the 'Son of Man'.

In accordance with the demands of the mainstream Hollywood product with epic and biopic cross-fertilisation that strongly defines aspects of the film, Ray's choice of Jeffrey Hunter offers the audience, at first glance, a straightforward matinée idol hero, of the type avoided by Scorsese, Stevens and De Mille. Hunter's Jesus is the Messiah of the secularised gentiles, the Adonis whose self-description as the 'Son of Man' in the Sermon on the Mount seems designed to cut through specifically Christian preoccupations for those in the audience to whom they are secondary or dispensable. From one point of view, Ray's interest in Hunter parallels the minimal interest in the real Jesus of, say, Correggio in the voluptuous *Noli Me Tangere* painting, or of Michaelangelo in his *Risen Christ*. In retaining an unambiguous sexual aura, Michelangelo's Christ belongs to a whole tradition to which Leo Steinberg has drawn attention, of paintings of Christ, either as infant or adult, sometimes flagrantly displaying an 'ostentatio genitalium', sometimes only codedly. By variously emphasising Christ's genitality Renaissance artists highlighted the mystery of the Incarnation. The naturalistic truths of these paintings, Steinberg argues, from the unselfconscious exposure of the infant's genitals to, in maturity, the dead Christ's touching of his genitals (for example in Ribera's *Entombment*), are a startling part of the conceptual meanings of the 'totality of a promise fulfilled'. In other words, by highlighting Christ's sexuality or sexual potential these paintings assert his incarnation in the fullest possible sense.

While *King of Kings* cannot possibly ever have dared to stress Christ's humanity in this way, it echoes the doubleness in other parts of the film by emphasising his humanity through his self-definitions as the 'Son of Man' in the Sermon on the Mount, through his youthful beauty, the faint sexual aura surrounding him in the scenes of his disrobing before flagellation, and in the Crucifixion itself, scenes attracting attention for their exposure of Hunter's immaculately shaved armpits. The irony is that through trying to remove by this prim act of depilation all threat of sexual connotation, exactly the opposite effect has been achieved, the absence of hair in the places one would normally expect to find it unavoidably drawing attention to its absence and to the mechanisms dictating its removal. Hunter's adherence to Hollywood 1950s torso-shaving patterns does not of course re-sexualise Jesus, but it does further place the role in the secular, idealised– heroic traditions of Hollywood masculinity. The effect makes of Ray's Jesus someone whose tenderness, self-sacrifice and renunciation of aggression and violence become all the more acceptable because espoused by a figure of male beauty idealised by the Hollywood cinema of that time. This is the sense in which ultimately Jesus can become not just a rabbi (Judas's first term of address to him), but, more significantly, the 'Son of Man', a humanised hero, commanding respect and admiration for his mission, with or without acceptance of its divinely-ordained inspiration.

The term 'Son of Man' has been variously defined as either a circumlocution in the interests of modesty or appearing in Daniel, 7, or Enoch, 1, as meaning 'suffering servant', with Christian interpretations favouring more eschatalogical significance. In *King of Kings* this phrase is allowed, because of its secular resonances. Like all Ray's male protagonists Jesus is a 'Son', struggling to find his masculinity, in the materialist male or 'Man' dominated culture of 1950s America.

In the Sermon on the Mount set-piece, Jesus twice refers to himself in this way. The reverberations of the phrase find their visual complement in the colour patterns of Jesus's dress in this and earlier scenes. Here Jesus wears red for the first time. In maturity he dresses first in white (also at his trial), then red, followed by brown and then white again. His costume colours fit into an intricate pattern established by the film, in which comparisons, contrasts and perspectives become visually stated. White, the colour of the lamb ('I am the good shepherd. The good shepherd lays down his life for his sheep' he replies in this scene when asked if he is the Messiah) is primarily identified with Jesus, but it is also the colour of Pompey's and Pilate's battle-dress, the shawls of the High Priests, the shroud protecting the inner sanctuary where the scrolls are kept, the veils worn by Herodias and Salome on their first appearance in the film on their journey through the Judaean countryside, and the dress worn by the adulteress, Mary Magdalene. In making the Romans and the priests wear white the film asks where purity lies: in Roman efficiency? the old Law? In making these women wear the same colour the film comments ironically on the corruption of sexual innocence and fidelity. While brown seems reserved both for more mundane moments (when Jesus goes home to fix his mother's chair) and for more serene ones (his Resurrection, brown rather than white reinforcing his identification with earth and nature, and perhaps incidentally bearing on patterns of scepticism), red, above all the colour of blood, of the Passion, is worn by Jesus for the first time following the death of John the Baptist. The spilling of the Baptist's blood foreshadows the Crucifixion, and Jesus's costume colour prefigures his own Passion.

Once Jesus is disturbed from his reveries by Peter, he begins to mingle in the crowd, the camera cutting between him and the group as a whole, spread out in vast numbers all over the Mount, or between him and little huddles of listeners. As he weaves in and out of the multitude, speaking the resonant words of the Beatitudes, the redness of Jesus, like a bloodstain, creates a visual metaphor of self-sacrifice for humanity, represented in microcosm on the hillside. The compassion symbolised by Jesus's red cloak is set off against the cruelty of the Romans, whose scarlet cloaks suggest a haemorrhage of tyranny over their conquered subjects.

As with the colour patterns, so too with Philip Yordan's dialogue: the film expects its audience to ponder the various resemblances and comparisons of speech. As Herod the Great lies dead, Orson Welles's voice-over intones, 'So Herod the Great, crushed by his many murders, self-crucified, fell dead.' The futile life of the corrupt ruler seems all the more wasted through application of a word, 'crucified', so highly charged with the significance of Jesus's supreme act of self-sacrifice.

Language, as used here and elsewhere by Jesus, retains all the plenitude of meaning accepted by tradition, but to the sceptic, for whom Barabbas is a sort of screen alter ego, words have at best only fleeting influence, futile without action. As Barabbas rejects Christ's seemingly Utopian promises, he echoes Antipas, who confessed himself the 'slave of words, the words of a king', when asked by Salome whether he would keep his promise if she danced before him, and in the process forces a comparison between Herod and Jesus, both kings. Neither Herod's nor Jesus's promise, in the eyes of Barabbas and sceptics in the audience, is kept. The fact that Barabbas, a sympathetically focused character here, is never wholly condemned for meeting force with force, as Ray balances his 1950s 'new man' tendencies with a need for traditional male attributes in the face of persecution, ultimately means, if only for the non-committed audience, that even the force of the Resurrection ending might be undermined.

Scepticism is deeply ingrained in this film. The few miracles that are dramatised are attributable as much to charisma as to divinity. This is the only one of the Christ narratives, significantly, to omit the raising of Lazarus. Jesus's eyes, at significant moments seen in extreme close-up (first meeting the Baptist, or curing the blind man), are used in complex patterns of imagery to suggest virtuosity in mind over matter techniques of the type discussed in Morton Smith's *Jesus the Magician*, which argues that Jesus learnt his magic in Egypt. In addition to the few seemingly psychosomatic miracles we do see, we have only reports of others: the feeding of the five thousand, the walking on the water, the calming of the storm, the dying child brought back to health. Instead of witnessing for ourselves their effect on the disciples, we only have the narrator's word that they were 'awed by his miracles', something that in heightening the film's scepticism prioritises the humanism of Jesus's ministry. Jesus's rebel at the Sermon on the Mount projects a version of masculinity as angry but also beautiful and feminised, the approachable 'Son of Man' who takes the place of the more forbidding, unknown, even absent father. As the Son takes the place of the Father, as *King of Kings* replaces *The King of Kings*, a double act of transgressive oedipal intertextuality takes place, De Mille's fatherly (though admittedly, unforbidding) Jesus giving way to the filial Jeffrey Hunter, a spiritual, devout version superseded by a more secular one. The accessibility of Ray's Jesus comes partly through the pastoral, studenty milieu of his relationship with his disciples (something taken further in Stevens), but partly also through identification with his mother (already foregrounded in invented non-Gospel sequences with Jesus and Mary Magdalene), who in the Sermon on the Mount can often be seen in close-up listening to Jesus in costume colours of matching red or black, her presence here, as at the Crucifixion, projecting an image of the suffering as well as the joyful, proud mother, asserting her influence over the son.

In what is, then, the most secular of all the film versions, an ambiance of ambiguity casts doubt, if one cares to look for it, on the apologetically Christian focus of the Gospels. Even the Resurrection itself (we see Christ and Mary Magdalene in the garden, but we do not see Christ subsequently) is presented through a somewhat stagey, formalised device, as the apostles line up on the Galilean beach for the unseen Christ's shadow to fall on their nets to make the sign of the cross. The apostles eventually exit from the frame to set off on their proselytising mission, the 'Shadow of the Galilean' readable either as historical reality or as Church propaganda.

7

An American pastoral:
George Stevens's *The Greatest Story Ever Told* (1965)

THE CALL OF THE WILD

> I was halfway across America, at the dividing line between the East of my youth and, the West of my future . . . — Jack Kerouac, *On the Road*

Although it includes many moments, both early on and during the later crucifixion scenes, that portray the savagery of Roman rule (for example the forest of crosses covering the landscape at the beginning of the film), *The Greatest Story Ever Told* is less interested than Ray's film in the social implications of Jesus's ministry, laying more emphasis on personal salvation, exploring through a more respectful, devotional rhetoric, spiritual issues involving self-determination and self-sacrifice. In one sense its title is a misnomer, 'story' suggesting allusive self-consciousness fitting more naturally the Ray film; in another, though, in the sense of the revival hymn's usage of the word ('Tell me the old, old story'), with its connotations of an often told tale, it is appropriate. Further, for all its emotive moments, such as when Jesus weeps at Lazarus's death, this Christ narrative acquires a more detached mode of expression than any of the others. With his Byzantine look, Max von Sydow makes Jesus a slightly unearthly figure, his otherness marked by Von Sydow's foreignness and identification with the European art cinema. At times, too, his unvarying costume of white robe and burnous (Ray's Jesus never covers his head, as Stevens's does), projects an image not just of light but also of unworldliness. In fact his first adult appearance, mysteriously materialising out of the urban shadows, stresses this otherness. All of this, coupled with moments like the multitude's chanting of the Lord's Prayer in one of the great outdoor scenes, makes the film resemble at times a church service. Where it exists, the over-voice commentary is theological (St John): 'In the beginning was the word, and the word was with God . . .', something that adds to the film's impression of ritual, great emphasis being given elsewhere to watchers or observers, as we, the audience, so often watch interior audiences watching Jesus. The film even begins and ends inside a church: Jesus's image first appears in a fresco, dissolves into the Palestine night sky, becoming identified with a star, and then an oil lamp flame, before the narrative finally gets under way. In a few dissolves we have a concise summary of the ecclesiastical history of Christianity: the son of a sky god descending in human form to save sinners. Given this controlling ecclesiastical structure, made explicit by the rhyming fresco images at the end, the rest of the film celebrates both the divine structure of the universe and, especially, the landscape which reflects it, exposing the corruptions and degradations to which, in the film's rhetoric, even after the covenant mortals have descended.

Avoiding the unnecessary distraction of concentration on the narrower historical circumstances of Jesus's ministry, the film dispenses with the history lesson at the beginning of the Ray film. As if exemplifying Nietzsche's notion that Jesus was the 'great symbolist', denying time, space and history, accepting only inner realities, the film refuses identification between events in ancient Judaea and modern Israel. No stereotypes equating Herod with ogrish Palestinians are attempted, the King of the Jews here defined as Idumean, not Arab. Even the traditional ambience of sexual debauchery underlining the corruption of Herod disappears. Perhaps 1960s relaxation of sexual morals meant that sex tended less to be identified with evil, so it disappears from a scene where it would have been irrelevant. The court mise-en-scène, so decadent in Ray, projects an image of stony austerity, eschewing too the self-indulgent decadence of Herodias's and Salome's erotic presence. In this film Salome is a far more shadowy figure, not pleading on her mother's behalf for the baptiser's head, while Herod (Jose Ferrer), rather than slave of the flesh, becomes a troubled politician, out of his depth in the atmosphere of spiritual unrest gripping his kingdom. Additionally, Barabbas (Richard Conte) has lost all the heroic stature given him by Ray, appearing only at the end in connection with his liberation at Jesus's expense. Judas (David McCallum), too, while not reverting to the more negative imagery used by De Mille, becomes an ambiguous character, the film seeming ill at ease in its need to include him in the narrative, any adherence to the strict norms of scapegoat stereotypes running the risk of diminishing the film's interest in questions of inner choice.

The ancient historical focus of the Gospels is worked in rather more quietly than in other Christ films, alongside the film's implicit interests in the world of 1960s America, where even minute details, like the Baptist's language, making the 'desert a highway for our God', possess a dualism anchoring the film in its own times, as the narrative attempts to widen the scope of its impact. At times, especially in outdoor shots, the look of *The Greatest Story* (shot in Utah rather than Israel) recalls the great big-sky Westerns of the Hollywood cinema, especially of course Stevens's own *Shane*. Often, as there or in the Ford pastorals, the screen is filled with sky, the characters reduced to diminutive silhouettes journeying across the horizon, as when the Holy Family return from their Egyptian exile, their presence barely discernible at the very bottom of the frame, the remainder of the image filled with billowy clouds proclaiming the infinity of the universe. There are even several minor echoes of the Western, like the inclusion of a minor character who must earn the group's respect before being granted full membership (Little James paralleling the Horst Bucholz part in *The Magnificent Seven*), or the assault by barbarians (here Herod's soldiers taking on the generic function of Apaches) on the lives of the holy innocents. Repeatedly, too, the camera prefaces key narrative moments with dissolving panoramas of landscape, sometimes merging Jesus's voice-over ('all the tribes of the earth shall see the Son of Man coming in the cloud of heaven, the power and the great glory'), with the landscape itself, as if the two were inseparably linked. The pace of the narrative is extremely slow, the film actually beginning with nine dissolves, its first two sequences depicting journeys as, in one of them, the Holy Family rides through a forest of crucifixes. Before the Sermon on the Mount, for instance, and in keeping with the meditative effects of the whole film, the camera stays with Jesus in long shot, remaining motionless as he speaks the eight Beatitudes. Stasis here, as in the straight-to-camera 'I am the resurrection' speech, is identified with certainty, slowness suggesting not just reverence but meditation.

These vast cinerama landscapes are often set off against intimate pastoral moments. As the meaning of life is questioned by the lake, the disciples throwing stones and watching their ripples disappear, the film because almost Thoreauesque, its reworking of the familiar pastoral images of Jesus's sayings recalling the descriptions of the Pond in *Walden*, that work so important in the more sober aspects of 1960s sensibility of anti-materialist self-cultivation:

> It is a soothing employment, on one of those fine days in the fall when all the warmth of the sun is fully appreciated, to sit on a stump at such a height as this, overlooking the pond, and study the dimpling circles which are incessantly inscribed on its otherwise invisible surface amid the reflected skies and trees.

Often, indeed, the film has the look and feel of a gentler road movie, as Jesus and the apostles, neo-Cynic Jewish itinerant philosophers, or a group of 1960s Thoreauvian counter-culture students, are seen wandering the countryside, earnestly debating the great issues of spirituality, love of God and one's fellows. Jesus himself uses 'on the road' imagery in his non-canonical words at the Last Supper: 'You who have been with me so long, who have given up all to follow me, to walk with me down all these dusty roads.' Day and night Jesus is often in conversation with the apostles – for instance when, shortly after rescuing Mary Magdalene, the group, by now significantly including her, is found discussing the question of Jesus's identity.

As Jesus and the apostles stretch out in the shadows of the olive trees for a rest, Jesus asks, formulating Christianity's most crucial question, 'Tell me, whom do men say that I am?' Various of them, including Thomas and Judas, offer cautious answers but, unprompted, Peter declares 'You are the Messiah, the Christ, the Son of the living God', as if moved to do so – like Christ himself when he uses pastoral imagery about grains of wheat in conversation with Andrew in the Garden of Gethsemane – by the bucolic surroundings, taking inspiration from the truths of the wilderness. The call of the wild made in this film, this time through Charlton Heston's rugged playing of John the Baptist, crosses the Isaiah-inspired conviction of the wilderness's provision of a necessary antidote to the poisoned charms of a city-bred culture with the time's contemporary version of pastoralism.

For a film that went into production in 1964, the appeal of the wilderness – quite apart from its evangelical American pioneering resonances – arises from the collective unconscious of a country, tortured by the tragedy of Vietnam, already at some levels raising a counter-cultural, partially Thoreau-inspired cry against the militarism of the ruling oligarchy. But the decision to go into the wilderness, for Jesus as much as for John the Baptist, and for all the others fleeing from the tumult of the city, undoubtedly raises questions about self-centred narrowness of vision. The flight from society, that Sartrean-perceived hell of human company, leads in the quest for salvation in solitude or asceticism to as many difficulties as solutions. Symbolically, and in a way drawing parallels between the American and Jewish nations, the answering of the call of the wild is even readable as desired detachment from the greater family of humanity. As Mettilius the Roman puts it in Gerd Theissen's *The Shadow of the Galilean*, '. . . just as the whole people once left Egypt for the wilderness. Doesn't that express contempt for humanity, rejection of foreigners and others, indeed rejection of a people generally?' The question there is rightly seen by the text's self-conscious narrator as insidiously harbouring the repetition of an age-old prejudice against the self-absorbed nation of the 'Chosen'. But there, as in the Gospel's themselves, and as in *The Greatest Story*, the response to the call of the wild is not to turn away from humanity so much as to be invigorated by it before returning to grapple with the pitiful illusions of the wayward multitude.

DEVIL IN DISGUISE

The wilderness clarifies the problem of evil for Jesus, for it is there that he confronts the Devil, who makes altogether six appearances in the film, although this is the first and in some respects the most important. In addition to this scene, he appears during the attempted stoning of the Magdalene; in Nazareth, outside Jesus's house; when Judas goes to the priests; as one of Peter's accusers; and in the crowd bellowing for Jesus's execution. The Devil, here, identified in these scenes with hypocrisy, treachery, bigotry and pride – all exemplified by the negative instincts and actions of characters whom he goads on in these scenes – contrasts sharply with other more charismatic incarnations in the various traditions of Western iconography. While the Ray film reduces him to a disembodied voice, thus avoiding allowing physical splendour to make evil doctrine more palatable, *The Greatest Story* evades pitfalls by having the Devil appear as a bald, ageing, jocularly sinister figure played by Donald Pleasance, an actor subsequently type-cast in horror or manic roles. What the film loses in subtlety here is soon recovered in the identifications made between the Devil's ubiquity and the communities of whom he becomes a natural projection.

Even in Hollywood, played by charismatic actors like Ray Walston (*Damn Yankees*), or Laird Cregar (*Heaven Can Wait*), Satan, as in Milton and Calderón, claims the audience's sneaking admiration. Such dangers are deliberately avoided here, the first appearance setting the tone. At a time of growing counter-culture revulsion against materialist and consumerist excess, it seems logical, where conventionally devout audiences might equate the diabolical with pride and rebellion against the creator, that for more socially critical Christians and others the Devil should rather be identified with materialism and its consequences. During their first confrontation, as Jesus climbs a steep boulder, his physical ordeals a visual image of his terrible inner struggle, Satan remarks, with a relaxed, cordial chuckle, welcoming Jesus into his desert shelter and venomous confidence: 'Long hard climb, wasn't it? Come on in, if you like. Some think the whole of life should be hard like that. An easy life is a sinful life. That's what they think. Not so. Life should be as easy as a man can make it.' Without the distractions of humour (Ray Walston's Satan), or elegance (Laird Cregar's), these disarming words of conviviality, coming against the background of a gigantic full orange moon, at once symbolising the enormousness of the universe and the more mundane glories offered by a fallen creature tempting Jesus to name his price (even the moon), are dramatically exposed for what they truly represent: the worshipping of egocentricity in a narcissistic culture, the overvaluation of purely bodily needs, the enslavement by the flattery of worldly success. There is a real sense, too, via this Satan, of evil's definition through images of the worldly, complacent, corporation man. There is no simple youth/age dichotomy here, since some of the film's positive characters (such as Nicodemus, Old Aaron) are older ones. The point is, rather, that evil is portrayed through images of comfortable, middle-class conformism. All of this is aptly given a visual image of physical degeneration, a Satan deprived of youth, glamour and charm, though not entirely without wily, seemingly genial rival values. In confronting Satan here, Jesus faces what for the film is the essence of evil, ready for its various spin-offs and consequences in the incidents that involve him from this point on.

Just as Jesus tells the disciples, 'the kingdom of God is here within you', so Satan's dominion knows no frontiers. As Jesus and the disciples in their peripatetic wanderings become the visual embodiment of enlightenment, so the presence of Satan in many different settings dramatises in a homely symbolism Nineham's argument that as the forces of evil were thought to be in the ascendant Jesus was sent, in the view of Christian apologists, to combat them with his ministry. In the partisan rhetoric of the Gospels, Satan is identified with Judaic officialdom and, even, with the Jews as a whole, where Jesus goes on to say that 'Ye are of your father the devil'. But, in so far as *The Greatest Story* avoids historicising its narrative beyond the demands of verisimilitude, and taking into account Hollywood's unvaryingly highly complex racial–religious sensitivities, the film is very much at one with 1960s ideals of meditation and inner change as the responsibility of the individual. Consequently, the film can hardly have considered adopting positions of sectarian or biased racial or religious commitment along the lines of John's inflammatory prejudices.

So, for every Caiaphas condemning Jesus the film presents a Nicodemus defending him as, avoiding bigotry, it focuses on unsectarian definitions of evil. Caiaphas, it is made clear, is a Roman appointee; an early scene shows us the High Priest's robes being handed over to the Romans; elsewhere Caiaphas is made to appear under Pilate's control: 'Governor Pilate will see the High Priest.' 'Concerning what?' 'Governor Pilate will tell you.' So

Jesus is condemned to death not by Jewish scapegoat figures – and the Devil's presence at the trial where his view prevails proves it – but because evil, in the film's delicately balanced judgement, is rooted in human nature.

Nevertheless, for all its universalising tendencies – Jesus is played by a Byzantine-looking Swede, the film shot in Utah, generic cross-fertilisation sought with the Western – the film cannot avoid its own historical determinants. Significantly, therefore, in contrast with Ray's 1950s-rooted narrative which excludes it, this film, more introspective, more otherworldly, in many ways dehistoricised, includes an episode conflating an allusion to Luke's Dives and Lazarus story about riches with Mark's and Matthew's story about the wealthy young man who seeks to follow Jesus, releasing a cluster of themes around the rejection of materialism, a set of preoccupations very much in tune with the mid-1960s proliferation of interest in alternative lifestyles, preference for country communes and pilgrimages to the (admittedly further) East.

SERVING TWO MASTERS

More than the other Christ narratives *The Greatest Story* highlights the necessary material sacrifices of Christianity. The story of Lazarus of Bethany in St John is used as much to exemplify such considerations as to celebrate Jesus's miraculous powers. Lazarus and his sisters, admirers of Jesus's teachings, are unable to go to the extreme lengths of finally severing their links with a comfortable way of life, in obedience to the call to 'follow me'.

The point is developed in one of the film's most alert, most complex scenes, its version of Christ in the house of Martha and Mary, a sequence projecting an image of a relaxed, domestic ambiance, where Lazarus and his sisters seem content to think that nothing more difficult is required of them:

> *Jesus*: You're not far from the kingdom of God, Lazarus.
> *Lazarus*: Tell me, would it be possible for me to go with you?
> *Jesus*: You are wealthy.
> *Lazarus*: Yes I am. You consider wealth a crime?
> *Jesus*: Not at all, but it may become a burden. For what does it profit a man to gain the whole world and lose his soul?
> *Lazarus*: Are you saying that a man cannot have both money and a soul?
> *Jesus*: I am saying that it is easier for a camel to go through the eye of a needle than for a rich man to enter the kingdom of heaven.
> *Mary*: My brother will go to heaven. He is a good man.

Jesus: Did I say he was not good? I said he was wealthy. Where a man's wealth is
  there is his heart also. A man cannot serve two masters. You cannot serve
  both God and money.
Lazarus: But I give my money to God. I give a third of all I earn.

The scene's dilemma, how to reconcile the ultimate demands of
Christianity with the American Dream's material promises, remains
unresolved as this section of dialogue gives way to Jesus's story about the
widow who gave all she had, the two pennies, eliciting Lazarus's query
'Who could do such a thing?' Although Jesus's teaching centres on a
woman's commitment, the scene exhibits a parallel uncertain attitude to its
women characters, simultaneously accentuating and marginalising them
within the renovations and constraints of its traditional liberalism
moderated by 1960s reformulations. So, while the discussion about ultimate discipleship involves only their brother, Mary and Martha remain
largely passive, even though absorbed, spectators. Replying somewhat
contradictorily that he is not against wealth, Jesus maintains nevertheless,
'A man cannot serve two masters'. When Lazarus replies, 'Who could do
such a thing?', Jesus, following a short pause, rises, not in the slightest
angered by the question, and moves off with the disciples, leaving Lazarus
and his sisters behind.

Lazarus has failed an ultimate test, but Jesus seems to recognise by his
refusal to condemn him that practical men like Lazarus and others are a
social necessity. Lazarus is the practical man without whom society would
collapse, and on whom the idealist depends for support, in the film's
contemporary sub-text the benevolent, socially-conscious businessman–
benefactor. Plainly such a man cannot respond to the call for total worldly
detachment. From a Nietzschean point of view this might be regarded as a
key moment in the Jesus story, where someone actually rejects the denials
of Christianity, refusing to dispense with honour and material advantage. If
Jesus and his disciples epitomise the determination to renounce the world
for the spiritual salvation of others, Lazarus represents the admirable but
less heroic drive to help others improve their worldly condition. Stevens's
1960s narrative, identifying powerfully with the mendicant, peripatetic life
of Jesus's group, still feels obliged to make space for Lazarus's benevolent
materialism.

The simultaneous foregrounding and marginalisaton of Martha and
Mary in the scene complements the film' complex overall attitude to
women. The Virgin Mary (Dorothy Maguire) clearly belongs to the wholly
domestic tradition of Holy Family madonnas. But the anonymous woman
praying for the Messiah's coming at the beginning of the film suggests more

active roles, in part acted out by Mary Magdalene, seen in close-up when Jesus instructs the disciples to teach, and who is presented as remembering Jesus's prophecy of the Ressurection, and then going to look for him at the tomb. Martha and Mary belong in one sense to the film's conservative drives, restricting them to the background as listeners not participants in the debate on spiritual demands. Yet even if excluded from centrality, their presence makes them not only nurturers/carers but an intelligent audience for Jesus's words. If the film is only able to make Mary register a momentary protest at their marginalisation (and then typically taking the form of a defence of her brother), it strives to see them in terms largely detached from the objectifications of sexual desire. The imposing mise-en-scène of male nudity – statues of Roman Gods and heroes like Mars, Hercules and Jupiter, prominent in Pilate's palace – not only symbolises pagan idolatry but male power, including the sexual, from the objectifications of which Christianity claims to offer women rescue. While women may face other dangers from ideological processes associated with Christianity – through oedipally motivated madonna and fallen Eve stereotyping – they are at least shown finding a role and purpose other than the wholly erotic, within the limits of what is available in biblical times. So Veronica wipes Jesus's face on the road to Calvary, Mary Magdalene joins the disciples, and is favoured as the person to whom Jesus first appears after the Resurrection.

So when Jesus raises Lazarus in this film, he does it not purely out of friendship for the dead brother but as a favour for his sisters, as if in doing so he acknowledges, at least as far as the film's dominant conservatism allows, the place of women, listening sympathetically to their requests in the new order of things. Here women, like pagans, (John Wayne's Roman soldier), blacks (Sidney Poitier's Simon of Cyrene) Jews and gentiles, all have a place, as the film seems to reply to the question Little James asks near the beginning of the film, 'Is it [i.e. Christianity] just for us or for everyone?'

The scene of the raising of Lazarus is one of the great set-pieces of the film. The importance of the scene is conveyed initially by a static, painterly tableau presentation, as the camera pulls back to long shot in another of the film's compositions reminiscent of one of the multi-levelled, rock-covered Mantegna paintings of scenes from the Gospels (like *The Agony in the Garden*). Sometimes, as here, through oblique reference, but elsewhere more directly, as when reverent parallels are made with Leonardo's *Last Supper* or when the Hallelujah chorus is used to mark the change from stasis to the explosive energy that sweeps over the onlookers who rush to spread the news of Lazarus's resurrection, the invocation of Western culture's textual landmarks imbues the film with an authority adequate to its grave thematics. Interestingly, Stevens claimed that he was attempting to create a 'sixties concept of Jesus Christ . . . For example, we're not going to thank Mr Da Vinci for his arrangement of the Last Supper. When the scene comes, we hope audiences will feel that it happened this way.' Yet often the effect is the opposite, something that even led the Broadcasting and Film Commission of the National Council of Churches to avoid, pointedly, giving the film an award. As the editor of the *Christian Advocate* put it, 'Stevens must have known that his characters were all lifeless, stereotyped, cardboard figures out of Sunday school literature . . . Presented in this deadly discursive fashion they lacked the power to command attention or demand decision.'

This response by slightly radicalised churchmen parallels more secular objections to the casting of stars in vignette roles. Felix Barber in *The Evening News* wrote:

> Good Time Girl Carroll Baker puts down her carpetbag to wipe sweat from the brow of Jesus; Shelley Winters has a brief attack of leprosy . . . No one blames Hollywood stars for wanting to arrange a little personal atonement. But couldn't George Stevens, the director, see that this sort of casting was death to sincerity and realism.

From their different perspectives both theologian and Fleet Street hack seem to be groping for an aesthetic of the Christ narrative that would be satisfied only by the grainy realism and anonymous characterisation of, say, a Pasolini, condemning Hollywood's equally marked traditions of anti-realism. But even if the film packs its conclusions with stars to try to recoup the vast budget, the effect of their glittering presence has the logic (at least from Hollywood's perspective) of contributing to its celebratory, respectful tone. It is as though the Greatest Story is worthy only of Hollywood's greatest actors. Seen like this, even John Wayne's Centurion speaking his 'Truly this was the Son of God' line (often viewed as wholly bathetic) has its tributary place. This pattern is repeated in the film's less popular allusions. If Leonardo is used by Buñuel as one of the ways through which to begin the deconstruction of European art and ideology, *The Greatest Story*'s allusions to Leonardo, Mantegna, Handel and others, whatever Stevens says, are designed to do the opposite: to find exalted forms for what it takes to be the greatest story ever told, a story for all races (orientals as well as blacks placed strategically in the crowd scenes along the way of the cross and elsewhere) and all classes, for all men and women, stressing the Christian message through the modernity of expression (gesturing perhaps towards apocalyptic nuclear holocausts, affirming inner values, formulating a spiritual anti-establishment message) of the last (Christ's) words of the film: 'Do not fret over tomorrow, leave it to fret over its own needs. For today, today's troubles are enough.'

8

From Main Street to mean streets: Martin Scorsese's *The Last Temptation of Christ* (1988)

TEXT AND CONTEXT

In its controversial history *The Last Temptation of Christ* has attracted more emotion than analysis. The film's difficulties, in all stages of development, are well known. Large-scale fundamentalist (Catholic as well as Protestant) opposition was the most visible of these. Less obvious difficulties sprang from other sources, not all opposed to the 'permissiveness' which made a film with such shocking elements – a subjective, doubting, sexualised Jesus – possible for the first time in mainstream cinema.

No life of Christ project is free of problems, bringing the spectre of the box-office failure attending both Ray's and Stevens's films. The public has consistently preferred the religious film in its less elevated forms rather than in its central one, the Christ film. The primitive American cinema may have produced approaching forty Christ films, but these were fragmentary pageants, predating full narrative film. By the time of the popular failure of *Intolerance*, with its Christ narrative as one of four stories, it is clear that in a consumerist cinema the religious film will have no exemption from market laws, and that the Christ film will be a rare phenomenon. This is both because of its severity and because it has obvious sub-generic limitations, incapable of variations like other genres. Thus, its limited output – four major films in over fifty years.

When the sensitivity of the subject to Christian as well as Jewish audiences is added, the barriers to making such films are so formidable that the will to refilm can triumph only in favourable cultural circumstances seeming to demand a new version. The 1980s, characterised by socio-religious volatility, were such a time, marked by increasing secularism, liberalisation of censorship, religious relativism, liberation theology and other socially-conscious modes of Christianity, and perhaps by not so much a resurgence of belief as a 'longing to believe'. Equally, these tendencies led to powerful counter-resurgences, often making their impact through the 'electric church' of television evangelism and religious conservatism.

While these provided the socio-theological context for a new Christ film, within the cinema three factors provided further determinants. Firstly, Pasolini's film, indisputably influential on Scorsese; secondly, the development, against conventional 'blockbuster' practice, of a 'rough' aesthetic of cinema – dominated by directors like Scorsese, Schrader and Altman – allowing the possibility of a Christ film conceived for a substantial minority rather than a mass audience; and thirdly, evidence within this cinema of the continuing need for dramatisation of religious meanings, albeit in secular contexts (for instance *Taxi Driver*, *Hardcore*).

But any Christ film in the 1980s, however opportune, faced specific contemporary problems, for escalating costs made such a project increasingly risky. The Christ Film also found itself in an aesthetic predicament. By the 1980s the old epic forms were over-predictable. Yet the exhausted model was the only one known. The Christ Film was the victim of a double-bind. Major innovations seemed called for, yet would be resisted by audiences over-familiar with old forms but unattuned to new ones. The solution – both economic and aesthetic – lay in the incorporation into what we call the American 'rough' cinema of some of Pasolini's deviant achievements. Not the least of these was to suggest that the conjunction of the Christ Film and the Epic was an historical accident rather than a necessity. Grasping this led to *The Last Temptation's* existence, with its relatively low budget and direction towards an audience already existing for post-studio auteurist cinema.

A third problem faced by *The Last Temptation* concerned only the minority audience within the greater one. The question here was the possibility of the film's falling between the conventional Christ epic and an ideal of a deconstructive version. By adapting Kazantzakis's major novel *The Last Temptation*, the film laid itself open to the reaction that when faithful it illustrated, and when it adapted it simplified. Likely to seem too radical to the larger audience, it ran the risk of being considered insufficiently radical by the smaller. Any adaptation of this work would face difficulties in transforming into a different medium a verbal artefact of remarkable richness. As Scorsese and Schrader have noted, addressing an audience unfamiliar with many of the novel's registers can lead to simplification: for example the omission of Matthew's rewriting of the events in the novel, which even includes Jesus's critique of his Gospel. The sense of loss created is the price of using such a powerful source. Yet its transposition into contemporary American cinematic modes is achieved with such force that the text acquires an authenticity of its own.

JESUS

> Listen you fuckers, you screw-heads, here is a man who would not take it any more, a man who stood up against the cunts, the scum, the dogs, the shits, the filth. — Travis in *Taxi Driver*

Radical instabilities

In his book *The Cinema of Loneliness* Robert Kolker explores how the narratives of *Taxi Driver* and *Raging Bull* compel an intense, 'discomforting' experience of an unstable protagonist's subjectivity: 'The viewer, made to gaze at the character in particularly discomforting ways, is made as well to gaze with the character himself, to see the world as he sees it.' The viewer/image relationship here is the antithesis of the traditional Christ Film which makes the viewer gaze at the protagonist in comforting ways and, while registering others' reactions to him, forbids access to his consciousness. To subjectivise Christ is to release questions not only disrupting traditional representations, in which the primary question is how others relate to Christ not how he related to himself, but of theology itself. However, this subjectivising is precisely what carries over from Scorsese's secular films into *The Last Temptation*, making its Jesus resemble the Travis Bickle and Jake La Motta of *Taxi Driver* and *Raging Bull* as much as the Jesus of De Mille, Ray and Stevens. Like Travis and La Motta, if not in their ultimate self-destructiveness, Scorsese's Jesus offers the viewer little escape from his tormented consciousness (in fact he is absent in only five brief scenes). This almost total occupation of the screen is the precondition of the film's intensely subjective feel, but what produces it is a battery of devices suggesting interiorisation, fully and semi-subjective point-of-view shots, and everywhere that typically Scorsesian 'subjectivising of the objective' (Mitry). Characteristically, Scorsese expresses the protagonist's turbulence through a nervously questing camera, which even in apparently conventional shot/countershot conversation sequences unsettlingly edges inwards as if propelled by an undefined interrogative obsession, strongly reinforced by the mass of verbal interrogatives throughout the film (Judas asking Jesus, 'What are you? What kind of man are you?'; Jesus questioning his mother after he rejects her, 'Who are you?' etc.).

In its dramatisation of Jesus's subjectivity the film particularly uses travelling point-of-view shots taken from unstable handheld cameras, registering highly emotive situations: for example when walking by the Sea of Galilee, Jesus hears footsteps following him. In all cases, the obvious comparisons are with the more extreme sequences of Travis cruising New

York. The lakeshore sequence is representative of the film's system: a single shot beginning objectively (though with unclassical characteristics such as the closeness of the camera, refusing the spectator comfortable distance), but then metamorphosing, without a cut, into a subjective shot as Jesus gazes into the distance, then reverting to an objective view of him continuing his journey. Such moments are paralleled by instances of aural subjectivity: the sounds of everything but the water bleeding away when Jesus meets the Baptist, the wailing ululations disappearing as Jesus raises Lazarus. Additionally, there is the interiorised voice of Jesus, spasmodically interrupting the flow of events in a typically unstable interrogatory form. The difference between such effects and Jesus's voice in bridging passages in Stevens is absolute. There external, heard by the disciples or other listeners, in Scorsese it is wholly private, heard by no one in the diegesis.

However individual, the Jesuses of De Mille, Ray and Stevens share a monumental externality. The shock of the *The Last Temptation* consists of its Jesus being so unmonumental. He is often alone or in intimate one-to-one relationships with others (even his trials reduced to a conversation with Pilate), whereas in the preceding films, except for the Temptation and Gethsemane, he is never really by himself.

Pasolini's influence over Scorsese is particularly visible where the Italian develops counter-representations based on camera intimacy, a rough style imitating documentary (as when the camera-onlooker is blocked at the back of the crowd in Jesus's trial scene), and other devices estranging the representations of Christ from convention. They are, however, in no way effects of interiority. The shock of Pasolini's verisimilitudes brings us closer to his opaque Christ's force, but motivations are as wholly obscure as in the other films, the use of point-of-view shots illustrating this. Though we are at times given Jesus's perspective, this is in neither a sustained nor a psychologically revealing way (and, in fact, variations in shot distance confuse the onlooker as to whether shots are subjective or objective rhetoric). In Pasolini what the device tends to signify is transparency itself, rather than any decodable psychology.

The Last Temptation presents a fragmented, almost schizophrenic Jesus. Even the signs of his possession by God are ambiguous, something like epilepsy, that could be madness or repressed sexual desire. He expresses God's invasion of him in contradictory similes (claws, a cool breeze). He wavers between accepting and denying his Messiahship, between identification with the law of the father and of the mother, between the sensual world and the unseen, between the spiritual and the carnal, and between opposed ways of overcoming injustice. The uncanny moment where he plucks out his heart is a paradigm of instability, the apocalyptic expressed through subversion of the Catholic iconology of the sacred heart.

This insecurity spreads over the film's narrative progression. Without visual or aural establishing procedures (the first shot is a fast sweeping forward track), it begins by abruptly dismissing the security of the traditional voice-over beginning, replacing it with a trope as taboo as the protagonist's subjective shot, Jesus's interior monologue, extra-diegetic authority replaced by a fragmented personal voice, adrift and uncontextualised, speaking incoherently of the external forces that possess him, ambivalent markers of sainthood or madness: 'The feeling begins, very tender, very loving. Claws slip underneath the skin and then tear their way up. Just before they reach my eyes they dig in. Then I remember . . .' Jesus's angst-ridden voice may have immediate charisma, but it does not, in the biblical phrase, speak as one having authority. Or rather, what authority it has comes from an embrace, not a denial, of radical doubt and incoherence.

Further on, Jesus's indecision is underlined by the fact that often he does not act but is acted on by others: when John tells him to begin his ministry; when Judas decides to approach the Baptist; and when the Baptist turns him towards apocalyptic destruction. This conversion leads only to further indeterminacy as Jesus's espousal of the Baptist's violence is immediately followed by the idyll at Martha and Mary's. When that ends with the revelation of the Baptist's death, Jesus's threatening appearance before the disciples ('I'm inviting you to a war') is contradicted by the healing of the demoniac, the raising of Lazarus and the joyful wedding at Cana. The commitment to apocalypse, present only in this later sequence of events when Jesus returns to Nazareth, becomes dominant again only in the first sortie to Jerusalem, but even here, because the narrative presents not one but two assaults on the Temple, Jesus's indeterminacy is again emphasised. In the second of these scenes, having committed himself to revolutionary martyrdom, Jesus's resolution disintegrates as he hesitantly waits for God's approval, and then interprets his stigmata as divine disapproval.

These indeterminacies – culminating in the fantasy descent from the cross – are echoed throughout the profuse detail of the film. To take one instance: like the De Mille film, *The Last Temptation* is prolific in its references to the animal world. But whereas the De Mille holds on to a stable, inherited emblematism of the animal (the Mother's doves, the lamb Jesus holds in the Temple) in the service of the human and divine, in *The Last Temptation* 'Everything has two meanings', as Jesus says of the serpents that come to tempt him. This is true of the opaquely symbolic lizards and snakes decorating the entrance to Magdalene's house; the framing and focus in the brothel scene centring attention on two lizards on a plant as she copulates in the background; the snake and lion (with the voices of

Magdalene and Judas) who utter truths that may be lies as well as deceits
that may be truths; the conversation about pity between Jesus and Judas
where Jesus says he sees God in the eye of an ant; the monkeys scampering
around the house where Jesus and the Magdalene honeymoon. In contrast
to *The King of Kings'* associations, *The Last Temptation* establishes a
bewildering indeterminacy, producing an unanthropomorphic nature, by
turns mundane, violent and beautiful. This is a book of nature for which,
however, there is no obvious key, one also retaining, despite the
screenplay's diminution of the book's interest in the topic, a Far Eastern
(the unexplained presence of the Indian prince in the brothel scene), as
distinct from a Near-Eastern, view of the interrelatedness of all creation.

Sexuality

> I was walking one hot summer afternoon, through the deserted streets of a
> provincial town in Italy which was unknown to me. I found myself in a quarter
> of whose character I could not remain in doubt. Nothing but painted women
> were to be seen at the windows of the small houses, and I hastened to leave the
> narrow street at the next turning. But after having wandered for a time without
> enquiring my way, I suddenly found myself back in the same street.
> — Freud, 'The Uncanny'

In controversy the film's issues have been simplified into total preoccupation with Jesus's sexuality. This is understandable since Jesus's
oscillation between desire for the Magdalene and for God is central, playing
into all other instabilities. Nevertheless, it has been discussed in reductive
ways, separating the sexual from complex theological implications, and, in
particular, divorcing it from the domesticity which, as much as the sexual
itself, is the ultimate temptation for the narrative's Jesus.

Christology's man/God definitions were solidified at Chalcedon (AD
451) in formulations steering between the tendencies of Arianism (too
God-centred) and Sabellianism (too man-centred). The most interesting
development of the 'truly-God and truly-man' dogma attributes to Christ
the potentiality to sin. Surveying the subject, Kelly points to one
formulation that Christ's nature 'was of the same nature as other human
souls and thus was susceptible to at least the initial stirrings of passion . . .
These did not involve it in any sin, but were the essential precondition and
merit of the Saviour's struggle against evil.'

The film is less radical than Kazantzakis's novel (which actually begins
with Jesus in mid-dream) in dramatising Jesus's inner self. The film, reser-
ving the shock of Jesus dreaming for the end, nevertheless finds ways of

indicating unconscious alongside conscious mentality. The invocation of Freud is doubly pertinent, in its relevance to discussion of a Christ endowed with what is now taken to be definitive of man – the unconscious – and in its parallel with the moment where Jesus, apparently travelling towards the desert monastery, finds himself near Mary Magdalene.

To dramatise the unconscious in a post-Freudian age is inevitably to highlight unconscious sexual and oedipal motivations. The title *The* Last *Temptation* underlines what appears an oddity to the modern eye in the Gospels' temptation accounts, their omission of the sexual. Patristic theology's taboo on the question of Christ's sexuality has a lingering influence, for there seems nowhere to be a post-Freudian theological consideration of the structure of Christ's personality. Interest in Christ's sexuality is not simply a contemporary aberration, for Milton in *Paradise Regained* implies dissatisfaction with the temptation account. Unable to alter his Gospel source, Milton nevertheless raises the question through a discussion among the devils which suggests that Christ could be tempted sexually. In fact Satan dismisses this, arguing that lesser heroes have been proof against beautiful women. But through the strategy of suggestion and cancellation, the topic surfaces.

What Milton hinted at, Kazantzakis, Scorsese and Schrader directly address. The film contains not only Christ openly discussing his sexuality but a temptation in which the serpent, speaking with Magdalene's voice, offers the sexual paradise and then, finally, the dream-enactment of Jesus's making love to and marrying Magdalene and then Mary, committing adultery with Martha, and polygamously fathering many children with the two sisters. Suggesting unconscious thought processes, certain travelling subjective shots define Jesus's consciousness as permeated with desire. His passage through Magdala to Magdalene's house is conveyed through a travelling subjective shot which lingers on a bare-breasted girl. Equally, in a similar shot, again attached to Christ as he strides through the Temple, the camera-eye notes not only the moneylenders but prostitutes and their clients just before the protagonist explodes with anger, suggesting that repressed desire complicates Jesus's reforming zeal. Even his early contact with God takes a form that suggests a close relationship to the sexual, as in one of his writhing fits he calls out the name not of God but 'Magdalene!'.

Sowing the seed

It is regrettable that a Dostoyevski did not live near this most interesting of all decadents. — Nietzsche, *The Anti Christ*

Some way into *The Last Temptation*, Willem Dafoe's Jesus goes public, hesitantly addressing the small crowd he has gathered round him: 'I've got something to tell you . . . uh . . . I'm . . . I'm sorry . . . but the easiest way to make myself clear is to tell you a story.' This unprepossessing apology leads into his version of the parable of the sower, inviting the film audience impossibly to imagine themselves as the sullen interior audience hearing Jesus's words for the first time: 'A farmer was planting in his field. Some seed fell on the ground and the birds ate it. Some seed fell on rocks and dried up. But some seed . . . some seed . . . some seed fell on rich soil and grew into enough wheat to feed a whole nation.' Paradoxically, the estrangement created by hearing the familiar words defamiliarised to what seem their origins can be produced only through an intertextuality which plays against the institutional versions of the parable, stripping them down until we feel the primary narrative beneath the literary elaborations such as Matthew's:

> Some seed fell on rocky ground, where it had little soil, and it sprouted quickly because it had no depth of earth. But when the sun rose the young corn was scorched, and as it had no root it withered away. . . . And some seed fell on to good soil, where it bore fruit, yielding up a hundredfold or it might by sixtyfold or thirtyfold. If you have ears to hear, then hear.

The feeling of authenticity generated against such a full version has, it must be stressed, no absolute validity. In finding the 'story' beneath the 'parable', the scene ignores in the interests of the illusion of primariness Jesus's debts to rabbinical discourse. So there is no single solution to the problem of language in the Christ Film, for the conservative rhetorics in the Ray and Stevens films have their own validity, as they move towards opposite effects to *The Last Temptation*'s, to ritual, a speaking of the words which embraces their deep-seated familiarity. However enthusiastically we may respond to the later film's iconoclasms, we cannot understand them naively as truer in language or anything else than the earlier films. This applies equally to the Pasolini film, often credited with a validity other Christ films lack but which has its own highly designed illusions of authenticity, Christ's hyper-rapid delivery as free from realistic markers of discourse as it ever is in Ray or Stevens. What can be asserted in *The Last Temptation* is a series of sub-versions performed on previous texts by which the film produces a compelling fiction of origins.

Even the narrative position of the first preaching scene is slightly deviant, placed *before* two crucial moments conventionally establishing Jesus's authority – the temptation and baptism. Authority denied at the structural level permeates down to the most particular, to, say, Jesus's paralinguistic hesitance, a deviance further emphasised by Jesus's interior voice when approaching with Judas – 'What if I say the wrong thing? What if I say the right thing?' – and by Judas's sceptical presence throughout what follows. Furthermore, the preaching is prologued by Jesus's disruption of the crowd's attempt to stone Magdalene, which leaves his audience sullenly frustrated, resistant to Jesus's first attempt to convey to others meanings which are unclear even to himself.

Dafoe's Jesus embodies incoherence overlaid with all the nervous intensity associated with Method acting. This de-iconicisation plays against a set of traditional filmic and pro-filmic images held in the audience's minds. In one respect only Dafoe's Jesus complies with, rather than disrupts them, as, instead of responding to the time's pressure to portray Jesus as Semitic, it provides another spectacularly unSemitic Christ. Yet it is too easy to see the director's final choice simply within the regressive syndrome in which it is caught up. The latter is, of course, one of the implications of Scorsese's statement that 'the minute I saw Willem Dafoe I felt comfortable with his face', but alongside this we should recognise that for Scorsese and his audience this Christ is the Christ not only of tradition but also of deep-rooted cultural imagination. Additionally, gains balance losses, since placed on such familiar ground every minor deviation stands out, whereas with an ethnic Christ much of the film's play of difference on the familiar would be lost.

Speaking of Dafoe, Scorsese distinguishes him from Jeffrey Hunter, arguing that in using a movie star for Jesus the makers of *King of Kings* 'are unable to deal completely with the human side'. The point is imprecise, for Dafoe is undeniably a star, but Scorsese is highlighting the kind of star he is: post-Method, unconventional, affiliated to the 'rough cinema'. In fact, in the context of his Christ, even his WASP–Aryan qualities are less than straightforward, visually relating him to the frailer, more human portrayals of the Flemish rather than of the heroic Italian Renaissance. (Notice his acute facial resemblance to the portrait of Tymotheus by Van Eyck.) That Dafoe is an actor/star of the schizophrenic rather than monophrenic kind is dramatised by the tendency of his roles to polarise. Thus, at one extreme there are Captain Elias, the good soldier of *Platoon*, who actually dies in a huge cruciform gesture; the FBI agent in *Mississippi Burning*; the military policeman in love with the nun in *Saigon*: all figures of virtue struggling in a flawed world. At the other there are the deranged, crippled ex-vet Charlie in *Born on the Fourth of July* and every American's dark doppelgänger, the sinister Bobby Peru in *Wild at Heart*, grotesque cameo parodies of the American Dream, Puritan lineaments still discernible underneath manic surface.

These polarities are clashingly incorporated rather than repressed in Dafoe's portrayal of Jesus, motivated by Jesus's struggle between love and destruction, with the second polarity most foregrounded in the frightening image of projected *ressentiment*, brandishing the axe and hellishly lit by flames as he preaches violent revolution to the disciples. Dafoe's Jesus, torn between enormous dichotomies, resolved only by the final catastrophe in which his sadistic–masochistic alternatives are transmuted into self-sacrifice, exhibits in this scene, as elsewhere, an extreme volatility, the antithesis of traditional iconic representation. Take, for instance, the moment in the middle of his preaching when he hears the laughter of two cynics and advances on them laughing himself, telling them that those who are laughing now will be crying later, a fluid sequence of changing emotions never resting in the stability of the remembered tableaux but which also denies the opposite certainties of reductive deconstruction.

As it develops into a shorthand, unceremonious version of the Beatitudes, the scene subverts the grand compositions of the Sermon on the Mount in Ray. There the scene was visually sublime, with Jesus looking down on a huge multitude-filled valley, its epic scale underwritten by the improbably huge audience. *The Last Temptation* denies its scene sublime perspectives, places Jesus and his audience intimately and democratically on the same level. Ray's smooth structural mobility is replaced by jagged editing and techniques imitating documentary urgency – fast pans, the camera's pretence at failure to predict Jesus's sudden movements leading to rapid reframing, and subversions of the iconic postures adopted by the Jesus of the other films, as when he stands, armed spread, palms open, in the most traditional of poses, and Dafoe's seraphic smile transforms it into an enigmatic or Nietzschean/Dostoyevskian 'idiot' variant. Ray's Jesus is also questioned by the crowd, but the difference is that he answers with almost metronomic authority. This Jesus can exude uncertainty, at times seeming to plead for approval and intimacy. Although in larger dramatic terms the Ray sermon ends with failure where Barabbas refuses to meet Jesus, the sequence per se climaxes with the Lord's Prayer, in contrast to the confusion of this scene's ending when the crowd rushes off in vengeful disarray, fundamentally misunderstanding Jesus's teaching, with music appearing now for the first time in the scene, not inspirationally underscoring the truths of Christianity, as in the traditional usage of the Ray sequence, but to signify accelerating clamour and chaos.

JUDAS MY BROTHER

> If, therefore, there is a doubt affecting his case, he is entitled to the benefit of that doubt. — De Quincey

It may be, as Frank Kermode speculates in *The Genesis of Secrecy*, that Mark's Gospel 'bred the function betrayal before the agent betrayal was identified'. From this Proppian perspective one can envisage that in 'an earlier stage . . . Judas had no part in the scene of the last supper' and that ultimately 'it is not unreasonable to conjecture that there was originally no Judas at all'. In a Roman/Christian Epic, *The Robe*, Demetrius, hearing Jesus is in danger, rushes off to warn him. He meets a mysterious stranger whom he asks about Christ. The stranger replies that he is too late, for Christ has already been betrayed. Questioned why, he replies:

> Because men are weak. Because they are cursed with envy and cowardice. Because they dream of truth but cannot live with it. So they doubt. They doubt, the fools. Why must men betray themselves with doubt? Tell them, the others. Find them and tell them not to doubt. Tell them to keep their faith . . .

Demetrius asks 'Who are you?', to receive the reply, 'Judas', at which lightning flashes, thunder peals and the stranger rushes away through a portal through which in the lightning we glimpse the tree from which the doomed suicide will hang.

In this appearance in *The Robe* Judas encompasses the momentary individualising of his function, the act of betrayal placed on a single individual, but in his generalisations about all men's apostasy he almost dissolves back into the function of betrayal. The midrashic invention of Judas's speech lists not only negatives but a curdled positive (dreaming of truth) which becomes a negative through the gap experienced between ideal and actual, with doubt, presumably the fate of all men, as its issue. And this Judas not only agonises over his doubt but transcends his own misery, thinking of others even as he moves towards suicide.

Whether or not our view of Judas demotes agent to function to the point where the agent can be said to have had no objective existence, such a deconstructive gaze enables us to see the agent-function in its moment of construction as character, as a proliferation of questions implicit in the designation of the betrayer opens up new narrative needs, first of all in the original Gospel authors, then in their commentators, later in the midrash of literary and film authors. Many readers will be familiar with the method by which the post-Mark Gospels built up their picture of Judas out of Old Testament sources, the palimpsest achieving fullest expression in John's

Gospel where Judas is not only known from the beginning by Christ as the betrayer but made purse-keeper, to establish his avarice. Thus he becomes an emblem of Pharisaic materialism, his very name made to mark his symbolic representation of the enemies of Jesus.

Thus to pass from traditional representation to *The Robe*'s is not to cross a divide marking off stable from unstable representations but to follow a continuum of invention, the originals taken from texts seen as prophecies; later ones from theological theorising; the latest from the mastercodes of history, sociology and psychology. Thus there is hardly a literary or cinematic view of Judas not prefigured in theological speculation. Even the wildest, Borges's story about the theologian who propounds a counter-theory of the Incarnation in which God becomes man not through Jesus but Judas is not that much more extreme than the Cainite sect who honoured Judas for his place in the divine plan.

Borges's story is the height of revisionism, Christ demoted by Judas. Less excessively, modern treatments of Judas have refused the symbolic polarities, seeking explanation rather than condemnation. De Quincey's essay (1857) marks the moment at which Judas is transformed. His ringing sentence sets the pattern for later versions: 'Not one thing, but all things, must rank as false which traditionally we accept about him.'

From De Quincey comes that dramatisation of the Judas of German theology, the Judas who is deeply committed to Christ's political Messiahship, betraying him to force him into action; and whose life might be interpreted as a 'spasmodic effort of vindictive patriotism and of rebellious ambition, noble by possibility in its grand central motive, though erring and worldly-minded of necessity'. As he comes down into cinematic representation, this view of De Quincey's is the central modern one, replayed in Ray, Stevens and Zeffirelli; flanked on one side by the traditional Judas who fits the world of De Mille's *The King of Kings* and Pasolini's *Matthew* and on the other side by Kazantzakis's and Scorsese's Judas, transformed from pariah into heroic 'brother' and beloved disciple.

The combination of St John and De Mille produced the most traditional film Judas: though surprisingly young and dandified, in other aspects a powerful stereotype of the avaricious betrayer, surrounded by minatory music, and indelibly negative characteristics. All later versions conflict with this archetype, though Pasolini's *Matthew* might seem exceptional. In one sense this is true for, faced with the problem of dramatising the barely-conceived pre-Johannine Judas of St Matthew, Pasolini in fact 'cheats' by lifting a pejorative account of Judas from St John (Mary's anointing of Jesus), reshaping incidents in Matthew involving the disciples into ones reflecting only on Judas. But in another sense Pasolini's Judas belongs to a modern context, addressing an art-film audience reading the film as the re-enactment of cultural archetypes not as simple assertion of them. Where Pasolini complicates the archetypes by lingering facial close-ups that deliver a semiotic excess of meaning, Hollywood's modernisations are more openly midrashic along the basic lines suggested by De Quincey. In these, as rather differently in Dreyer's version, Judas is brought within the tradition of complex psychologised villains of later classical Hollywood.

Scorsese's Judas (Harvey Keitel: edgy, street-wise, quasi-criminal in various Scorsese films) has thus a complex set of origins. His outlines derive not only from Kazantzakis, and from the speculative theology which influenced him, but also from the American cinema, from the characters and relationships within Scorsese's and Schrader's films with their secular versions of redemptive quests, and finally from the Judas figures of Ray's and Stevens's films. Our point here, though, is less to search for minute influences than to establish a broad congruence in the film presentations of Judas which lies behind Scorsese's film. In Ray, Rip Torn's Judas is a sympathetic figure divided between two masters, his 'betrayal' a means of forcing Jesus's hand. Here neither avarice nor ambition as motivations survive in any form. Ray's boldness contrasts with Stevens's cautious constraint, too traditional to reinterpret as much as Ray, too sophisticated simply to return to origins. Consequently, David McCallum's anguished Judas projects opaqueness, highlighted by numerous close-ups, often of him looking at Jesus, that are finally indecipherable. If the handling of the spectacular raising of Lazarus scene, where Judas alone of all the spectators is positioned looking away from the miracle, suggests an inability to see the divine before him, the betrayal scene more than half counters pejorative connotations with his confusion and his moving statement of his love for Jesus. Further, in Stevens's major invention in this area, Judas is allowed a death not by hanging but by casting himself into the holocaust, an act which cannot but connect him tragically with recent history.

Keitel's Judas, bullish and obdurate, traditional only in his red hair, raging with anger and scorn, spitting, and buffeting Jesus when we first see them together, is even more foregrounded than Torn's. In the film's second half he is almost invariably at Jesus's side, Jesus's symbiotic second self, the voice of protest politics to Jesus's more metaphysical questing. His entry into the narrative presupposes, in its angry intimacy, long – indeed on the symbolic level eternal – acquaintance. Ordered by the Zealots to kill Jesus, he is drawn into uneasy alliance and unwilling loyalty by Jesus's charisma. But, equally, Jesus keeps Judas by his side as a kind of conscience and assurance of psychological and physical strength against his own weakness ('You can't leave me. You have to give me strength'). By omitting most of the novel's concentration on the other disciples, the film makes Judas even more pre-eminent, not only in his own scornful view ('I'm not like those men . . . They're weak . . .') and in Jesus's ('Of all my friends you are the strongest') but inevitably in the spectator's, with Peter, especially, diminished in comparison.

This pre-eminence and closeness to Jesus are visible throughout, but particularly in the series of intimate conversations between Judas and Jesus. These are presented not as guru–disciple encounters but, crucially, as volatile compatibilities, the closeness of the speakers mirrored by their own physically touching one another, with Judas arguing for the political Messiahship, Christ for inner transformation. The boldest, most moving image of their affinity (something leading Jesus to force the ultimate sacrifice of betrayal from Judas) comes when the camera looks down on Jesus asleep in the protective embrace of his friend 'my brother'. The sense of their inseparability – spirit to matter – in these scenes is augmented by the refusal of the shooting style to fragment the pair as they argue, to present first the one and then the other in conventional shot/reverse shot. Instead the frame gradually includes, with increasingly fewer exceptions, the two figures in relationship. Elsewhere, after Jesus's early private experiences, Judas is almost constantly at his side, marching with Christ, Peter and sometimes Magdalene, usually carrying a staff making him look forcefully apostolic, another unsurpation of Peter's role. Very often we are made aware of Judas's brooding presence, behind or beside Jesus in the frame, as in the first preaching scene.

Though John, Philip and Peter enter Christ's house as, in his fantasy, he lies on his deathbed, the scene's climax is reserved for Judas's entry with bloody hands from recent fighting with the Romans, and his harshly moving judgements of Jesus's apostasy. His words drive Jesus back in shame to the cross. Judas's obdurate strength is never allowed wholly to dissolve away into Christ's more inner-world concerns, remaining in tension with them, adding to that quality of speculative incompleteness contained within the film's heroic movement.

THE END

The Crucifixion

Those outraged by *The Last Temptation* were especially exercised over the film's last section, the representation of Jesus's imagined conviction that he is not the Messiah, only a man who allows himself to be removed from the cross into a life of domesticity. However, the temptation to renounce his messianic calling is finally resisted when Jesus returns to the cross, recognising in the seductions of a normal life (not just sexual intercourse with Mary Magdalene, but a huge brood of children and the comfortable clutter of family existence) the last and most powerful, because so seemingly innocently desirable, of the temptations stage-managed by the Devil.

While Jesus locked in sexual embrace represents the focal point of outrage for fundamentalists and many non-fundamentalist believers, its meaning can be judged only through the narrative and other contexts to which it belongs. The narrative sequences of the film's ending are reducible to three elements: firstly, the Crucifixion; secondly, Jesus's temptation by sex and domesticity; thirdly, the place of Paul in the history of Christianity. In the scenes around the Crucifixion Scorsese remains true to Hollywood traditions that play intertextually with the great European paintings of Christ's sacrifice, though his choices (such as Bosch, da Messina, Grünewald) all have a certain shock element. What he takes in reworking the stations of the cross from Bosch's Ghent *Christ Carrying the Cross* – a painting which looks to the cinematic eye as though it has been taken through a telescopic lens – is, firstly, the sense of Bosch's Christ almost suffocated in the middle of the frame by the faces of the mob, and, secondly, overwhelmingly sadistic, the facial expressions of those characters. The reworking of Bosch suggests a desire to emphasise the grotesque ubiquity of human cruelty. The flagellation is portrayed with extreme brutality, and throughout the film Scorsese shows no hesitation in dramatising explicit cruelty in what is easily the most violent of all Hollywood Christ narratives (e.g. in the scene of the Zealot's crucifixion with the close-up of nails hammered into flesh, the shriek of agony when the first hammer blow is struck, the blood splashing on to the face of Jesus). Though the Ghent painting does not represent its characters as the human/animal hybrids of *The Garden of Delights*, their expressions emphasise dehumanisation. The point is carried over into *The Last Temptation*, where Scorsese's version of the Bosch painting is in one respect actually more extreme, omitting the original's presence of the positive figures of the good thief and St Veronica.

The bloodbath images of Passover sacrifice draw attention to the ritualistic excesses of pre-Christan Judaism but they are only one aspect of imagery stressing violent human instinct. The Bosch-inspired faces crowding Jesus seem delighted by his agony. After its initial high-angle perspective – as we look down on him carrying the cross down a narrow alley – the film places Jesus in full frontal shot, head crowned with thorns, blood dripping on to his face and chest, his face contorted by suffering. In front of

him stand two women, the one on the left grinning, the one on the right
seemingly free of all trace of human sympathy. More onlookers are grouped
behind, a figure at the left pointing contemptuously at Jesus. Throughout
this sequence which moves in slow motion, all natural sounds are suppressed, allowing Peter Gabriel's patchwork of Arabic, North African and
1980s rock music, here extremely *lento* and carried by a lamenting solo
voice, to emphasise the sombre mood of grief. With its wailing Middle
Eastern strains, the music complements the orientalised ambience of the
mise-en-scène, costumes, and Semitic physiognomies.

From one perspective, all these (influenced by Pasolini's 'archaic–
arbitrary' in *Oedipus Rex* and *Medea*) represent the film's attempts to create a
world of difference, an ambience subverting the de-orientalised Western
view of Christianity's origins. From another, these affirmative, anti-
parochial processes are in danger of conforming to the familiar negative
stereotypes of the 'orientalist' perception of the Middle East. Although
Scorsese claimed to have wanted to avoid directly contemporary meanings,
nevertheless, for all the anti-traditional detail, the main characters (Judas,
Magdalene and of course Jesus) retain their American nobility, while the
mob embody the equivocal force of the negative stereotype.

The negative stereotype, given a specifically Arab expression in Ray,
here acquires a wider complex of meanings of otherness represented as the
primitive, dark, irrational crudities of the Middle East, in acts as alienating
as female tattooing or the barbarity of stoning adulteresses. At one obvious
level these practices are associated with ancient Jewish culture, but at
another they are invoked as traditions perhaps no longer Jewish but still –
and where not literally, then figuratively – alive in the cultures of the
Middle East. The appeal of Jesus to a new law, his affirmation of God's love
for all men and women, thus assumes not only eschatalogical but also
cultural significance. Tatooing, for instance, with all the mixture of fascination and revulsion it provokes, is given a highly visual impact through its
presence on the faces and bodies of the women in the film. While the
Romans bear the brunt of guilt for Jesus's execution, and while in other
scenes, say the stoning of Magdalene, unSemiticised participants share in
the urge to violence, there is no doubt that many of the film's historical Jews
or more accurately the Easterners with whom they were once historically
identified, are shown to collaborate with primitive relish in Jesus's victimisation. The behaviour of the crowd, seen from Jesus's perspective on the
cross, emphasises the point. One man there seems especially animated,
thrusting hand gestures of defiance directly at the crucified Jesus. As he
gesticulates, his gesture takes on a generically Middle Eastern form. The
film does more than its predecessors to create an ambience of difference,

succeeding far more than the others in de-Westernising too parochial a view of Christianity, and it might also be argued that the generalised Middle Easternness also partly functions as an evasion of unfavourable representations of Jewishness. Nevertheless, eclectically creating a mishmash of Eastern imagery, the film seems at times in danger of presenting much of the primitiveness and violence of the world Jesus encounters in terms of a universal that when interrogated is in a wide sense culture-specific, deflecting on to the Middle Eastern world vices as much the province of American mean streets as anywhere, seemingly bearing out in the process Edward Said's remarks about Western appropriation and distortion of Eastern realities. So for instance the exposure of the Middle Eastern repression of women, which naturally gains most of the audience's disapproval, may hide the less overt imprisonments the narrative itself imposes.

Domesticity: brides of Christ

The last temptation, the domesticity Jesus lives out in fantasy with Magdalene, and then after she dies with Mary and Martha, has like all the others been set up by the Devil. The sexual, familial, female-centred life must be renounced by the exceptional man for higher values. That is the narrative's heroic logic, but constrained by the mixed pressures of the source novel, the troubled representation of women in Scorsese's other films, and 1980s American post-feminist tensions, the film's handling of it is especially significant, through images of women more heightened, and more heightenedly problematic, than in other Christ Films. The emphatically masculinised vision shared by the authors of both film and novel is consistently expressed through the film's males. But not only do the men see the female wholly as body to the masculine mind, the women themselves, Magdalene, Mary and Martha, all describe themselves in these terms as well. In reworking their sources Scorsese and Schrader resist mitigating their male/female, mind/body polarities (presented not as good versus evil but, at least for heroic males, as greater good versus lesser good), an approach never granting that women, like men, may have religious or ascetic drives capable of superseding the biological. The limitation of the film's portrait of women is less disdain of female sexuality (Barbara Hershey's Magdalene hardly represents that), more an inability to figure women as other than sexual, as female *and* spiritual, so that it shows no interest in seeing Magdalene in the light, say, of the Nag Hammadi discoveries of Gnostic Gospels in which she plays a more important spiritual role than the male disciples. So, even though celebrated as sexual being, like the other women, she is ultimately portrayed as biological trap for the hero, the male never correspondingly representing the same threat for the spiritual woman. A striking instance of this occurs when, after making love with Jesus, the pregnant Magdalene is seen bathed in a strange light raptly contemplating her belly, her hand, like a talon, stretching across it threateningly. Reaching beyond Jesus's subjective vision to objective presentation, this is in keeping with the torments of all Scorsese's protagonists. Like Travis and La Motta, Jesus experiences sexuality as intense conflict, drawn to it and repelled by it simultaneously. Placing the hero within the greater creative pattern of the Christ narrative, the conflict can, for once, in heroic assertion, fashion his schizophrenic turbulence and sublimate his tormented sexuality into achievements denied the secular heroes. But, at the same time, the problems raised by the female characters are never satisfactorily engaged.

Scorsese's own account of the changing of the Devil's disguise as he lures Jesus away from his destiny on the cross, from the novel's androgynous boy to a pre-adolescent girl, hardly touches the disguise's significance – that the Devil is a woman yet again – with the additional meaning that, given the dualistic distrust of women's sexuality and overvaluation of their purity which Scorsese's films dramatise from the culture at large, the innocent, pre-sexual girl is the most powerful advocate, the most seductive disguise of all.

The dream the Devil provokes in Jesus releases a complex of conscious and unconscious desires, including both positive and negative views of domesticity and women oscillating between celebration (Magdalene in the wedding procession) and misogyny (the Devil prompting Jesus to even further sexual activity, with insultingly reductive lines like 'There's only one woman in the world', 'She's Magdalene with a different face')

Here as elsewhere women are presented ambivalently. Earlier on, their dignified place in the new order is asserted by the presence not only of the Virgin Mary and the Magdalene but also of Mary and Martha at the traditionally all-male Last Supper. When Jesus is on the cross, he calls for his women relatives and friends, who are loyally there for him. On the other hand, the fierceness of Jesus's rejection of his mother exceeds narrative necessities.

In the dream-sequence women are healers. When Jesus comes down from the cross his wounds are tended first by the girl/angel and then, before making love, by Mary Magdalene. Great though the sexual attractions of Barbara Hershey's Magdalene are ('Oh Jesus, just nod your head and we'll be in bed together'), they are seen only as part of the domestic life (Magdalene gasping that they will have a child as she climaxes with Jesus). This is the ambience of healing, sexuality and domesticity to which Jesus is powerfully drawn but which he finally rejects. Immediately before encountering Paul, Jesus is seen on a family outing with his two women and six children. The elder girl carries a wooden doll that looks like a portrait of her father, an image signifying the temptation for Jesus to make of himself no more than an ordinary *paterfamilias*, the ego-ideal for his children, rather than master-figure for all humanity. The heroic–spiritual quest in its Christian version has traditionally resisted such temptations, but Judas's stern reproach, pushing Jesus back to the cross, is typical of the film's view of the domestic world as only the concern of women and children.

St Paul: printing the legend

The Last Temptation at its conclusion reserves a place for St Paul, in a way paralleled by George Moore's novel *The Brook Kerith* (1916). There Moore's Jesus, surviving the Crucifixion, returns to the Essenes, repenting what he now sees as his Messianic arrogance. Later, practising a religion more Far Eastern than Judaeo-Christian, he meets Paul who refuses to believe that he is the Jesus whom Paul calls the resurrected Messiah: 'Paul ... seemed to have forgotten the man walking by his side. He is rapt, Jesus said to himself, in the Jesus of his imagination.' In its last pages the narration leaves Jesus to follow Paul on his missionary travels, intimating that the future of Christianity lies with the apostle. Both Moore and Kazantzakis, and Scorsese and Schrader in their use of Kazantzakis, dramatise, though in terms less completely hostile, the antichrist's ferocious perception that the apostolic 'dysangel' perverted the original 'evangel' to invent institutional Christianity.

The film acknowledges for the only time in a Hollywood Christ narrative Paul's shaping of Christianity's destiny. In a startling contemporary inflection, his evangelical vision is given the specifically American appearance of the hell-fire Bible-belt preacher. Harry Dean Stanton's wasted, end-of-the-road Paul is moulded on the great American Bible-thumpers (as well as the charlatan blind evangelist, Asa Hawks, he played in *Wise Blood*, 1979). He projects through the filters of films like *Repo Man* and *Paris, Texas* and their disinherited worlds the historical Paul's conviction that Jesus was the apocalyptic deliverer. The historical Paul seems to have been committed above all to the notion of *kerygma*, removing Jesus from historical contexts, turning him into a universalising saviour for whom all mankind, not just Jewry, was 'the chosen'. So Stanton's Paul inherits the 'I was a sinner' rhetoric (Acts, 26: 10–11), plays on the emotional responses of his audience (Acts, 20: 36–7), and, above all, like the real Paul, has no interest in the real Jesus, only his resurrection.

Before Jesus and his family come across him, Paul is given the 33 AD equivalent of a Baptist or Methodist pulpit setting as he delivers the familiar rhetoric: 'I killed anyone who broke the law of Moses, and I loved it!' Whereas St John says that the Chief Priests resolved to do away with Lazarus, here it is actually Paul who kills him (an invention of the film). He wallows in the detailed description of the sin – here sadistic violence, elsewhere, naturally, sex (though the whoring, never mentioned by the historical Paul, is added) – primarily so as to titillate the sinners with lurid wickedness before settling for the burdens of piety. When Jesus challenges Paul, on his distortion of the realities of Jesus's life, Paul's reply summarises his commitment to faith and the Resurrection: 'Their only hope is the resurrected Jesus. The resurrected Jesus saved the world, and that's what matters . . .' But this film, refusing to gesture to a resurrection, with typical force makes Jesus himself, of all people, question Paul's rhetoric.

The film leaves open the question of the divine order of the universe – since Jesus only ever doubts his part in God's plan, not God's reality – while asking why the institutions, rituals and even falsifications are necessary. The answer seems to be that human frailty requires examples of individual heroism and sacrifice as inspiration for its salvation. But there is a whole world of difference between the Scorsese Jesus's struggle and the falsification fostered upon him by this desperate Paul. There is a world of difference, too, between this post-modernist film's critique of Paul's method – shorthand for a whole society's fabrication and acceptance of the easiest forms of spiritual consolation – and, say, in a more secular context, the relatively untroubled toleration of such procedures in a film made in less questioning times like *The Man Who Shot Liberty Valance* where a previous character was also more interested in 'printing the legend' than in confronting 'the painfully strange features' of a uniquely remarkable man, who, the film leaves it up in the air, may be resurrected or may not, but is certainly the Nietzschean Christ in the most positive terms, the Christ of the moment, not of the Resurrection.

'*My* Jesus is much more important, much more powerful', Scorsese's uncompromisingly eschatalogical Paul proclaims. With the historical Paul's 'rabbinical insolence' (the Anti Christ's characteristically hostile phrase) redeployed in the service of mainstream American evangelism, the cross to which Jesus is nailed in Paul's fevered imagination is constructed not by a revenge-inspired discontented underclass but by potent forces in a society still horrified by the prospect of redefinitions of its convictions. In no other Hollywood film about Jesus has it really been possible for audiences so forcefully to feel that, for all his charisma and inspirational heroism, Jesus may simply not have been the Son of God.

Part three

THE ROMAN/CHRISTIAN EPIC

19 *Ben-Hur* (1925): Judaeo-Christian humanity (Ramon Novarro as Judah) offsets hard-hearted Roman discipline (Francis X. Bushman as Messala)

20 The arena in *Spartacus*: microcosm of a cruel unChristian world celebrating the triumph of matter over spirit

21 A balcony of Roman connotations in *Quo Vadis?*: the bad infant Emperor, the predatory Eagle, the hyper-masculine guard, Petronius's ironic hedonism, the lustful Empress, an austere Seneca

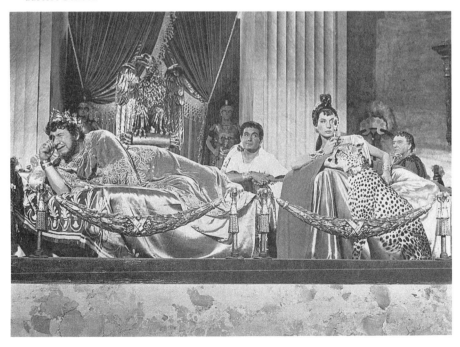

22 Sheikh Ilderin (Hugh Griffith), Hollywood's 1950s Biblical Epic image of the Arab as, at best, shifty rogue

23 Roman soldier and (crippled) Christian maiden in *The Robe*. Miriam imparts her faith to Marcellus (Richard Burton)

24 *Demetrius and the Gladiators*: the Robe as sign of Lucia's (Debra Paget) translucent serenity and Demetrius's (Victor Mature) agonistic ecstasy

25 Demetrius, the slave, and Messalina (Susan Hayward), the mistress, of desire

26 Victor Mature in close-up: within rugged features a softened, epicene sub-text to 1950s norms of masculinity

9

The poetics of the Roman /Christian Epic

THE CANON

The following films constitute the centrality of the third sub-genre, the Roman/Christian Epic: *Ben-Hur* (Niblo, 1925); *The Sign of the Cross* (De Mille, 1932); *The Last Days of Pompeii* (Schoedsack, 1935); *Quo Vadis?* (LeRoy, 1951); *Androcles and the Lion* (Erskine, 1952); *Salome* (Dieterle, 1953); *The Robe* (Koster, 1953); *Demetrius and the Gladiators* (Daves, 1954); *The Silver Chalice* (Saville, 1955); *Ben-Hur* (Wyler, 1959); *The Big Fisherman* (Borzage, 1959); and *Barabbas* (Fleischer, 1962). These films differ from their generic neighbours in terms of narrative, character, chronology and geography. So:

(i) They no longer have a strictly scriptural source as do the Christ and Old Testament Films.

(ii) They place invented non-biblical protagonists within the world-historical crisis of the beginnings of Christianity as a religion of gentile conversion.

(iii) Geographically they centre on Rome, looking forward to the institutionalisation of Christianity as the state religion under Constantine.

(iv) They are dated almost invariably between the death of Christ and circa AD64, the first persecution of Christianity in Rome.

These categories may be more complicated than appears when the dominant paradigm is stated. For instance, in (ii), though the protagonist is usually invented (like Judah Ben-Hur in *Ben-Hur*, Basil in *The Silver Chalice*), (s)he may be replaced by a peripheral New Testament character subjected to reformulation, whose narrative may infract rules (i) and (ii). Examples are Salome and Barabbas. In *The Silver Chalice* Simon the Magician, developed from the character in Acts, is foregrounded enough to become the narrative's anti-hero. In an exceptional case a major New Testament character, Peter, occupies the foreground in *The Big Fisherman*, but he is surrounded by plots featuring invented characters. Equally, category (iii) includes chronological variations. *Ben-Hur* begins at the birth of Christ and ends on Easter Sunday. *Salome* begins during Christ's ministry and ends untypically at the Sermon on the Mount. Conversely, a narrative may start shortly before (*The Robe*) or at the moment of (*Barabbas*) the Crucifixion, and then progress. Or it may begin considerably after (*Quo Vadis?*, *The Sign of the Cross*, *The Silver Chalice*, *Demetrius and the Gladiators*, the first three in the favourite Neronic period). Finally, in category (iv), although Rome is always a literal site (Pompeii is really Rome plus volcano in *The Last Days of Pompeii*), variations may occur. It can be the sole setting (in *Quo Vadis?*, *The Sign of the Cross*, *Demetrius and the Gladiators* – except for memory flashes back to Judaea in the first and last of these). But sometimes Rome is one of two or more places (in *The Robe* where it alternates with Judaea, and *Ben-Hur* which is mostly set in Judaea but where, as in *Barabbas*'s non-Roman settings, Rome's power is omnipresent).

A definitive mapping of the sub-genre includes films with various extended family relationships. For instance, *The Sign of the Pagan*, set circa AD 450, falls well outside the definitive period but inflects the Christian/Roman pagan opposition into one opposing later Roman Christians with non-Roman pagans led by Atilla the Hun. Contrastingly, *Spartacus*, dramatising events in the late Roman republic predating Christianity is, as we shall argue later, touched by Christian meanings, while, conversely, *The Fall of the Roman Empire*, is a Christian era (circa AD 180) narrative without reference to Christianity, with Marcus Aurelius an alternative moral centre. Yet the total expulsion of Christianity is as impossible here as in Fellini's *Satyricon*.

The central films also have important resemblances to other Hollywood ancient-world films which do not treat the rise of Christianity but are equally committed to the spectacular reinvention of past civilisations. Beyond Rome, Egypt figures most prominently (as in *The Egyptian*, *Land of the Pharaohs*, and both De Mille's and Mankiewicz's *Cleopatra*).

Finally, there are areas beyond Hollywood offering relevant comparisons, either in treating similar material from Christian history (such as Rossellini's *Augustine of Hippo*) or ancient-world material just prior to the rise of Christianity (Fellini's *Satyricon*).

As in the other sub-genres, the television mini-series has been the primary life in the 1980s of kinds of films no longer prolific in the cinema, and here Franco Rossi's *Quo Vadis?* and Cooper's *Anno Domini* are important versions. The last, the popular double of Anthony Burgess's novel *The Kingdom of the Wicked*, points to a final element in the formation and continuing history of the sub-genre, its source in, and interaction with, literary fictions. Wallace's *Ben-Hur* (1860) and Sienkiewicz's *Quo Vadis?* (1896) are the founding fictions of the cinematic sub-genre, mediated through stage adaptations, *Ben-Hur* (New York, 1899; London, 1901) and *The Sign of the Cross* (1896). And when the cinematic sub-genre, if not its television equivalent, seems exhausted, sophisticated new literary versions have arisen, ironically deconstructing the old literary and cinematic treatments. Here the key texts are Burgess's *The Kingdom of the Wicked*, Gore Vidal's *Julian* and, above all, with its labyrinthine ironies, Montheilhet's reworking of *Quo Vadis?*, *Neropolis*.

THE FALL INTO HISTORY AND THE SHADOW OF THE GALILEAN

> To be able to talk with a man who talked to Christ our Lord! — Pomponia in *Quo Vadis?* (LeRoy)

One of the sub-genre's lesser products, *Salome*, ends by replacing the conventional seal on the narrative's completion, 'The End', with the words 'This was the Beginning'. The conceit plays with our knowledge of the arbitrariness of any story's cut-off point. But what is true of any narrative – that its closure is unreal because history continues beyond the frame – has a privileged meaning when the film ends with its leading characters, a Roman officer and a Jewish princess, attending the Sermon on the Mount. 'Beginning' here implies not only the continuing flux but the initiation of a new order of being in the new covenant reinterpreting past history as a progress towards that point, and all future history as conditioned by it. And yet that immediate future history – the content of the Roman/Christian Epic – produces anxiety as well as confidence. Though the typical Christ Film ending counters the terrors of history's flux with promises of a solacing eternal presence, the Roman/Christian Film necessarily re-encounters the chaos of secular history.

One of the most striking manifestations of this is the convention that allows the presence – but only at the margins of the narrative – of the Saviour: that is, Christ appears not only very briefly but also in a very curious way, sometimes literally at the margins – the edge of the screen – as with the detached hand and arm of Jesus that move suddenly into the frame several times in the 1925 *Ben-Hur*. Any devotee of the sub-genre can recall instances from a catalogue of memorably evasive tropes – feature-dissolving long-shots; reverend synecdoches of hand or foot; calculatingly unrevealing angles; shots set up from above or behind; the shadow, or if substance, substance obscured, of the divine actor. The 1925 *Ben-Hur* illustrates almost the full grammar of such euphemism. As the Romans stop with their prisoners at a site identified by an intertitle as 'A Carpenter's Shop by the Nazareth Road', a hand working a saw enters right. When Judah sprawls on the ground, the hand puts down the saw, dips a bowl into the well, then enters the frame again, accompanied at one point by a sandalled foot and an arm that touches Judah's face. Afterwards, as soldiers and prisoners leave, the hand again guides the saw. Years later, the same hand enters left, first at the stoning of the adulteress, then to resurrect a mother's dead baby on the Via Crucis, and then to cure Judah's mother and sister. At the Crucifixion a nailed hand in close-up clasps and unclasps. The only unsynecdochal shots of Christ view him from the back, as in his trial, or obscured, as in the Last Supper tableau where Judas is positioned to block audience access to his features.

There is no question of this being only a primitive convention that later films bypass, for more than thirty years later Wyler repeats these moments, and there are similar incidents in *Salome*, *The Big Fisherman* and *Barabbas*, the latter loosening convention enough to show Christ face-on in medium long-shot in the trial scene, but ostentatiously refusing the close-ups that the logic of proximity demands. In *The Silver Chalice* even Basil's sculpture of Christ's head is filmed from the side at an obscuring angle.

All this contrasts with the Christ film's close-up depiction of Christ, so that the convention is not a generic prohibition on the unimpeded representation of Christ. It is active only in this sub-genre and can be explained only by underlying structures in the Roman film. The world of the sub-genre resumes the processes of history, presenting a milieu in which Christ is asserted as the dynamo of historical change, but now only by unseen influence. While some of the films' protagonists actually see Christ 'in the flesh', more do not. So for most their situation already approximates to that of the modern believer or agnostic. Without immediate access to Christ, they must rely on his reported words and their own interior perceptions against the frequent comments of others that Christianity is a madness or 'beautiful dream'. Here the underlying text is John, 20: 29, 'Blessed are they that have not seen, and yet have believed'. Thus the importance in the films of the declining few who have been eyewitnesses to Jesus, and the scene where Peter (*Quo Vadis?*, *The Robe*) or a surrogate (Titus in *The Sign of the Cross*) give their precious, almost extinct 'I was there' testimony.

The sub-genre foregrounds secular characters of whom faith in things unseen is required, for whom eyewitnesses are now disappearing, who, even when they are witnesses, like Barabbas, may not be able to believe, or, like Demetrius in *Demetrius and the Gladiators*, be capable of apostasy. In films where the whole or much of the narrative is set after the Crucifixion, there is an equally sparing use of ways of structuring Christ's presence back into the films, through dreams, flashbacks, fantasies, miraculous appearances, and so on. There are very few instances of this: Gallio's Crucifixion nightmare in *The Robe*, Christ's appearance to the dying Marius in *Pompeii*, Demetrius's flashback to the Crucifixion, the vignettes brought to life by Peter's preaching in *Quo Vadis?* (Christ borrowing Peter's boat to preach in, the Last Supper, etc.). Not only are these fragmentary but they are dominated by identical effects so that, whatever the eyewitness sees, what the audience sees is Christ obscured. An apparent exception where Christ is shown face-on in long-shot in *Quo Vadis?* turns out to be a tableau based on Da Vinci and thus a representation of a representation, not an unmediated view. This sequence even enacts an aural version of the prohibition, for though Christ's lips move, the words heard are Peter's reportage.

At one with the more obvious demotion of Christ's presence in these narratives and consituting a redoubled marginalisation, the conceit of the obscuring of Christ is thus far from arbitrary. Whatever the characters see of Christ's features, the audience, sunk even deeper into historical movement away from the Christ moment than their narrative surrogates, are not allowed impeded vision, for the withholding expresses their distance from the events. Similarly, the films seldom attempt to extend the age of miracles into post-Gospel history. In contrast, on the rare occasions when something like a miracle happens in these films (other than those performed by Christ, as in *Ben-Hur*), for instance where Peter cures Demetrius in *The Robe* or a little girl in *The Silver Chalice*, it may be only a psychosomatic healing. Elsewhere the age of miracles seems indubitably past. The lovers in *Quo Vadis?* may be saved, but nothing intervenes to save their fellow-believers. The only indubitable remaining miracle is faith itself. Hence the camera's fixation on the Christian characters' faces as they register their apprehension of the divine: uplifted head, inward and upward directed eyes, ecstatic smile, all the touching poverty of the outward and visible semiosis of contact with the unseen transcendental.

THE VOICE OF HISTORY: PROLOGUES TO WHAT IS POSSIBLE

> This is the story of that immortal conflict — Prologue, *Quo Vadis?*

Most typically the Roman/Christian Epic begins with a prologue in which the voice of history defines over a montage of synecdoches of Roman power the significance of the world-historical contest to be enacted. *Quo Vadis?* may be taken as a paradigm.

This is the Appian Way . . . Imperial Rome is the centre of the Empire and undisputed master of the world. But with this power inevitably comes corruption. The individual is at the mercy of the state . . . There is no escape from the whip and the sword. That any power on earth can shake the foundations of this pyramid of power and corruption, human misery and slavery, seems inconceivable, but thirty years before this day a miracle occurs. On a Roman cross in Judaea a man died to make men free; to spread the gospel of Love and Redemption. Soon that humble cross is destined to replace the proud eagles that top the victorious Roman standards. This is the story of that immortal conflict.

This overseeing voice of history comes in various inflections. Here, as in *Spartacus*, its rhetoric speaks in median American accents an accepted version of historical truth. Indeed, in *The Sign of the Pagan* the voice is so commonplace, so lacking in the markers of authority, that one wonders (it is, however minor, a film by Douglas Sirk) whether America's appropriation of the past in its own image is fleetingly subjected to parody. Conversely, the voice of history may locate itself in the past, in a British voice with connotations of old-world knowledge that America lacks. This happens in *The Fall of the Roman Empire*, with its Gibbonesque echoes, and is varied in the 1959 Wyler *Ben-Hur* where Britishness combines with tones of apostolic wisdom in the prologue voice of Finlay Currie, who later appears as Balthasar in the narrative. *Ben-Hur*'s use of Currie, where the voice at first comes as the pure voice of History but is later attached to a character in tune with destiny, is halfway to the complex effect in *The Robe*. There the prologue is delivered by the hero (Richard Burton) as he strolls around Rome, a moment to which we shall return and, of course, another use of Britishness.

This (always male) prologue voice, however placed in terms of nationality, age or class, intones a forceful, moralising rhetoric usually positioned beyond the flux of events, from a perspective in which competing forces are polarised and destiny clarified. Rather unsettlingly, perhaps because of its non-Christian context, *The Fall of the Roman Empire* threatens more relativistic approaches: 'the Fall of Rome, like her Rise, had not one cause but many. It was not an event, but a process spread over three hundred years.' In fact the narrative both disappoints and relieves by running counter to this opening, clarifying history into a moral perspective that tends to absolute oppositions and single causes. The more typical opening of *Quo Vadis?* lays out in binary antagonism oppositions from whose encounter the ultimate dynamic of history will be born: Conquering Rome/Conquered Judaea; Empire/Slavery; Power/Helplessness; the Whip and the Sword/Suffering. Unencumbered by post-Nietzschean doubts of the virtues inherent in suffering and slavery, the opposing terms are absolute. Briefly the voice of history pretends that in the limited perspective of the moment it sees only an impasse. Escape from the cruel hierarchies seems 'inconceivable'. Only 'a miracle' could make an absolute reversal possible. But the periphery contains a road (the way of the cross) more important than the centre's Appian Way, and the execution of an apparently insignificant criminal is to be the central event of history. The irony parallels numerous moments within the films' narratives where characters, trapped within limited views, make remarks seemingly at one with the irrefutable tide of events but which, for an audience positioned with destiny, resonate with irony. 'When I have punished these Christians', boasts Nero in *Quo Vadis?*, 'history will not be sure that they ever existed.' On the contrary, in the greatest irony of history, the 'humble cross' is about to 'replace the proud eagles'.

As the prologue to *Quo Vadis?* is spoken, images unfold expressing the implacability of Roman power. Through an idyllic pastoral landscape soldiers and chariots approach. The rhythm of the succeeding shots and the movement of the legions within the shots form an unrelieved momentum from screen left to bottom right. By the fifth shot the glamour of the military parade is exposed by the revelation of the cost on which it is built. Children impassively watch slaves being whipped along the road. Close-ups emphasise the reality of their suffering. Further shots concentrate on soldiers whipping them and on the savage aspect of the standard bearers in their panther head-dresses. In the 1925 *Ben-Hur* the oppositions are relayed through antithetical titles and images: 'Pagan Rome was at the zenith of her power. The tread of her legions shook the world and from every land rose the cries of captive people praying for a deliverer'; 'Jerusalem the Golden, conquered and oppressed, wept in the shadow of her walls.' In the 1959 version the oppositions are the meanings of two buildings, 'the fortress of Antonia, the seat of Roman power' and 'the great Golden temple, the outward sign of an inward and imperturbable faith'. In *Spartacus* (as in *The Robe* and *Quo Vadis?*) slavery is defined as the cancer destroying Rome from within. The pre-prologue title sequence in *Spartacus* reveals the fragility underlying apparently immutable Roman power as the last of many imperial busts, all marked by expressions of pitiless masculine arrogance, begin to crack apart, the camera actually moving into an eyehole to begin the narrative. In *The Robe* the prologuising voice of history, presiding over images of Roman power and decadence, is rather complicatedly the voice of the hero, Marcellus Gallio (Richard Burton). In its multi-facetedness, first it is the voice of the character, Tribune Gallio, complicit at this point with Roman oppression, celebrating it in a wearily ironic way. But, in counterpoint, his *anomie* suggests the judgement of history, which the audience already knows, and which Gallio will come to perceive as he moves from Roman soldier to Christian martyr.

In the prologue to *Quo Vadis?* the Christian events alluded to in other prologues are actually fleetingly dramatised in shots of Christ being whipped like a slave and hustled along the Via Crucis, moving diagonally upwards from left to right, an inserted movement that runs counter to the prevailing forward, downward diagonal thrust of the soldiers. In the visual irony this produces, Christ stumbles in the opposite direction to the relentless march of secular history.

Since the films position the audience with destiny, there is a temptation which they find hard to resist, to identify the historical process with dominant values. These are not only Christian, which are assumed to have absolute superiority not only to Roman values but also to all rival religions of the day, such as the Eastern goddess cults, but, more specifically, Christian values as interpreted by mainstream America of the time, not only the constant imposing of a contemporary interpretation of Christianity upon the historical narratives but also the persistent use of historical events as sites for airing contemporary concerns and analogies.

Nowhere is this better illustrated than in the prologue added in 1943 to the re-release of De Mille's *The Sign of the Cross*. Here, prior to the narrative proper, American military personnel embark on a Flying Fortress mission over occupied Rome to drop leaflets rather than bombs. In this additional sequence there is an overt instance of the whole genre's way of reading ancient in the light of modern history, for Nero in his burning of Rome is openly compared with Hitler ('For Nero thought he was master of the world. He cared no more for the lives of others than Hitler does') and the Germanic provenance of the barbarians makes them forerunners of the Third Reich. The group in the plane, a microcosm of Christian America, containing both Protestant and Catholic chaplains, and among others 'Hoboken', the turret-gunner, representative of sceptical but superstitious secular man, but, significantly, no black or Jew, flies to the defence of a civilisation identified with a (white) Christianity. While we may agree that the invocation of a 'just war' was, if ever, justified against the Nazis, we should still be aware of the way the prologue collapses the values of primitive Christianity into those of later Christianised states, and 1940s America in particular. Although the prologue only shows the Allies dropping leaflets, the belligerent rhetoric given to the spunky stereotype of a Catholic boxing priest ('When did we ever duck a fight?') is presented as identical with the attitude of the early martyrs ('who refused to believe that might makes right'). The extremity of the wartime situation makes the appropriation more blatant than usual and forces a major contradiction to analytic notice. For the earliest Christianity no concept of a just war existed, so rather than the analogy proposed, the truer one would be its reverse, that the Allies should accept passive martyrdom from the new Nero. As elsewhere the radical difference of the past is difficult for the American cinema to apprehend, but in its defence the same might be said of the dominant culture as a whole and its versions of Christianity.

PROLOGUE INTO PLOT: ROMAN SOLDIERS, CHRISTIAN MAIDENS AND OTHER VARIATIONS

Salome and *Barabbas*: narrative and sub-genre

Salome (1953) and *Barabbas* (1962), similar in that they both use minor New Testament figures, also mark extremes of difference in the sub-genre. The earlier suggests by its date and casting (Rita Hayworth as Salome) the more than usual dominance of star vehicle conventions. The later film's attributes potentially distance it from the earlier – a late date; high art source (Pär Lagerkvist); a prestigious screenwriter, Christopher Fry; a director, Richard Fleischer, of interesting output (*Mandingo* and *The Boston Strangler*); its Italian–American production basis suggesting variations on the dominant Hollywood model – and announce revisionist possibilities. But put so, the asymmetry of the comparison may well be exaggerated. *Salome*'s director, William Dieterle, was an even more distinguished film maker, and *Salome* is notable for highly-wrought colour and compositional effects. At a certain point difference returns to similarity; the conventional text reveals unexpected sophistication, the deviant text reveals itself governed by convention.

Dieterle's film keeps the outlines of the biblical narrative. Yet it also makes extraordinary changes when it has Salome perform her dance for Herod, not to gain John the Baptist's head but in an unsuccessful attempt to save him. On John's word, she also accepts Christ as the Messiah. These narrative turnabouts can perhaps be explained as dictated by Hayworth's star persona of the good–bad girl par excellence. On the other hand, the film's second major invention, Claudius the Roman officer (Stewart Granger), is a basic convention of the Roman/Christian Film, allowing the typical Roman soldier/non-Roman maiden love plot. In this instance, the usual woman-converts-man mechanism is reversed as Claudius converts

Salome to John's teachings and, through them, to Christ's. This is achieved through a narrative premise in which ingenuity outweighs verisimilitude, the Roman's (to say the least, unlikely) friendship with the Baptist. The wildly inventive state that *Salome*'s narrative attains owes nothing to the revisionist traits operating in a film like *Barabbas* but is the product of an intersecting mélange of conventions – deformation piled upon deformation, though each with its own logic – producing an exhibition of the sub-genre's intrinsic interests, motifs and themes, though at the cost of historical plausibility.

Conversely, *Barabbas* deviates by pressing as much towards the art film as popular generic expectations allow. To have an elderly hero (Anthony Quinn), with, after the beginning, no sexual life at all, goes powerfully against the sub-genre's erotic conventions. *Barabbas* is also unique in having its hero remain to the end in a state of unresolved doubt. The film stays faithful to Lagerkvist's novella of anguished agnosticism as it traces Barabbas's wanderings from his release at Christ's expense to his eventual death by crucifixion in Rome where he is condemned for incendiarism, having joined the Christians in the mistaken belief that they have set fire to Rome. Given these deviant aspects, where it is reshaped by generic demands resisted elsewhere is very interesting. Two elements particularly stand out. First there is the transformation of the hare-lipped girl (Barabbas's ex-mistress) into Silvana Mangano. At an obvious level star demands dictate that the character will become an inflection of the star. Thus her death by stoning becomes a moment of martyrdom more consonant with the ecstatic, semi-sexualised female martyrdoms of *The Sign of the Cross* than with her bathetic book-death. 'She snuffled out her faith in her Lord and Saviour . . . she spoke even more absurdly and thickly than usual, because of standing in front of so many people and being nervous. And they showed clearly that they were ill at ease, that they thought it was embarrassing; some turned away in shame.' The film reworks this blurring of central oppositions. Even where the hero remains perpetually unresolved, oppositions of a clarity the source denies make the film's effects here more akin to the narrative of Stephen's martyrdom (Acts, 7) than to the dissonances of modernist story-telling. Barabbas, as sceptical man, may not wholeheartedly believe in what she says, but the beauty of her belief must contrast absolutely with the blackness of other parts of the film. The hero, in this quasi-modernist inflection, may be unable to choose, but the choices must remain absolute.

Another reshaping invents heightened external actions into which the book's inward-looking preoccupations are placed. So whereas the novella's Barabbas is released from the mines because Sahak's Christianity impresses the overseer, in the film their release is caused by a mine disaster killing everyone but the pair. The modulation is into spectacle, but it would be hyper-puritanical to call this mere sensationalism. In fact the film's changes fully support the powerful underworld darkness/light oppositions of the whole narrative. This reshaping is followed by the invention of Barabbas's gladiatorial career when, now in Rome, he and Sahak are forced to become gladiators, Sahak, because of his Christianity, refusing to fight and being executed, Barabbas, because of his inability to believe, becoming a successful gladiator. The transformation transposes the novella's themes into yet another hellish environment, the arena's theatre of cruelty, presided over by that figure of exemplary Roman sadism, the chief of the gladiators (Jack Palance).

The *Quo Vadis?* plot

The paradigm plots of the sub-genre derive from the novels *Ben-Hur* and *Quo Vadis?*. Unlike *Salome* and *Barabbas*, with their fictions created around minor New Testament figures, these exhibit the fullest (historical novel) characteristics of the sub-genre, placing invented protagonists within the conflicts caused by the founding of Christianity, alongside both fictional and historical individuals.

In the *Quo Vadis?* plot, a love relationship between a pagan Roman male and a non-Roman Christian female takes place against the early Roman persecutions. Their love enacts at the most intimate level the contesting and merging of the opposing ethics. The male, a soldier, is identified with Roman inhumanity. He pursues the woman sexually. She resists but, despite abhorring his values, falls in love with him. The highly-wrought scene in LeRoy's *Quo Vadis?* where Lydia (Deborah Kerr) prays to Christ both for Marcus Vinicius's conversion and for her own desires, renders the whole complex of desire and restraint, the licit and illicit, the spiritual and the sensual, very forcibly. As their relationship grows, the Roman soldier's desire changes from lust to a wish for marriage. However, his unreconstructed attitudes reassert themselves, and they part. Drawn back by his love, he is won over to her Christianity. Arrested for her beliefs, she is condemned to the arena with the other Christians. He decides to join her. They marry. In alternative possible endings they either embrace martyrdom together or are rescued, as in the novel. This resumé covers the two films that most obviously derive from the novel, De Mille's *The Sign of the Cross* and LeRoy's *Quo Vadis?*. But its structures govern in multiple transformations significant elements of other films (most notably *The Robe* and *Demetrius*).

Christian maidens

The woman is from the beginning identified with Christian spirituality. Deborah (Pier Angeli) in *The Silver Chalice* is even the grand-daughter of Joseph of Arimathea. Lydia in *Quo Vadis?* is first seen by Marcus Vinicius (Robert Taylor) emblematically lighting lamps and indeed holds a taper thoughout their first meeting. Mercia (Elissa Landi) in *The Sign of the Cross* has a name that is obviously symbolic, like Lucia's in *Demetrius and the Gladiators*. Marcus Superbus first meets her drawing water from a well, with all the accompanying biblical connotations. Varinia (Jean Simmons) in *Spartacus*, not a Christian but functioning as a Christian maiden, is also associated with the symbolism of the water pitcher, as she is in *Androcles*.

Both Lydia and Mercia (and Diana, again Jean Simmons, their Roman equivalent in *The Robe*) are sentenced to death for their beliefs, only Lydia of the three escaping martyrdom. In this they fulfil the early Christian pattern of virgin martyrs. Indeed, Lydia's mode of execution (though she survives it) is clearly based on that of the martyr Blandina who was tossed by a bull. In the novel *Quo Vadis?* the power of the bull and the nakedness of the female victim underline the sadistic sexuality of her ordeal. The LeRoy version may stage the scene more decorously, but the situation and the flimsiness of Lydia's costume retain the scene's basic sexual and sadistic ambience.

This, however, is not the only sexualisation that takes place. The virginity of these martyrs, of such interest to early Christians, would have little appeal to the audiences of these films. So the Christian maiden is transformed into the sub-genre's virtuous but indubitably sexual heroine who leads the pagan male to the higher sexuality of romantic Christian monogamy. As such she represents not the overcoming of sexuality emblematised by her original, but rather a good sexuality set in opposition to the perverse desire of the sub-genre's equivalent of Film Noir's temptress, the Empress (Poppaea)/Patricia Laffan in *Quo Vadis?* and Claudette Colbert in *The Sign of the Cross*, and Messalina/Susan Hayward in *Demetrius*), typed by rapacious sexuality and flagrant signs of decadence like Poppaea's pet leopards. When in *The Sign of the Cross* Claudette Colbert realises that Fredric March prefers Elissa Landi, she is directly identified with her leopards when their roars on the soundtrack coincide with her angry expressions of frustrated appetite.

The actresses playing the redemptive sexual woman comprise a complex oxymoron of sexuality and purity, though in the case of Lucia (Debra Paget) in *Demetrius* the role can become simply emblematic and almost asexual. These actresses tend to be British (or European), whereas the Roman soldier can be British or American, yet another variation on the multiple encodings that Britishness has in the Biblical Epic. Here Britishness conveys aloofness and aristocratic reserve. But alongside this, Kerr, Simmons and Landi all project a certain sexual fervour, with Deborah Kerr's fecund hips and breasts emphasised by the camera and the discreetly diaphanous outfits she wears. In her case the repeated joke of Nero's echoing of Petronius's unlikely judgement of her as 'Too narrow in the hips' verbally underlines the contrast her body makes with her slightly haughty face. 'Mostly blues, I think', says Acte as she dresses Lydia in Nero's 'House of Women' (blue suggesting the celestial Madonna), but it is in delicately passional pink that we first see her. In revealing phrases Poppaea scornfully describes Mercia both as 'baby-faced' and as 'a Christian wanton', and it is precisely this crossing of the Christian and the highly sexualised, the innocent and the erotic, that is characteristic. Both Lydia and Mercia notably fall in love at first sight, which suggests that somehow the apparent opposites of romantic sexual irrationalism and Christian sexual rationalism have been fused, with romantic love displaying a secular version of sudden grace and conversion (and, as we shall see, its own version of immortality). Mercia, occasionally heaving with desire, flirts outrageously with her Roman about his sexual reputation, and the pitcher which they break during their verbal foreplay later becomes a fond reminiscence for the pair, its symbolism underlining the triumph of monogamy over virginity. If Landi's hair is often haloed by numinous lighting effects (compare the halo-like silver headband worn by Deborah/Pier Angeli in *The Silver Chalice*), she also wears a gown whose general decorum is compromised by an effect more associated with Mae West, piping that unmistakably defines her genital area. Similarly in Jean Simmons's religious roles (including Sharon Falconer in *Elmer Gantry*) there is always a certain *discordia concors* between the conflicting signs of submissive spirituality and of voluptuousness that are characteristic of both star and character-function.

Roman soldiers

The paradigm plot matches the Christian woman with her antithesis, the Roman male, his hyper-masculinity stressed by his Roman military costume, predominantly steel and leather, emphasising machine-like hardness, and with the sword hung at the front more than the side, boasting an unregenerately phallic sexuality in the machismo conflation of weapon with organ. In Sienkiewicz's original the 'vindictive, ferocious soul' of a hero who kills his old slave in a fit of rage is more brutally expressed than in the films where such excesses are given more moderate expression in the patriarchal arrogance of Marcus Vinicius (Robert Taylor) in *Quo Vadis?* and Marcus Superbus (Fredric March) in *The Sign of the Cross*, and moderated even more in other versions of the same character (for instance Marcellus Gallio/Richard Burton in *The Robe* and Claudius/Stewart Granger in *Salome*), the softenings a constituent of the desire to modulate between concepts of masculinity and femininity in such a way that traditional masculine characteristics connected with aggression and dominance may be retained in some measure even while being criticised and feminised.

Fredric March's entry in *The Sign of the Cross* gives the filmic version of the Roman hero at his at least half-endearing extreme, careering into sight in a chariot, flailing a huge whip with which he immediately strikes out no fewer than six times, arrogantly amused by Mercia's plight when he first sees her, roughly aggressive and superciliously courtly by turns. Robert Taylor as Vinicius woos Lydia poetically when he first sees her, but characteristically assumes she is a slave and later even forces her into what amounts to slavery when he and Petronius manipulate Nero into giving her to him as a gift. However, like Fredric March, Robert Taylor is shown as not really criminal, for when he has Deborah Kerr in his power he does not finally use it. The audience is plainly meant to find his attitudes reactionary – 'Well, I don't know a thing about philosophy, and lovely women shouldn't have the time to think that deeply' – while at the same time enjoying aspects of his masculine forcefulness. As we pass from the potentially redeemable to the irredeemable, Crassus (Laurence Olivier) in *Spartacus* gives us the character in its deadliest unmovable form, a suaver, more articulate version of Romans throughout the film wedded to power – the sadistic killing machine played by Jack Palance in *Barabbas*, Ernest Borgnine in *Demetrius*, the brutal centurion in *The Robe* and many others. Here Crassus's only true love is the sadistic mother-whore Rome. As he tells Antoninus: 'There is only one way to deal with Rome . . . you must abase yourself before her. You must grovel at her feet.' Occasionally such characteristics may be transferred to non-Roman characters, for instance in *The Silver Chalice* to both the leader of the Sicarii and Simon the Magician (Jack Palance) with their 'Nietzschean' hatred of religion which 'saps men of their virility and courage', but even here the Roman connection tends to remain strong because it is ultimately a Roman world in which they live and act.

Omnia vincit amor

This dominating love plot structure where opposites meet and resolve is repeated across the sub-genre. Its advantages as a convention are obvious. It charges the films with erotic interest, but an erotic interest that draws into intimate conflict opposing ideologies in their most personalised form.

The convention alludes to historical reality. Compare I Corinthians where Paul instructs Christian spouses married to pagans what their behaviour should be – Christianity under threat from intermarriage, but also, by a happy conjunction of faith and sexuality, spreading as its consequence. In the films' ideal pattern, through love of the Christian woman the male loses his reprehensible attributes – violence, arrogance, contempt for the female, while the female (in a movement opposite to early Christian romances where the burgeoning saint rejects all suitors for the love of Christ), through love of the man accepts enjoyment of the body, softening what is seen as too puritanical a concept of Christianity.

In the 'model' plot, although the female accepts the male without demanding conversion (though, naturally, she wants it), conflicts arise within the relationship. Thus Vinicius is jealous of Christ's influence over Lydia, while Marcus Superbus presses Mercia to abandon her co-religionists for personal happiness (as the Captain does Lavinia in *Androcles*). The situation is further complicated when the amoral attractions of the Empress tempt the hero. The clash of ethical perspectives is given in an extreme form in *The Sign of the Cross* when Marcus Superbus mocks Mercia in front of his partying Roman friends and Antaria's erotic dance, 'The Naken Moon', is interrupted by the hymns the Christians sing as they are transported to the arena. Eventually, however, despite or through such affliction, the couple are reunited.

This central love relationship admits significant variation. For instance, in *Pompeii*, where the hero's relationship with an adopted child replaces the primary love plot, erotic miscegenation is deflected into the relationship between Marius's son, Flavius, and the slave girl, Clodia. In *The Robe* both male and female lovers are Roman and it is the soldier who first becomes Christian, while the woman occupies what is usually the male role of attempting to turn him away from the foolishness of Christianity, and herself only slowly moves towards belief. This recalcitrance, however, is the only negative aspect of the Roman male that Diana shares in her pagan inflection of most of the values associated with the Christian woman (which she eventually becomes). In *Spartacus*, on the other hand, with its pre-Christian but allusively Christianised setting, neither lover is Roman. Varinia here embodies a spiritualising femininity, under the influence of which Spartacus (Kirk Douglas) reconceives his rebellion as a transformation of society in which not only women but the arts (represented by the poet Antoninus/Tony Curtis) have an influential place. So while the rebels' campsite is a training place for the army of liberation, it is also a place of families and feminine presence. Once, early on, when the insurrectionists free some slaves, Spartacus scornfully remarks that there are too many women. A white-haired grandmother turns on him, arguing incontrovertibly that 'if woman was made out of man, it is through woman that man came to be'. Spartacus acknowledges his mistake and embraces her.

As noted, where the plots are closest to the Sienkiewicz original, the Empress's lust obstructs the hero's progress towards the heroine's Christianity. In fact, when spurned, she revenges herself by planning the destruction of the heroine. In *Demetrius* Messalina has this role, coming between Lucia and Demetrius and attempting the destruction of the hero, who is not Roman but takes on, at times, 'Roman' values both as gladiator and lover, just as in *Spartacus* the hero, in all other senses anti-Roman, is 'Roman' in his initially unreconstructed masculinity. In *The Robe* Caligula reverses the sexes in his spasmodic desire for Diana and his coming between her and Marcellus, and the roles are similarly reversed in *Spartacus* when Crassus forces Varinia into a sexual relationship but fails to win her away from the memory of Spartacus. Like Atilla in *The Sign of the Pagan*, content to force the wife, Ildico, who will not even speak to him, Crassus forces himself on Varinia who punishes him by the coldness with which she enforcedly gives herself. A 'director's cut' of *Spartacus*, just released at the time of writing (November 1991), contains a previously censored scene in which Crassus makes homosexual overtures to Antoninus, an example that must stand for many of the further transformations of the functions and motifs outlined above.

The Petronian perspective

Only one of the films deriving from Sienkiewicz, LeRoy's *Quo Vadis?* retains what is perhaps the novel's primary consciousness, Gaius Petronius, poet, hedonist, amorist and sceptic, confidant of Nero and uncle of Marcus Vinicius. But even if he is given concrete form only once, in Leo Genn's detached urbanity the character brings into focus what exists fugitively in other films, a powerfully appealing alternative view of events from the perspective of pleasure, irony, aesthetics and self-gratification. Apart from Petronius the viewpoint may or may not have other fleeting representatives in the films (Claudette Colbert's often sympathetic Poppaea in *The Sign of the Cross*; implications of a more reasonable hedonism within the distorted desires of Nero and Messalina), but it exists as a constant possibility of interpretation poised between the demanding super-ego of Christianity and the self-destructive id of the Emperor.

Petronius, both as literal character and as ironic viewpoint, is highly complex, a field of multiple ambivalances. Among other things, he acts out a parallel to Marcus Vinicius's and Lydia's love in his attachment to his Spanish slave, Eunice. Like Vinicius he moves to a higher ethic than slavery (finally giving Eunice her freedom), a form of monogamy seen as superior to promiscuity or polygamy, debates about which run through the sub-genre. Examples are found in the exchange that Martian (Jeff Chandler) has with Atilla in *The Sign of the Pagan* (*Atilla*: 'These Romans [i.e. Roman Christians] have a strange custom: they take but one wife.' *Martian*: 'A good wife can be all things to a man. Or he can marry four hundred times and not find a good one among them') and Judah with Sheikh Ilderim in Wyler's *Ben-Hur*. But Petronius's love is presented as purely carnal and aesthetic as he constantly celebrates Eunice as a piece of living sculpture. The text clearly wants to distinguish morally between Vinicius's and Lydia's spiritualised sexuality and this unspiritualised version. Petronius's banquet is a secular parallel to the Last Supper with its host farewelling his friends amidst a decor of flowers, orchestra, food, drink, etc., representing his exquisite values, and with the physician's letting of his blood paralleling/parodying Christ's giving of his. The difference, from the film's overt Christian perspective, is that it contains no promise for the future, in spite of Eunice's claim that 'Love such as I feel cannot ever die'. Petronius can triumph over Nero only in wit, not in fact, still treating Christianity as he dies as a subject of speculative agnostic wit. At one and the same time the film declares his cultured, ironic view inadequate, yet implicitly allows it to criticise the salvationary metaphysics of Christianity.

Lovers and martyrs

Changed by love, the Roman soldier finally commits himself to the Christian woman, aligning himself with the persecuted Christians. But the narrative in this genre, as if slightly infected by the Petronian viewpoint, hesitates to move towards too absolute a conclusion. There is a charac-teristic stutter which allows for the presence of scepticism. While the woman, as in various martyrdom accounts, becomes heroine and teacher, consoling and confirming (as when Mercia, in *The Sign of the Cross*, per-suades the frightened boy, Stefan, to face the arena), the soldier confesses he only half believes. 'I believe in *you*, not this Christ', says Marcus Super-bus, though later, with the promise of immortality, he finds himself 'happy' and 'full of strange hope'. Similarly, Vinicius to Lydia: 'You would never wish me to pretend, would you? That I feel myself a Christian? . . . It's proven good, full of courage, right here . . . but there are many things I cannot believe . . . understand.' Lydia's reply, it seems, is sufficient: 'Christ is within you, Marcus. You feel Him more strongly than you know', for when he is forced to watch her in the arena a prayer to Christ rises to his lips. In *The Robe*'s playing out of the conversion scenario, where the roles are reversed, Diana follows a similar trajectory, and in *Salome*, without any martyrdom, the Princess is converted via the Baptist and her lover to Christian belief. *Demetrius*, though, is a variant of the dominant pattern, with the hero converted (or rather, re-converted) by wordless contact with Lucia. The last moments of the drama of conversion may resolve into either a 'happy' ending with the lovers free together, or martyred in the para- doxically 'happier' ending. In *Spartacus* there is an exceptional finale where the hero is 'martyred' but the heroine survives to present to him beneath the cross the son who will inherit the unspoken Christian future.

The *Ben-Hur* plot

The second *ur*-plot is less obviously generative than the first but demands consideration, not only because the 1925 and 1959 versions of *Ben-Hur* are so central but for similarities with the *Quo Vadis?* plot that it pursues amidst differences, and for its various elements that are often joined with other narrative formations (for example the encounters with Jesus in the Holy Land in *The Robe* and *Pompeii*).

Wallace's novel tells of a young, aristocratic Jew who, in meeting again with his childhood companion, Messala, now a Roman Officer, finds friendship impossible because of the Roman's arrogance towards the Jews. An accident endangering the life of the governor is blamed on him, his mother and sister are arrested, and Messala condemns him to the galleys, his mother and sister to prison. On the way to the galleys Judah encounters Jesus, though the reader has been made aware of the birth of the Messiah, at the beginning of the narrative nearly thirty years before. In the galleys Judah suffers what becomes in the films one of the great spectacles of Roman sadism: the exhausted rowers, chained to their benches, whipped by savage overseers, their hopeless labours controlled by the inhuman thud of the *hortator*'s drum. When pirates attack, Judah in escaping rescues the Roman commander, Quintus Arrius, who takes him to Rome and adopts him as his son. Returning to his homeland, Judah searches for his mother and sister while also planning military support for the Messiah. Re- encountering Messala, he defeats him in the great chariot race that becomes the kinetic centre-piece of the two films. (In the films Messala, played first by Francis X. Bushman and later by Stephen Boyd, dies; in the novel he survives crippled.) When he finds that his mother and sister are lepers,

Judah is persuaded by his sister to search out the young rabbi (Jesus) known for his miraculous cures. When Judah and Jesus meet again on the Via Crucis, Jesus refuses his offer of military help but cures his mother and sister. As the novel ends, Judah, converted to Christianity, decides to help his co-religionists just beginning to suffer persecution in Rome.

Like the *Quo Vadis?* plot *Ben-Hur* develops, more modestly, the sub-generic love-relationship; here not between a Roman and a Christian but between two Jews (Christians by the end of the narrative). But it involves similar metaphorical oppositions, since Judah, though fiercely anti-Roman, becomes like his enemy Messala in seeking revenge (i.e. 'Roman' in the larger sense alluded to above), while Esther is identified with peace and reconciliation. The source novel, however, differs from Sienkiewicz's in its anti-eroticism, brusquely rejecting such concerns when Judah visits the Grove of Daphne. Though he is briefly tempted by its world of erotic pastoral, duty easily prevails. The novel and the first film complicate the (hardly passionate) love plot with a second female who threatens to seduce the hero (paralleling the Empress of the *Quo Vadis?* plot), Iras, the Egyptian. In *The Silver Chalice*, which combines elements of the *Quo Vadis?* and *Ben-Hur* plots with the Grail legend, Helena (Virginia Mayo), the sensual pagan antithesis to the Christian Deborah, fills out the duality experienced by the (in this case neither Roman nor Jewish but, like Demetrius, Greek) hero, Basil (Paul Newman). Curiously, the Wyler film omits Iras, perhaps in part because Judah is played by Charlton Heston who is, as we remark below, more the iconic lawgiver than the lover. The film seems almost comically aware of this when Judah, listening to Ilderim rhapsodically describing his horses, thinks he is talking about his wives, and then displays his own polygamous affection for the equine team, which rather surpasses what he shows to Esther.

Another way in which the *Ben-Hur* narrative parallels *Quo Vadis?* is in its renovation by the feminine of modes of culture perceived as excessively masculine. In all the versions a notably fatherless Judah breaks with his Roman alter ego Messala, a warrior-figure of huge masculine pride. Through Messala's revenge Judah loses his wholly female family. He gains a second father, the Roman Quintus Arrius (Jack Hawkins in the Wyler version), not corrupt like Messala but nevertheless patriarchal and militaristic. Renouncing his status as Roman and son, Judah breaks with this surrogate father to return to Judea to search for his mother and sister, and for Jesus, seen initially by Judah as another warrior-patriarch until he reconceives him in a partially feminised altered ideal. Thus beneath his nationalistic commitments and his desire for revenge, the story's drive in all its forms (but especially in the films) is towards the reuniting of Judah's matriarchal family. More than the love plot with Esther, it is the hero's recovery of the female group that is the counterweight to the love plot of the *Quo Vadis?* films. Both *Ben-Hur* films culminate in tableaux where the hero is surrounded by the three women, mother, sister, and future wife. The narrative's desire for feminisation is captured in the novel's remarkable description of Jesus, not an effect able to be repeated in the films but influencing them and displaced elsewhere.

> The head was open to the cloudless light, except as it was draped with hair long and slightly waved, and parted in the middle, and auburn in tint, with a tendency to reddish-golden where most strongly touched by the sun. Under a broad, low forehead, under black, well-arched brows, beamed eyes dark blue and large, and softened to exceeding tenderness by lashes of great length sometimes seen on children, but seldom, if ever, on men . . . The delicacy of the nostrils was unusual . . . and when it was taken into account with the gentleness of the eyes, the pallor of the complexion, the fine texture of the hair, and the softness of the beard, which fell in waves over his throat to his breast, never a soldier but would have laughed at him in encounter, never a child that would not, with quick instinct, have given him its hand and whole artless trust: nor might anyone have said he was not beautiful.

Clearly this is an excessive verion which in the films usually modulates into a careful balance of feminine and masculine, as when Deborah in *The Silver Chalice*, visualising Christ for the sculptor Basil, notes that 'his mouth was sensitive and kind', but quickly adds that 'there was no weakness in it' and that it was 'strong and firm', having already stated (for the masculinely short-haired 1950s) that 'He did not wear his hair long as most people think'. All this bears close relation to what we have analysed in the 1927 *The King of Kings*. It takes slightly different forms in source and films; in the novel, for instance, Iras, the corrupt female, who identifies with the hyper-masculine Messala, mocks Jesus's 'woman's face'. But the concern is active in all three texts, tracing the positive feminisation credited to Christianity. At the same time, over the sub-genre, such suggestions coexist with contrary ones, so that a male dominance, properly softened but not destroyed, is preserved. Though led to Christianity by her in *The Sign of the Cross*, Marcus Superbus eventually leads Mercia to martyrdom, and in various other ways traditional hierarchies are simultaneously softened and restored. For instance, though in many of the films females lead by example, in only one case do we see a woman in the role of public teacher, and there, in *The Robe*, Miriam is crippled and thus disqualified from the usual femine roles. In *Spartacus* it is a son to inherit the future that Varinia wishes to have and whom she displays before the dying Spartacus; and in LeRoy's *Quo Vadis?*, when, in prison and about, it seems, to die, Lydia tells Marcus

Vinicius that she wanted to have a child by him, she says 'I would love to have given you a son.'

'WE'LL MEET AGAIN': CHRISTIANITY AND ROMANTIC LOVE

> He has imagined a heaven, and has left entirely out of it all his delights, the one ecstasy that stands first and foremost in the heart of every individual of his race – and ours – sexual intercourse. — Mark Twain, *Letters from the Earth*

Typically the Roman/Christian Epic sets up contrasts in the erotic, ending with the triumph of a Christianised sexual love over baser forms. But sometimes something in excess of this is dramatised, a heightening that merges spiritual and erotic love to the point where Christianity's promise of eternal life is interpreted by the lovers as their passion's continuation, not its extinction.

Throughout the sub-genre there are various suppressions, especially of the idea that earlier Christianity, or at least the 'over-achieving' martyrs, existed in an apocalyptic fervour heralding the last days (something only the television version of *Quo Vadis?* accentuates) and therefore devalued sexuality. One of the limits of the Hollywood cinema's archaeological passion is reached here. Despite its elements of puritanism and funda-mentalism, it is difficult to think of a culture less like radical early Christianity than twentieth-century America, with its materialism, its belief in the goodness of (at least prescribed and controlled) sexual love, and the family.

So, rather than being an impediment to salvation, sexuality is divided into a bad, though fascinating, kind (Roman licentiousness), occasionally a higher pagan eroticism (Petronius and Eunice in *Quo Vadis?*), and a trans-cendent form fused with the idea of Christian love itself. Sienkiewicz's novel is the immediate source of this last, but is more archaeologically exact in showing the conflict between the erotic and the radical asexuality promi-nent in early Christianity. In the novel Lygia (changed to Lydia in the film) feels guilty about betraying Christ for Vinicius. Crispus, a harshly world-negating Christian, is unattractively presented in his lack of sympathy for Lygia but does state the harsh view, though it is rebuked immediately in Peter's reference to the marriage at Cana. Peter's attitude here is a toleration rather than celebration of carnality, but, later, *eros* and *caritas* are characteristically (con)fused when Vinicius, Peter and Paul talk:

'I have been told that your doctrine takes no account of life, of human joys, of happiness . . . Is it really so? Do you, then, regard it as a sin to love, to feel joy, to desire happiness? Are you enemies of life?' . . . In reply Peter said: 'We bring with us love' and Paul of Tarsus added: 'Though I speak with the tongues of men and of angels, and have not charity, I am become as a sounding brass, or a tinkling cymbal.'

This scene ends with Peter blessing the lovers – 'Love ye one another in the Lord and for his Glory, for in your love there is no sin.' The three views articulated correspond to three different strata of Pauline sexual theology – uncompromising demotion of the sexual (I Corinthians, 7:1); pragmatic acceptance (I Corinthians, 7:9); and a more positive view of marriage based on the analogy of Christ and the Church (Ephesians, 5:25). But the novel develops a fourth view, a transcendent sexual love which somehow stems from Christ. 'Believe me, Vinicius,' says Lygia, 'it was Christ who brought you to me.' Vinicius's conversion is explicitly based on his hope that their marriage will continue after the resurrection:

'And when death shall have closed my eyes . . . I shall find you again, my beloved. And that this doctrine is the best of all doctrines, both my reason tells and my heart feels by instinct' . . . Lygia had listened with her blue eyes fixed upon him – a pair of eyes that in the moonlight looked like mystic, dew-bespangled flowers. 'Yes, Marcus, all that is true', she said as she pressed her head yet closer to his shoulder.

The doctrine is the 'best of all doctrines' because it prolongs a spiritualised sexuality's raptures into Paradise, merging Christian immortality with sexual immortality. In *The Sign of the Cross*, awaiting martyrdom, Marcus asks Mercia, 'There, with this Christ, we can always be together?', and she replies, 'It's true', something given almost identical formulation in LeRoy's *Quo Vadis?* when Marcus Vinicius asserts that he and Lydia must be married 'so that it will be that way when we are together again'. Almost immediately Peter marries them with words of soaring unorthodoxy: 'May he who blessed the marriage at Cana bless you also. Love one another from this moment forward as man and wife in his Holy Name, the name of the Father, the Son and the Holy Ghost. In this life and the next, now and forever more.'

The implications here suggest why the apparently 'happy' ending of *Quo Vadis?* is somehow less satisfactory than the 'unhappy' ending of *The Sign of the Cross* and *The Robe*. In the latter the lovers' martyrdom fuses the triumph of Christianity with the ultimate myth of secular love, the ecstatic *Liebestod* of *Tristan und Isolde*, where death in fulfilment avoids all the depredations of age and decline. Whereas both novel and film versions of

Quo Vadis? save the Christian couple for domesticity, *The Sign of the Cross* and *The Robe* end in the consummation of martyrdom. Diana's white costume in *The Robe*'s court scene is bridal, while her and Marcellus's execution, in an amatory conceit which calls up Cupid's as well as Caligula's arrows, is to take place in the palace archery fields. Walking hand in hand down the aisle, Burton and Simmons are irresistibly like a bridal couple. Moments before, Diana has said to Caligula: 'Sire . . . Marcellus is my chosen husband. I ask to go with him . . . as for me, I have found another King. I want to go with my husband into his Kingdom.' The ambiguity is perfectly poised. Is her other King Christ or her husband? Does she mean, go with her husband into Christ's kingdom, or into her husband's kingdom? Whichever, or both, their surroundings become the sky, signifier of ambiguous immortality, real or desired.

ORIGINAL SCENES:
THE DISAPPEARING JEW

> In that he saith, A new covenant, he hath made the first old. Now that which decayeth and waxeth old is ready to vanish away. — Hebrews, 8:13

Unhabitual readers of The Acts of the Apostles may be surprised by the absence of the conflict with Rome that dominates later Christian apologetics and, eventually, Hollywood's versions of early Christianity. Its persecutors are orthodox Jews, so that the Romans, to whom Paul looked for protection, tend to be marginally positive figures. It has been suggested that the New Testament's treatment of the Romans (above all Pilate's unwillingness to crucify Jesus) is calculated to appease the power which, before the persecutions, Christians had every interest in cultivating. In Hollywood's presentation the reverse is true, and (at least on the surface) every effort is made to establish the Romans' guilt. But the corollary of this is not, as in the Christ film, that Jewish figures are presented in mitigating circumstances, so much as that they are not presented at all.

The absence of this difficult history – involving persecutions of Christians as heretics by Orthodox Jews and the beginnings of Christian anti-Semitism – and the consequent emphasis on the conflict between Christianity and Rome have explanations in the dramatic potential of the clash between pagan empire and Christian future. But other factors add reasons for the excision of Jewish contexts. Just as Christianity embarrasses Judaism by marginalising it into merely the precursor of Christianity, so Judaism embarrasses Christianity by refusing to die and insisting upon its

Judaic origins. Consequently Jewish material in these films ·is avoided, firstly, to cover the scandal of origins, and secondly, immediately and pragmatically, to avoid conflict with Jewish organisations sensitive to anti-Semitic representations. Additionally, the powerful Jewish presence in the film industry would hardly have wished to present the Jews as persecutors of Christianity.

Looking at the two literary *ur*-texts and the cinematic reworkings of *Ben-Hur* and *Quo Vadis?*, the repression is easier to achieve in the latter than in the former. *Quo Vadis?* is set in Nero's Rome, where there is no need to present Christianity as anything but wholly formed. But the *Ben-Hur* narrative is unavoidably involved with Judaism's passage to Christianity.

The absence of Jewishness in the Sienkiewicz-derived films makes the appearance in LeRoy's *Quo Vadis?* of Abraham Sofaer's violently Semitic-looking Paul extremely curious. Both here and in *The Sign of the Cross* the novel's connection between the Empress Poppaea and Judaism is omitted, yet here suppressed material erupts physiognomically. In this 'return of the repressed', it is notable that the narrative still carries out a marginalisation of this Jewish Paul. Lydia wants Paul to marry her and Marcus Vinicius. This is prevented by the Roman's refusal to share her with 'another man' (i.e. Christ). When the marriage takes place it is the patriarchal Finlay Currie, playing a Peter completely without ethnic connotation, who performs it, achieving both a revelation of suppressed Jewish roots and their eventual supercession, with Paul disappearing from the narrative. If Sienkiewicz's novel has traces of anti-Semitism, they lie not in the historically plausible suggestion that Roman Jews aided the persecution of the Christians but in the omission of any explanatory religio-political context, leaving only a free-floating malevolence as motivation. Montheilhet, revisiting the narrative field in his novel *Neropolis*, even has the Chief Rabbi of Rome write a letter which compromises the Christians. But this happens within a context of Christian/Jewish rivalries, in which not only Christian claims over Judaism but Judaic objections to Christianity are articulated, in a situation too irony-laden to encourage prejudicial responses.

Only in the late *Barabbas* are Jewish/Christian conflicts briefly dramatised, at the narrative's beginning, though a marginal (and non-conflictual) instance occurs in *The Silver Chalice* when the leader of the Sicarii speaks scornfully to Simon the Magician of 'pious Jews dedicated to the Law of Moses and those others who follow Jesus' and Deborah's father, Aaron, who has not followed his father Joseph of Arimathea's conversion, briefly opposes her Christianity. By the mid 1980s the television mini-series *Anno Domini*, adapted from Burgess's *The Kingdom of Wickedness*, centres on both Jews and Christians who remain committed to their respective religions, though the popular piety thought necessary for the mass mode dictates that one character's conversion from Christianity to Mithraism is omitted (an omission typical, as Robin Lane Fox reminds us, of Christian-oriented treatments of pagan/Christian relations). The television series also omits the novel's sceptical finale, the eruption of Vesuvius. In another 1980s televison mini-series, *Masada*, the Roman/Jewish conflicts of the immediate post-Christ era are dramatised, but just as Jews all but disappear in the Roman/Christian Film, so here there is only a single reference over several hours to Christianity. But in the earlier films, despite the high profile that Judaism actually had in Rome, and despite *The Robe* and *Salome* placing part of their action in Palestine, Judaism is all but invisible. For instance, when in *The Robe* Marcellus revisits Cana, the Christian community he finds is completely unmarked by controversy, and where Jewish references are made it is in the context of an unproblematic transition from past to future.

With the *Ben-Hur* narratives the case is different, as the title and hero's name signal. Judah passes through stages of Jewish nationalist commitment, diminished in the second film version but pronounced in the novel and the 1925 film, where, until late on, he interprets the Messiah's coming nationalistically, actually offering Jesus the armies he has recruited. Even where the conflict between Jewish and Christian versions of the Messiah is softened into a more generalised struggle between the forces of love and *ressentiment*, there are difficult negotiations to be made. The novel's opening espoused an evolutionary view of religion, bringing together the three wise men of the Greek, Egyptian and Hindu traditions, all aspiring towards the higher monotheism and all recognising their religions' fulfilment in the Jewish Messiah. At the end of the novel (significantly omitted from both films), Judah, converted to Christianity, dedicates his fortune to building catacombs for the Roman Christians. The films prefer a vaguer metamorphosis, celebrating the 'young rabbi' with hints, but no direct statement, of the resurrection, the conversion implicit in details like Ramon Novarro's discreet abandonment of his skullcap in the 1925 version. The Wyler film inherits a more pressing set of background circumstances which include guilt over the Holocaust and pro-Israeli feeling in America. While militant Jewish nationalism (celebrated in *Exodus*, 1960) is played down in order to de-emphasise Christian/Jewish differences, Jewish elements are highlighted elsewhere, as in the replacement of the earlier film's blonde-ringleted Esther (May McAvoy) by the Israeli Haya Harareet, not only classically Semitic-looking but a more active character who debates questions of love and revenge with Judah. From a Jewish viewpoint this has negative aspects, since she is presented as naturally gravitating from a revenge-centred Judaism to a Christianity identified with love. However, the film's desire can hardly be other than to present the evolutionary superiority of Christianity, but in ways avoiding overt conflict, and honouring Judaism as much as possible within those terms. So Judah is shown observing Jewish customs (as distinct from laws alien to the non-Orthodox-Jewish majority) which can be positively imaged, washing himself before meals and touching the *mezuzah* at the entrance to his house. And when he prays before the chariot race he wears a skullcap and shawl, praying to Jehovah not for revenge but for forgiveness for the revenge he is about to commit, thus softening the opposition between the God of *ressentiment* and the God of Love. There is a notable moment after the family's apparent conversion where, entering his house, he straightens the *mezuzah*, implying the renovation of Judaism, rather than its abolition, by Christianity.

The Wyler *Ben-Hur*'s desire for reconciliation extends to the *Ben-Hur* narrative's fourth realm, the Arabs, represented by Sheikh Ilderim. It is Ilderim's horses that Judah drives in the chariot race, and in all the narratives the Arab expresses an aversion to the Romans equal to the Jews'. In a less constrained version of the Jewish–Arab concords in *Exodus*, the Wyler *Ben-Hur* has a moment of intense rapprochement between the Semitic enemies when Hugh Griffith (a jocose but not unsympathetic Arab) pins a star of David on Judah before the race, saying 'The star of David shine out for your people and my people together and blind the eyes of Rome'. It is an equivocal moment, involving desire for Jewish/Arab reconciliation but also wish-fulfilment on the part of Jewish Americans that the Arabs should accept the *de facto* situation of Jewish colonisation of Palestine. And, significantly, while Hugh Griffith is amiable, he is still a grotesque visual stereotype of the hooknosed, shady dealer, the Arab taking on a version of the Shylock look.

EARTHLY POWERS: THE EMPIRE OF THE SENSES/THE EMPEROR OF I SCREAM

> But in those days all I knew was how to suck, and how to lie still when my body sensed comfort, or cry when it felt pain. — Augustine, *Confessions*

There is one central figure so far only glancingly observed, though, unlike his opposite, far from hidden at the margins of the screen. To the scandal of responsible history, a mist of mythology muffles his outline, just as it obscures his opposite's. He is the Emperor of Rome – Nero, Caligula, the prince of this world, the bearer of the Mark of the Beast. However much the legend is deconstructed, the urge to print it is overwhelming. Historians remind us that for all their political ineptitudes, Caligula and Nero were popular with the masses, probably not surpassingly vicious, and that many of the stories of their perversities were oppositional propaganda. Further, the most famous story, that Nero burned Rome, is agreed to be a sensational fabrication. But this story, combining dictator, perverted idealist and mad aesthete, epicurean experimenter beyond good and evil and sadistic enemy of Christianity, serves so many purposes that it becomes a necessary fiction. Its pull is so powerful that even that most intelligent of post-modernist historical novels, *Neropolis*, feels that outright resistance to it is novelistically self-defeating, and that the best strategy is to print the legend, but in a form complicatedly playful rather than absolute.

In *Jokes and their Relation to the Unconscious* Freud noted the attractions great criminals and comedians have for their observers, who admire in them the narcissism that most adults unwillingly surrender to the reality principle. The Roman Emperor in these films, and as often as not this means Nero (bypassing the more conventional reality principle operators such as Tiberius and Claudius in *The Robe* and *Demetrius and the Gladiators*), combines, in an unholy trinity of narcissism, the criminal, the comedian and the infant. The pre-eminence of the last is visible in the tantrums and delusions of immortality of Caligula in *The Robe* and *Demetrius*, but above all in Laughton's and Ustinov's incarnations of Nero in *The Sign of the Cross* and *Quo Vadis?*, both actors swathed in puppyfat, babyfaced and chubbily androgynous, lolling on their cradle-thrones as they refuse adult disciplines and swing precipitately between demanding rages and fits of sentimental generosity. Indeed Ustinov is first seen in an unmistakably foetal position, while Laughton sucks his thumb as he discusses with Tigellinus the threat of Christianity. The Emperor (and in Rossi's television *Quo Vadis?* Klaus Maria Brandauer is their worthy successor) refuses to relinquish the narcissistic reign of infancy, convinced of his own immortality as he deals out life and death to the whole world. Ustinov, in particular, is both highly comic and almost unbearably emotionally febrile, always on the brink of tears, whether of rage or pleasure, most excessively where he receives news of Petronius's suicide. Here posed in an androgynous nightgown in a child's crawling position on his bed, he first of all rages – 'I shall never forgive him for this! Never! . . . Without my permission!' Then, told of Petronius's letter, he unbends into lachrymose sentimentality – 'His last thoughts were of me!' Finally, when he reads Petronius's insults, his anger finds relief in vengeance that childishly-animistically treats Petronius's possessions as the man – 'Destroy his house! Burn his books! Slaughter his animals! Kill his servants!' The Emperor as gangster-child is further illustrated in *The*

Fall of the Roman Empire where Commodus (Christopher Plummer) makes an extraordinary appearance when the doors in the belly of a mother goddess open to reveal the prince of disquiet inside. Commodus, like so many gangster figures, plays out in the narrative the original mother-loving, father-hating drama. Although in both *The Sign of the Cross* and *Quo Vadis?* the Empress Poppaea also represents untrammelled female desire, she is in relation to the Emperor chiefly a depraved mother figure: for instance when in *The Sign of the Cross* she plays nurse to Nero after his 'delicious debauchery' and in *Quo Vadis?* where she teases and controls Nero with deferred gratification of perverse pleasures in store for him in the torture of Lydia.

In his most outrageous manifestation, as Nero, the Emperor is almost always the emperor–artist, something immediately established in *Quo Vadis?* where Ustinov is first seen composing a poem, while Laughton at the beginning of *The Sign of the Cross* recites his epic on Troy's destruction within complex visual compositions that view burning Rome through a foreground of ornate musical instruments, thus visually symbolising the triumph of aesthetics over morality. In *Quo Vadis?*, as Nero waits for Lydia to be gored, he improvises verses in which the aesthetic of sadism is disturbingly dominant – 'Upon these lilies I heap now / Red roses upon red / A bloodied tide shall surge / Upon her milkwhite flesh.' Like other things connected with the Emperor, his artistic excess points in several directions: a warning against the confusion of aesthetics and politics, a reminder for a utilitarian society of the dangers (at once feminising and brutalising) of the aesthetic. But its greatest suggestiveness is its coexistence with other infantile traits, so that Nero's composing and performing are a bathetic–triumphant, wholly amoral recapturing of the infant's prattle, the pre-logical sound-patternings and associations of the child's projection of itself over the world.

Mincingly epicene, precious, displaying large elements of stereotyped effeteness and coded homosexuality, the Emperor, defying moral ordering in all else, also tends to defy the orderings of sexuality, in this the bad child of the id as opposed to the good child of religious discourse, the bisexual Freudian infant, its drives as yet unchannelled by the oedipal moment. Hollywood films of the period avoid literalising such meanings, but give them heavy coding, in contrast to the literary texts where Nero's bisexuality is overt (discreet in Sienkiewicz, prominent in Burgess, foregrounded in Montheilhet).

The world connoted here has its exteme cinematic expression in Fellini's *Satyricon*, outside the Hollywood cinema. A moral reading of the gender structure of the Roman/Christian epic might see Rome as exemplifying polar perversities of order/disorder: on the one hand, a rigid phallocentrism gone mad, and on the other the effeminate world of breakdown, orgy, mother goddesses, bisexuality. Against these the sexual politics of Christianity are represented as softening, without emasculating, the hardness of the male, and freeing the female from imprisonment by the body and pagan servitude. But implicit in the Hollywood films, and explicit in *Satyricon*, is the rebellion of the id against the laws and divisions of Western civilisation's super-ego, Judaeo-Christianity. Fellini's *Satyricon*, attempting to imagine a world without Christianity, invents a site where power and pleasure (frighteningly) hold sway. Here, symbolic of the dissolution caused by the plunge back into the childhood before the parent Christianity, is the bisexuality of the protagonists, the narrative turning on Ascylto's and Encolpius's pursuit of the boy Giton, and the theft of the androgyne-god.

In the overt moral structuring of the Hollywood films the emperor–infant is a grotesque exemplum of the consequences of godless unconstraint. His end in *Quo Vadis?* is penitentially terrible, amid gasping loneliness, underlying all the oedipal motifs and transgressions, the sudden appearance of the stern phallic mother in the shape of his abandoned mistress, Acte, commanding him to the discipline of death. But subterraneanly the Emperor is not only, like the gangster, an outlet as well as a punishment for the audience's narcissistic fantasies, he is also the condemned, yet in some sense secretly approved, persecutor of the super-ego Christianity, crushing and bleeding its martyrs, and finally feeding them to the wild beasts, representatives of the feral appetites they condemn.

10

The Robe and
Demetrius and the Gladiators

THE ROBE (1953)

Novel and film

The Robe (1953) was one of two films quarried out of a Lloyd C. Douglas novel about events immediately following the death of Jesus. The other was *The Big Fisherman*. Two other films with a contemporary setting, also heavily preoccupied with religion, the versions of *Magnificent Obsession* by Stahl and Sirk, were based on another of his novels.

Douglas (1977–1951), a Lutheran then Congregationalist minister, eventually a full-time writer, was a hugely successful popular novelist. Both *Magnificent Obsession* (1929) and *The Robe* (a best-seller between 1942 and 1945, and again with the release of the film), sold over three million copies. Reviewing the novel, Edmund Wilson responded in a divided way, finding Douglas's prose on the one hand 'an almost unrivalled fabric of old clichés, yet at the same time exhibiting what can only be described as old-time Christian feeling . . .'. The story of Marcellus, the Roman tribune who with his slave Demetrius attends the Crucifixion, is converted, and dies a martyr's death with his beloved, Diana – the narrative centring on the robe worn by Christ before his execution – fuses within its popular devotional mode themes of love, duty, religion and the clash of Roman decadence and Christian idealism in a way clearly susceptible to transformation into the cinematic language of the sub-genre.

Cinemascope

> I inhale great drafts of space . . . – Walt Whitman, *Song of the Open Road*

The Robe, the first film made in Twentieth Century Fox's Cinemascope process, created enormous interest through its combination of the filming of a well-known novel and the new format with its promise of visual – and indeed, with stereophonic sound, aural-wonders for cinemagoers with appetites whetted by current experiments with 3D and Cinerama.

The opening seconds of the film render ultra-dramatic this moment of technological history, focusing on the long-awaited curving strip. The scarlet curtains, background for the credits, open in a movement that seems interminable, exposing an apparently limitless expanse to the spectacle-starved television viewer.

The images that follow are understandably preoccupied with what Barry Salt called rather 'frieze-like processions' moving slowly across the screen – the power, riches, loot of Rome, military standards, marching feet, trains of slaves bearing elephant tusks and other treasures. A more sophisticated demonstration of big screen resources is made when Marcellus, back to the audience, walks towards the Forum, the sides of the screen masked by pillars receding as he advances, gradually disclosing the panorama of the marketplace. To reinspect such images is to recognise the film's relative mastery of wide-screen composition, grasping as it does the two most important elements of Scope aesthetics – new possibilities of meaning by relationship along the horizontal, and what Charles Barr defined as potentialities for the creation of depth. In the second place (scotching prejudices about the format's fitness only for photographing snakes) *The Robe* pursues diagonals as well as horizontals, recovering depth with multiple planes within the image. What begins as display, lines of people wandering across the screen, eventually becomes, in a film of external and internal journeyings, an embodiment of more intimate narrative concerns, especially when they are transcended in the final images, where, after all the criss-crossings of the characters' pilgrimages, Marcellus and Diana, face on, filling the screen in semi-close-up, walk towards the audience, abandoning the horizontal for forward and upward.

Cinemascope enhances *The Robe*'s themes in two ways. The first gives the visual compass that the destinies of nations and ideologies demand. Reformulating Eliade's division of sky gods into warriors and lawgivers, Frank McConnell draws attention to the cinema's equivalents in secular and religious epics. Generally religious epics enact the revelation of the Law, or, in the case of the Roman/Christian Film, the overcoming of a warrior culture by the higher law, its representatives triumphing by passive rather than active heroism. *The Robe*'s cinemascopic panoramas, contrasting the Roman and Palestinian worlds, create massive oppositions that displace the battles of the secular epic on to a more conceptual plane – relieved only by occasional flurries of fighting. These landscapes, resonating with para-doxical meaning, could be realised in ordinary screen terms, but Cinemascope's contours give them more epic connotations. However, the wide screen is also capable of intimate effects as well, of finding correlatives for the inward journeying of its characters whose individual destinies are shaped by, and help to shape, the narrative's larger movements.

An example set against the larger landscape occurs as Marcellus and Demetrius travel towards Jerusalem, Roman soldiers clearing a path through the local population. A travelling shot accompanies Demetrius striding on food, after which Marcellus and the Centurion appear on horseback, spreading across most of the screen from the left as they halt and talk. This and following images are constructed to present detailed views of the landscape behind them, a monotonous, upwardly-sloping stretch of ground dotted with trees and, initially, rather indeterminately moving people and animals straggling across it, contrasting with the Romans' determined one-way progress towards the city. On the newly expansive frame several planes are clear: the two Romans in the foreground; behind them, the landscape with its desultorily moving population; behind it, the horizon with figures distantly silhouetted across it; and beyond that the expanse of the sky.

Packed with naturalistic detail, an unprepossessing outskirt justifying the Centurion's remark 'Jerusalem's no pleasure resort at its best!', the frame also demands further interpretation of a kind biblical films inherit from traditions of iconography in Christian art. The two Roman overlords – pitiless, hyper-masculine Centurion, Burton with his look of sullen romantic dissatisfaction – dominate the lower world; behind them are the locals (now predominantly sweeping towards the city), associated by their position in the landscape with the element of earth; behind them are figures dotted on the hilltop, potentially associated with the celestial, but hardly released by their position against the sky, since they seem to be traders moving downwards towards the city. Against this backdrop suggestive of human duality, Marcellus and the Centurion converse idly, their words ironically pointing to significances these powerful men fail to grasp.

> *Centurion*: . . . The feast they call the Passover. This is when their soothsayers tell them their Messiah will come.
> *Marcellus*: The Messiah. What's that?
> *Centurion*: Redeemer. Son of their God. And general trouble-maker.

As they start moving again, the composition is further complicated by the rapid contrary movement of people just behind and in front of them, not into but out of the city. In a change of angle as the riders reach the city gates, the screen clearly divides into two spaces along the diagonal, the left-hand inner dominated by the Romans moving citywards, the right-hand outer filled with people rushing past the Romans, in a tumultuous counter-movement observed by Marcellus and the Centurion.

When we view from their perspective the crowds rushing into the landscape (though an earlier camera movement has followed the crowd of its own volition, as if expressing a desire out of the Romans' control), we also see, in a subtly altered landscape image in which the sky is more dominant, Jesus's followers descending diagonally from upper left (the sky) to right (the earth). While the two Romans move into the city, Demetrius enters the frame looking transfixedly off-screen – it must be Jesus producing this effect – then following Marcellus, but slowly, reluctantly, walking backwards. He stops, gazing at off-screen events, until we realise that Jesus has now entered Jerusalem. Another slave urges Demetrius into the city, but Demetrius remains transfixed by the look his new master has given him.

An example of Cinemascope's enhancing more intimate moments occurs later when Marcellus, frenziedly seeking Demetrius and the robe, passes by Miriam's house. Miriam is the young crippled woman to whom Jesus, en route to the wedding at Cana, has given faith and a voice (with which she has already sung to a rapt audience an account of the women's discovery of the Resurrection), but not new legs. Miriam's function is to inspire Christians in adversity and to show the handicapped (1953 is still the age of polio) that serene contentment is possible. She is also a slightly questionable figure within the sub-genre's themes of positive feminisation: on the one hand vitally involved in the Church's mission; on the other crippled, so that she somehow suggests a special case, that a healthy woman would not be usurping so active a role. The film seems to want to present her positively, to assert that women should have a major active religious role, and yet it also conveys something like the opposite as Miriam plays her vital part in Marcellus's conversion.

Unlike the earlier scene, this is intimate and semi-static, taking place in Miriam's garden, from which she has called to the bewildered Marcellus, who has just seen Jonathan give away the donkey Marcellus gave him. Peeved at this action that makes no Roman sense, Marcellus enters Miriam's garden, a grotto-like scene in which the young woman (dressed and posed to suggest the Virgin Mary) sits rather like an apparition, looking like a disembodied wimpled head and shoulders until the approaching camera shows that she is reclining in a litter. Pulled in by her question, 'Why are you so angry?' (Romans, we assume from Burton's constant aggressive angst, react with frustrated anger to anything outside their understanding), Marcellus engages in a conversation with her in which she suggests – an idea he angrily rejects – that Christ could help him; and argues in the face of Marcellus' scepticism, that Jesus took the better course in not physically healing her.

Structured around the flow of their encounter, the scene ends unresolved as Marcellus departs searching for Demetrius, but leaves the audience feeling Miriam's profound effect on the Tribune, something shown moments later when, confronting Demetrius, he breaks down.

The scene is visually built around Marcellus's movements around the motionless Miriam, whose stasis (in one sense pitiable, in another representing immovable faith), is reflected in the stone structures surrounding her in the garden mise-en-scène which contrast symbolically with the great stone structures of the Roman sites. The small drama of these movements – distance, Marcellus's hesitant approach, closeness as they sit together, renewed distance as he moves away, false rapprochement as he starts to return at her mention of 'The Big Fisherman', his abrupt departure – because of the extended frame, can be composed with both characters in the picture. This is so even when, at the beginning and the end, they are separated by large distances, thus establishing a sense of the characters' importance to each other even though they are strangers. More subtly, use of Scope expresses the changeability of their encounter, not just by their placement in the frame but by inwardly tracking camera movements that can convert a frame from one in which characters are coming closer together to one where they are again at opposite extremes of the image. The format's ability to keep horizontally or diagonally distant figures easily within the frame also means that when this scene, built out of two-shots, culminates in a series of alternating single shots of the characters, the variation impinges meaningfully. Briefly together, Miriam and Marcellus must resume their destinies alone, Miriam not really lonely because of her faith, Marcellus still trapped in isolation.

Naming Names

> *Mr Stripling*: Are you a member of the Writers' Guild?
> *Mr Maltz*: Next you are going to ask me what religious group I belong to.
> – HUAC Hearings 1947

As with all these films, Christian material is shadowed by contemporary allusion, and *The Robe* as much as any we discuss makes coded reference to early 1950s American politics.

By the time *The Robe* was in production, there had been a second assault on Hollywood by the House Unamerican Activities Committee (March 1951 to mid-1952), directed more at actors than the writers attacked in 1947, demanding that figures like Sterling Hayden, Robert Taylor and

Larry Parks, in a key phrase, should 'name names' with Communist Party connections. In the Hollywood climate which had already produced films like *I Married a Communist* (1949), a film about conflicting ideologies, however historically distanced, that included a ruler urging a law-enforcement agent to infiltrate subversives, in words almost identical with 'name names', seemed designed to suggest coded connections with the off-screen politics of 'the Great Fear'. 'I want names, Tribune, names of all the disciples, of every man and woman who subscribed to this treason. All of them, no matter how much it costs, or how long it takes. You will report directly to me.'

Undoubtedly the screenwriter Philip Dunne (known as a liberal) has inscribed, and Henry Koster, the director, dramatised, an allusion to contentious current events within the historical narrative, one with no source in the novel where Tiberius's command is to 'learn what is to be known'. A second verbal allusion does in fact come from the novel, when Marcellus replies to Caligula with 'Sire, it is I who am on trial here, not you! Though he did not invent these words, we might well feel that Dunne, in redeploying them, perceived their similarity to the screenwriter John Howard Lawson's famous HUAC statement in 1947, 'I am not on trial here, Mr Chairman. This Committee is on trial here before the American people.'

How many of *The Robe*'s audience picked up these allusions we cannot know, but in 1953, the year of Arthur Miller's *The Crucible*, such meanings were in the air. The film's fragmentary parallelisms hardly amount to a sustained analogy, which would have been unlikely as well as, in blacklisting times, inadvisable. The allusions, though poweful, appear only fitfully through a context presenting hyperboles of tyranny hardly encouraging identification with American political life but gesturing at the enemy whose growing military powers were confirmed just before the film's release with the Russian hydrogen bomb test in August 1953. As with almost all the emperors in these films (Tiberius being a rare exception), realistic political perspectives vanish. Historians may cautiously reappraise Caligula, but this has no influence on the film's compound of the Roman historians' monster of corrupted absolute power, Christian legend's godless emperor and the totalitarian dictator threatening America embodied in the outrageous histrionics of Jay Robinson's Caligula.

Retaining the foxy, jerky grimacing described in the novel, Jay Robinson adds a sneering, over-precisely enunciated speech, taking the Englishness of epic villains to self-parodying limits in sounds like the 'o' in 'Gallio', a vowel so elongatedly distorted as to become another of the signs of artifice the film creates, with a certain satirical indulgence, around him. Robinson

does not walk. He strides and postures hyper-dramatically, suggesting a
self-conscious revelry in play-acting his role of the master of human
destiny. His gaudy capes (scarlet, indigo, tangerine), constantly swept back
with hand or shoulder, complement the extreme theatricality of his Rome
as represented by the Alma-Tadema-ish watercolour look of its exteriors
and the dehumanised interiors of the palace. Caligula and his objective
correlatives, the theatrical mises-en-scène of Rome, form together an
image of the Christian conviction that without Christ all the world is a
play-acting frenzy.

In a context where political realities are subsumed into the theatrical-
demonic, the fragmentary parallels seem a clear lesson that democracies
must not imitate the enemy. At other points, though, especially where they
involve Tiberius, things are less clear cut. Caligula is too crazy to be
plausibly related to the American scene. But the old Emperor Tiberius
(Ernst Thesiger) is at times as anciently avuncular, for all the British/
American differences, as the ageing Eisenhower himself. Indeed he is given
words that momentarily underline the connection when he reminds
Marcellus of his own military past: 'I fought in Iberia with your grandfather.'

Though representing the enemy, Tiberius seems at least halfway a
representative of reason. Before disappearing from the narrative, he is a
pillar of sanity beside Caligula and the temporarily insane Marcellus.
Tiberius' faults are clear in his interview with Marcellus: an unremitting
political sternness, a rigidified respect for self-control, and a refusal to allow
women significance. When Marcellus breaks down and Diana moves
towards him, Tiberius almost violently orders her to leave him, a clear
assertion that Roman manhood needs no feminine succour. Here he is
clearly a creature of repression, but, from an only slightly shifted angle
these attitudes might have seemed to audiences not so much unspeakable as
just exaggerated, versions of what in a more moderate form many
Americans might think it dangerous to abandon in the minatory Cold War
world. After all, when Caligula orders the condemned lovers to 'go into
your Kingdom' it is hard not to feel that alongside the theological and
romantic there is a strain of American imperialist meaning as well. Equally
there is a doubleness about Tiberius's rhetoric as he articulates his
nightmare of incipient collapse: 'When it comes, this is how it will start.
Some obscure martyr in some forgotten province. Then madness, infecting
the legions, rotting the empire, then the finish of Rome . . . man's desire to
be free. It is the greatest madness of all.' Narratively Tiberius is trapped in
worldly-wise misapprehension, misunderstanding the future, identifying
change with disorder rather than a new order. But as we watch the old

Machiavel venting his unease, there is a curious half-familiarity to the rhetoric which comes – however much it is pinned to the context as an expression of reactionary fears that are to be condemned – from its echoing of fears invoking the domino theory that influenced far more than the extreme right at this moment of the uneasy ending of the Korean War, the politics of 'brinksmanship' over Quemoy and Formosa, and the development of the possible doomsday strategy of 'massive retaliation'.

Somewhere underneath the overt rhetoric of the text are stirrings of a countertext in which the Roman view doesn't seem so unreasonable, and the Christian subversives become upholders of the status quo against not, of course, the falsely accused liberals but the new subversive Rome. But here we are dealing with echoes of echoes. The flickering HUAC motif is never forced to the point of concrete decision, to name or not to name, since at the trial Caligula seems more interested in entrapping Marcellus than getting him to inform. At any rate, not only does the contemporary political critique fade away, but, before that, it tends to an equivocation in which what the film rejects with its left hand – surveillance, investigation, police-state manoeuvres – it recovers with its right, the need to remain vigilant before the communist menace.

Epic Burton: semiotics and role

> I love the great despisers, for they are the great venerators and arrows of longing for the other bank. — Nietzsche, *Also sprach Zarathustra*

Even in his masterful words introducing Rome as the film begins, Marcellus is marked as semi-alienated from the culture of which he seems the arrogant embodiment. Passive irony becomes violently fraught as his role in the Crucifixion begins his propulsion towards Christianity. Where in other genres desire for union with the beloved is the agent that leads beyond self-imprisonment, here it is religion, though inevitably romantic love plays a part. Diana in *The Robe* is secondary, but her feminising influence operates even before Marcellus gets to Palestine, softening him into receptivity to new influences. This process of change plunges him into madness after the Crucifixion as he psychologically resists the new man – a process which on his return to Palestine is marked by a series of meetings with the feminised and marginalised; with the old man Justus, the child Jonathan, and Miriam, before he fights and defeats that remnant of his old allegiances, the Centurion.

His disorientation is signalled by the loss of his brutally elegant military uniform. This happens when he appears on his return to Palestine disguised as a cloth merchant, in order to find the robe which, in the novel's deference to Hollywood, has changed from brown to scarlet, not just an effect of the film's glossiness but also creating contrasts with the inhuman Roman military red. While as late as his audience with Tiberius his uniform remains crisply in place, instability breaks out elsewhere. Marcellus's voice and language undergo a crisis. From the powerful Churchillian tones characteristic of Burton's delivery, the voice becomes, at crucial moments, higher pitched, hysterical, unsteady, especially when he repeats his nightmarish post-Crucifixion catchphrase, 'Were you out there?'

With its awkward, cheek-turning attitudes to heroic masculinity, Christianity often seems more fertile ground for the conversion of these films' Jean Simmonses and Deborah Kerrs than for the stroppy macho maleness characteristic of Burton's screen roles. As Melvyn Bragg's biography notes, Burton was drawn to epic parts, seeing *Alexander the Great* and *Cleopatra* after *The Robe* as further attempts to solve the problems of the genre, but his inherently aristocratic qualities never entirely lose elements of a desperately poor and proletarian toughness. The exceptional man is also the rugby-playing, beer-drinking boyo from the valleys, an angry youth too, his pock-marked face providing the visual evidence of an under-privileged background, for which his tough, devil-may-care gestures are in part a revenge. Like Plutarch's Antony, Burton, even in *The Robe*, a film that sees him develop friendships with slaves and Christians, is the man who 'likes to drink like a good fellow with everybody, to sit with the soldiers when they dine'. The moody hero is also the man who in *The Robe* trusts a newly-bought slave, who has just tried to escape, to make his own way home, in this gesture, however paradoxically, showing generosity and a touching desire for friendship. Burton's Marcellus matches aristocratic heroism with the spirit of working-class democracy. Yet, contradicting this approachability and social ease is Burton's immovable aura of solitude, a feature of crucial relevance to his role as Marcellus.

Even though the Burton character invariably becomes emotionally involved, he is persecuted by a contradictory need for solitude. 'Trust no one and learn how to be alone', Philip of Macedon instructs Alexander, advice every Burton character heeds, even in *The Robe* where Marcellus's involvement with Diana is rarely detached from an ultimately solitary journey of self-discovery and spiritual salvation. The isolated, soul-searching characters Burton plays derive great advantage, Bragg argues, from social as well as metaphysical anguish. Burton is an outsider socially, whether on home ground in the proletarian settings of South Wales, or in Rome, or anywhere else in the heroic roles that, despite the surface bonhomie, leave him ill at ease in the company of his peers. Metaphysically, too, Burton exudes sunken-cheeked anguish. Like Jimmy Porter in Tony Richardson's version of John Osborne's famous play, he wants 'everything and nothing'. Burton's characteristic alientation matches the role of Marcellus well, the character's pre-Christian 'anger', the sign of metaphysical as well as societal dis-ease, having its most expressive form in his unconcealed loathing of Caligula but positively pointing towards the Christianity which seems to offer him an escape from solitude. Burton's more usual way of transcending alienation is through romantic love, his Bronte-esque stature as a screen lover pre-dating his involvement with Elizabeth Taylor in *Cleopatra*, reaching back to the scowling, tormentedly handsome Heathcliff figure of his first role in *My Cousin Rachel*.

My Cousin Rachel's director, Henry Koster, also directed *The Robe*, and although the latter tones down eroticism it still allows sexual desire a certain scope through Marcellus's involvement with Diana. Delivering love lines softly, without fuss or mawkishness, Burton nevertheless suggests an alluring sexual energy. Arguably, in a film with primarily Christian concerns, Burton's vibrant sexuality makes conversion to a faith predicated on denials of instinct, in the setting of a society celebrating their opposite, all the more poignantly ambivalent.

Diana (Jean Simmons), like Marcellus, is set apart by her sensitivity from imprisoning Roman values. But charming though she seems, in no need of redemption, the film wishes, at least sometimes, to see her in the light of the claim that Christianity has rescued woman from pagan servitude and placed her equal with man, at least in the sight of God. Though moving apparently freely in exalted circles, Diana is still controlled by external forces, most clearly the power Tiberius has to decide whom she will marry. Diana's structural subservience as a female in the Roman system is underlined by a telling detail of colour in the mise-en-scène. As Tiberius interviews Marcellus, she wears a loose-fitting dress with a trailing yellow over-garment significantly matching the colour of Tiberius's toga, placing her in his intimate orbit of power. The implicit argument by colour here, by varied implication elsewhere, is that while the pagan world imprisons even the freest woman, the Christian world frees her. This is an argument open to dispute on two counts: firstly, the considerable freedom of upper-class Roman women, and secondly, the early retreat feminist theologians have noted from the revolutionary egalitarian aspects of Christianity, so that even *The Robe*'s Miriam would soon be an unlikely figure.

Diana is interestingly contrasted with Miriam, the other young woman with whom Marcellus comes into significant contact and who is involved in his conversion. While Miriam, representing the new order (with its own equivocal attitudes to women) is, for all her virginal prettiness, almost wholly desexualised, Jean Simmons remains, despite her own virginally demure aspects, a highly eroticised star. The sexual-romantic vitality of Burton and Simmons is both deployed and constrained by the narrative, satisfying both the audience's desire for the triumph of romantic love and its needs for self-denial. Finally, as healthy, attractive characters they give credibility to Christianity as a religion for normal people, in no way the preserve of the odd or unfortunate, to which Miriam marginally belongs. So, though the spectator may fleetingly wonder if a reconstructed Marcellus might possibly become romantically involved with her, the film retains traditional allegiances to concepts of sexuality and female glamour in its generic romantic-couple formulations of the new, and Diana, not Miriam, is the natural partner for Marcellus, because of, more than despite, the contradictions that attend her.

Some of these are powerfully displayed in traditional religious symbolism when she takes her leave of Marcellus as he sails for Palestine for the first time. In a sequence of eight cuts, elegantly deploying the Scope format to surround the pair with images of death and immortality, Diana remains on the dockside while Marcellus moves between dock and ship, finally, after their embrace, looking yearningly at her as his ship departs. As the sequence begins on board, the powerful flame of the dockside brazier is conspicuously visible, present in the background throughout. After Marcellus is told that Diana is waiting to see him, he and the audience see her moving silently, wraithlike in the night mist, her ghostliness a fitting image of future release from the corporal enslavements of pagan antiquity. Looking rather like Miriam in her blue Madonna-like shawl, Diana declares her intention of acting as an intercessor for Marcellus with Tiberius, and then, when Marcellus asks her why, shyly declares her love for him. The moment brings into play a number of unresolved ambiguities hovering between the secular and the spiritual as the characters begin to take on new roles, Marcellus as Chistianised lover, Diana as mediatrice. As often across the whole genre, *The Robe* activates through its virtuous women (here Miriam and Diana, a virgin goddess too) various appeals to the psychological potency of the cult of the Virgin Mary, so that Diana's promise of secular intercession between Marcellus and Tiberius's 'divinity' is shadowed both with metaphysical allusion and the psychic fantasy of the restoring mother. As the pair stand embracing in the nocturnal mist, their mutual expressions of romantic love – though neither of them has yet heard of Christianity – are in the process of Christianisation. As the scene ends with the ship moving across the frame, our view and Marcellus's is of Diana who stands embodying the qualities of the ideal Christian bride-mother (demure, self-effacing, compassionate, ethereally sexual), though with the added qualities of star-system beauty, a neo-platonic beacon, like the flame still symbolically burning, of Christian love and truth.

DEMETRIUS AND THE GLADIATORS (1954)

The Robe 2

Demetrius and the Gladiators was rushed into production even before the release of *The Robe* to exploit interest in Cinemascope. The film, with a new director, Delmer Daves, begins by recycling the last moments of its source. As Caligula rages and Diana hands over Christ's garment 'for the Big Fisherman', new shots are inserted so that Messalina (Susan Hayward), who will play a major part in the new story, now appears among the audience at the trial.

Gladiators: 'Morituri te salutant'

> Being a Christian these days in Rome is anything but dull. — Demetrius in *Demetrius and the Gladiators*

A film entitled *Demetrius and the Gladiators* sets up definite expectations – the sub-human mob (including women and children; De Mille has some mordant family-outing vignettes in *The Sign of the Cross*) howling for blood; the no-exit terror of mortal combat; the merciless thumbs-down followed by the stab in the throat for the loser. Of all the Roman cruelties which the films place against Christian virtues, the arena is the most representative. In four films, *Pompeii*, *Barabbas*, *Demetrius* and *Spartacus*, the contrast is drama-tised by the Christian, or quasi-Christian, hero being forced to enter the gladiatorial *ludus*, school for sadism rather than souls, image of everything that Christianity claims to transcend.

It would be ingenuous to deny the films' interest in the sadism of public combat to the death. The baleful Roman institution stands as a paradigm of man's depravities, snuff movies, but not at a celluloid remove, and sanctioned by the state. Michael Grant's book *Gladiators* speculates on its meanings. Psychoanalytically viewed, however shocking, it is hardly sur-prising, for both Freud and Stekel emphasise man's destructive drives.

Grant adds two psycho-social explanations for the massive release of these impulses in Rome: firstly, the Roman father's absolute power which set up a circle of sadism, with the aggression suffered by the child repeated by the victim who 'relieves his own latent fears by doing to another what he fears might be done to him'; secondly (via Erich Fromm), that sadism arises from 'unconscious attempts to escape from intolerable, helpless isolation', a diagnosis applicable to conditions 'in the vast Roman world' where 'these symptoms became accentuated, permanent and ubiquitous. Millions of people felt shiftless, unsupported, unlooked-after, lost – and above all bored. The plunge into religion was one compensatory reaction. But another was immersion in sanguinary sadism.'

Again, it would be foolish to deny that part of the Hollywood cinema's driving pleasure principle resides in enactments of sadism and masochism. But it is too easy to assert that in these films religion merely serves as a screen for them, as if religion were merely the formal rather than subtantial occasion of their display. This is not to stick at the point made by critics of Christianity, of the religion's sado-masochism, but to say that the excesses of Roman cruelty – the id at its most aggressive fuelled by a perversely authoritarian super-ego – are part of the deep meaning of the sub-genre. Even Rossellini's *Augustine of Hippo*, though too austere to show the arena, has the mob's noise on the soundtrack, aurally if not visually reminding us of the darker recesses of instinctual man. As for the accusation that the presentation of the gladiatorial world is as attractive as repulsive, this is undoubtedly true. However, if sadism and masochism are inescapable psychic components, both films and audiences might be expected to react equivocally, allying themselves with the civilising values of Christianity, yet also finding regressive attractions in the arena, even forbidden pleasure in instinctual revenge upon the demanding super-ego's representatives. Further, it might be asked whether a culture so rooted in Social Darwinism as the American can validly disown so vivid a microcosm of the indivi- dualised power struggle.

The major source of information about the games in the films is Sienkiewicz's novel whose authenticity the films minutely imitate. What- ever else is distorted, the brutal arena world is relayed with fascinated factuality, and where we might suppose invention, say in the pre-fight banquets and sexual favours for the fighters in *Demetrius*, or in De Mille's perverse battle between barbarian women and pigmies in *The Sign of the Cross*, there is usually a basis of fact. Sienkiewicz's great description gives a balefully atmospheric catalogue of events – morning crowds outside the amphitheatre; the taunting of the starving wild beasts; the dawn sounds of the Christians singing hymns; the arrival of the trainers, followed by the naked, oiled gladiators, admired by women in the crowd; mules pulling wagonloads of coffins; and the arrival of figures dressed as Mercury and Charon to dispatch the wounded; most of them aspects recreated by the films.

An area, though, which the films claim as their special province is the gladiatorial school, that terrifying microcosm of an ultimately competitive society. In *Demetrius*, *Spartacus* and *Barabbas* part of the spectacle lies in the display of the technics of the brutalising process that turns men into efficient killers. The films are also fascinated by a society where sadistic impulses are so untrammelled that women indulge them fully. In *Spartacus* Kirk Douglas and Woody Strode are made to fight for the pleasure of aristocratic women who order that the fighters should wear 'just enough for modesty'. Like Poppaea in *Quo Vadis?* and *The Sign of the Cross*, Messalina in *Demetrius* is an *aficionada* of the fights, showing an almost orgasmic pleasure as she watches.

By placing the Christian Demetrius in this environment the narrative sets up an ethical and narratological dilemma. Ethically, will Demetrius fight? Not to fight means having his throat cut. A Christian is forbidden to fight, but Demetrius is enough of a Samson to make the denial a torment, as when Dardanius (Richard Egan) assaults him to see if he will turn the other cheek. If Christianity teaches one to suffer even such insults, surely it is unmanly. But how can Christianity be wrong? (The conflict, via Shaw's irony, is given comic twists in Robert Newton's half-reformed strongman in *Androcles*.) The unresolved dilemma is temporarily shelved when Glichon the Nubian King intervenes threateningly with '*I* am no Christian!'

The narratological dilemma is closely related. The film invokes the total pacifism of primitive Christianity, not later theologies of just wars and self defence, and thus potentially unsettles viewers used to concepts of allowable violence. So how is the narrative to keep its generic pact to give us Demetrius fighting the gladiators? It solves the problem ingeniously, first by having Demetrius and Glichon pretend mortal combat in the hope that both of them will be spared; then when their plan fails, having them really fight to the death, a death, however, averted when Demetrius refuses to kill Glichon. The film's greatest outburst of violence happens only when, having lost his faith at the apparent death of Lucia, Demetrius returns to the arena no longer a Christian and kills his five enemies in a pagan fury of revenge. But on his third visit to the arena, forced to face Macro, the champion gladiator, his faith has been restored. He refuses to fight and Macro prepares the death blow. Only external circumstances can rescue Demetrius. Macro and Caligula are assassinated by the Praetorian guard and Demetrius is saved.

The situation involves a familiar paradox. The ethic of non-violence triumphs, but through the violent actions of others. The state becomes a more just kingdom, with Claudius, in an historical fiction, friendly to Christianity, but only after the tyrant's violent overthrow. Demetrius and Christianity, even though they do not initiate it, benefit from an action forbidden to them. (In *The Robe* when the Christians rescue Demetrius the fighting is implausibly shown not to cause casualties.) These tortuous negotiations are the sub-genre's version of a dilemma running through the Hollywood cinema, the popular art of a society existing in enormous contradictions of idealism and violence. The central action genres of the American cinema, the Western and various forms of crime film, act out parallel ambivalences. The difference is that in the Roman/Christian film the Christian ethic behind other genres is foregrounded, and for all the evasions and half-truths with which it is approached, inescapably at the centre. The false solution of the dilemma in *Demetrius* is far more than the single film's.

Erotics

> The impulses of nature and the impulses of the spirit are at war with one
> another. — Augustine, *Confessions*

The Robe untypically avoided the erotic. Marcellus's libidinous past is asserted at the beginning, but his relation with Diana starts on a romantic height in her declaration of undying childhood love for him, and never descends. It also differs in omitting the frequent complication of the pagan woman's sexuality. *Demetrius and the Gladiators*, while giving formal recognition to Demetrius's spiritualised love for Lucia, makes little attempt to disguise its interest in Messalina's embodying of the unmediatedly sexual – not as a drive capable of being transformed by religious precepts but as their opposite.

Demetrius's erotic temptation, fall, and recovery echo Samson's, and Philip Dunne, re-narrativising *The Robe*, would have remembered Victor Mature's role five years before, just as there would have been memories of Susan Hayward in *David and Bathsheba*. Here Hayward plays Claudius's wife Messalina, a name synonomous with sexual licence, like Susan Hayward's, at least where she is the transcendent type of Hollywood's 'bad girl', the Barbara Graham of perhaps her most memorable role, the good-time girl and secular sexual martyr, wrongly executed for murder in *I Want to Live*.

Her antipodes, the Roman Christian Lucia, is played by Debra Paget, whose bland oval face, suburban daughter prettiness and guileless eyes offer little competition. Lucia, as her name indicates, emblematically represents Christian light, and has, admittedly, her share of courage, creating the disturbance which allows Demetrius to hide the robe, and gaining entry to the gladiatorial school with the courtesans. But her wholesomeness is presented unenticingly. Often she looks desperately childlike, especially in the shots where she stands hand in hand with Demetrius while the Roman soldiers search for the robe. And lying comatose after her rape, she clutches it like a security blanket, suggesting a regression to childhood that evades the problems of sexuality. She means so little emotionally to the narrative that she is unseen, unmentioned at its close. Her secondariness is reminiscent (as is Messalina in the other direction) of the patterns of Film Noir, another instance of generic intertextuality in the Biblical Epic.

As Messalina, Susan Hayward is everything that Lucia is not. Her knowing half-smile constantly comments on a world she interprets as wholly carnal. Certain distinctive performance characteristics, very much at one with the wrong-side-of-the-tracks, sexually abrasive parts she often plays, form a piquant association with the actress's prettiness. These (more indulged here than in her restrained Bathsheba) include heavy breathing highlighting a heaving bosom, 'bedroom' eyes that look shamelessly out from under sleepy lids, and a habit of sly side-glancing. Amongst profuse hand movements, a pose with her hands in front of her touching each other is redolent of narcissistic interest in her own tactility. Lastly, her characteristic pose for the camera is an exaggeration of the 'skewed frontality' convention of Hollywood acting, with the head turning to look or speak provocatively while the carefully posed body remains static, suggesting a promise of sexual *jouissance* but no symbiosis of body and mind, rather the head controlling the uses of the pleasure machine. These gestures' slightly coarse obviousness seems to lie behind dismissals of her acting ('She was good, gutsy, entertaining fun . . . but what she does should not really be labelled good screen acting').

Dyer's discussion of Lana Turner (another 'bad' actress) demonstrates how Sirk in *Imitation of Life* manipulates what might be considered the actress's faults, and the principle is extendable to Hayward. If the signals she gives off are tainted with banality, the shuffle of actressy poses matches the social type visible in her performances, and here transposed on to the historical seductress, the woman who uses her sexuality for advancement in a culture where women's quickest route to power is through men's desire, and whose air of sulky discontent suggests a world of dissatisfactions never quite allayed by erotic activity. Allusively Film Noir's 'tiger lady' in

Demetrius as she conceives the idea of setting the tigers on the reluctant gladiator, she simultaneously fulfils and parodies the metaphor, like Babs in *I Want to Live* when, arrested, she poses snarling for the photographers with her toy tiger. At least once in *Demetrius*, as she orders Demetrius to leave the vase she has broken on the floor, Barbara Graham's demotic pierces through the Empress's more cultivated tones.

Messalina's primary function is to portray the allure of a wholly unspiritualised eroticism. However, as the narrative continues she seems to split into several not easily compatible aspects. Libidinous and vengeful, she suddenly announces herself in love with Demetrius, claiming desperately that she will become a Christian if he saves himself. Earlier she has been allowed a defence of herself – rather radical for the early 1950s – as the product of the male culture around her when she asks Demetrius if it is any wonder she behaves as she does. And at the closure she admits her sexual excesses and promises a reformed future as Empress (which even for audiences unaware of the real character's historical fate may seem so unlikely that irony may be read into the situation). This melodramatic changeableness, verging on incoherence, is the result of a split apprehension of Messalina and what she represents – a carnality both desired and disavowed by protagonist and audience.

'Ay, but to die . . .'

The last enemy that shall be destroyed is death. — I Corinthians, 15:26

There is a temptation to try to resolve everything in a film like *Demetrius* into social meanings for which the religious content is merely a screen. But like other works of art with religious content *Demetrius* has metaphysical concerns which obviously take a particular social and historical shape, only the concerns themselves are not reducible simply to displacements of other matters. They demonstrate what Weber called 'intellectualism': 'more particularly the metaphysical needs of the human mind as it is driven to reflect on ethical and religious questions, driven not by material need but as an inner compulsion to understand the world as a meaningful cosmos and to take up a position towards it.' Thus the metaphysical question of the meaning of death haunts the characters in the film, presupposing an equal concern in the audience.

Demetrius's narrative is constructed around Caligula's attempts to recover the robe which he believes holds the secret of immortality. In dramatising his quest's climax the film equals Suetonius in inventiveness by having Caligula prosecute a bizarre experiment in which he kills a prisoner and attempts to resurrect him with the magic garment. Caligula, who even in *The Robe* seemed hardly interested in pursuing Diana, here shows her no interest at all, directing all his propensity for excess towards securing the immortality he believes the robe will guarantee. By comparison with Caligula, Messalina's interests are far more carnal, but even she is haunted by the question. Providing pre-match banquets for the gladiators allows her to attend these occasions where they couple with prostitutes and where she can respond to the nuances of an extreme occasion, the 'Marriage of Life and Death', as Caligula puts it when opening the games, an inspection of the sexual act under the shadow of *Thanatos* – the threat of death the experimental condition that may reveal the meaning of life. Hence her questioning of the brutal trainer Strabo as to whether a gladiator thinks of the woman he makes love to or of impending death. Strabo, a type of animal man, simply answers 'the woman', adding that a fighter never thinks he will be the one to 'get it'.

Even Messalina's sceptical, scholarly husband Claudius shows interest in the Christian belief in immortality, remarking several times on it in his ruminating way, though his interest later seems primarily in its usefulness. And, of course, the topic interests Demetrius profoundly. Very early in the film Demetrius's vulnerability on the subject of death is signalled. As a plasterer puts the last touches to Marcellus's and Diana's tomb, he confesses to finding it hard to find a meaning in their martyrdom, and accepts only with difficulty Peter's consolatory explanations. This prefigures later events, for it is Lucia's rape and seeming death at the hands of Dardanius which causes him to lose his faith.

The Biblical Epic (even the Old Testament Epic) identifies Christianity (and Judaism) with personal immortality and is untouched – superficially, anyway – by theological deconstruction that might consider the Resurrection as a metaphor for psychological rebirth. The Christians, as Caligula keeps saying with incredulous envy, believe they will live for ever. The consequences of not believing this are demonstrably terrible, as in Demetrius's case, since without it the world is the world of Caligula where any horror is possible. Despite its assertions of 'faith' in immortality, the film remains equivocal, proclaiming immortality but in a not-too-subterranean way counter-asserting the difficulties of such a belief in the face of a seemingly non-providential universe. Although such perceptions are always 'proved' wrong, doubt is given a subsidiary voice within the overall victory of faith.

When Claudius becomes emperor the film swerves away from metaphysical speculation towards pragmatics. Claudius looks at religion in terms of political utility. He observes that Demetrius possesses what Rome has lost – 'faith'; the implication being that societies without belief in what President Eisenhower called 'faith in the deathless dignity of man' fall into decadence and powerlessness. This analysis of Rome again sounds a warning for 1950s America as it faces the irreligious religion of communism in a Cold War where 'the forces of good and evil are massed and armed and opposed as rarely before in history' (the same inaugural address). Saying early on that he believes in 'nothing', Claudius does little thereafter to dispute that. His allowing the Christians religious freedom seems due less to his religious feelings than to Christianity's value as a social cement. It is hard not to see this as a representation of pragmatic American political behaviour which in its rhetoric of Christianity owes less to religious belief than to a belief in the social efficacy of belief.

The Nubian King

> Cursed be Canaan; a servant of servants shall he be to his brethren.
> — Genesis, 9:25

Glichon the Nubian King (William Marshall), a secondary but symptomatic presence in the film, shadows its protagonist throughout and is finally twinned to him at the close. When Demetrius arrives at the gladiatorial school, Strabo introduces Glichon as the 'King of the Swordsmen' and later says that he has been such a successful fighter that he is about to be freed, something that makes his unwillingness to kill Demetrius even more noble. Obviously, being a Nubian, he is black, which links him to various figures in other Biblical Epics of the period, for instance the King of Ethiopia (Woody Strode) and his sister, and the Nubians who accompany the Israelites on the Exodus in *The Ten Commandments* (1956), Woody Strode's gladiator in *Spartacus* who refuses to kill the hero, and Sidney Poitier's Simon of Cyrene in *The Greatest Story Ever Told*.

Much of Glichon's role would have ethical significance even without his colour, for he is the natural Nietzschean aristocrat who turns to Christianity as a higher ethos. But his negritude creates further meanings, the appearance of such black characters in religious epics of the time raising the question of why they now start to appear in inflections that are very positive compared with, say, the brief emphasis on a black spectator of the Roman Procurator's parade in the 1925 *Ben Hur*. There amidst the hostile Jerusalem crowd a young black man, mounted on an ass, quips, 'Bray a welcome, Bombo, for your brother, Gratus.' This character is certainly placed on the right side, against the Romans, and thus assured of audience sympathy; but he is so much the cretinous stereotype of the black man (to be laughed at as much as with) that the effect is uneasy. Viewed from today, the more positive figures of the 1950s and early 1960s may look stiffly conceived in the liberal imagination, but they embody important shifts in representation, responses to changes visible even in the conservative Eisenhower first administration, culminating in the Supreme Court ruling (May 1954) against the Plessey Ferguson decision with its mythology of 'separate but equal'. Godfrey Hodgson, writing of the origin of the dramatic changes in white/black relations in the 1960s, highlights the effect of the great exodus of blacks from the South into the Northern cities.

> The sudden emergence of millions of black citizens into the very centre of the national stage confronted American society, in an unexpectedly urgent and concrete shape, with the dilemma that Gunnar Myrdal had foreseen in 1944. It would no longer be possible to qualify the tenets of the American creed with a muttered sotto voce mental reservation . . . The American ideals of equality, abundance and constitutional democracy must be extended to black people, or they could be guaranteed to no one. It fell to the 1960s to wrestle with this dilemma. But it had already been posed by those northbound bus passengers in the 1940s.

Undoubtedly the growing emphasis on black themes in 1950s Hollywood is illuminated by Hodgson's words. Arguably, even more than other kinds of films, the religious film felt under pressure to grant positive representation to blacks since questions of the perceived reality or hypocrisy of Christianity were at stake. The late 1940s had seen important Protestant and Catholic reaction to growing tension over segregation within religious institutions themselves, as in 1946 the Federal Council of Churches formally renounced segregation, and in 1947 the Catholic archbishop of St Louis used the threat of excommunication to end segregation in parochial schools. Also, in complicated forms, there is a tendency in American culture to see blackness as closely related to Christianity: positively, recognising black suffering as the type of the Israelite captivity and Christian patience, qualities embodied in the negro spiritual (compare Pasolini's use of 'Sometimes I Feel like a Motherless Child' in *Matthew*), but, less positively, often identifying blacks with childish simplicity, so that they are seen as having a relationship to religion simultaneously more authentic than whites' but also inferior in its credulousness.

Glichon may not be played by an actor as well known as Woody Strode, whose gladiator in *Spartacus* acquires meanings from the actor's persecuted black soldier in *Sergeant Rutledge*, but William Marshall is none the less impressive. An enslaved Nubian King, his fate becomes a hyperbole of the American black's ancestry, torn from authority in his own environment and condemned to slavery in another's. But (the film argues) however much America has mistreated him, it differs from Rome in offering Christianity and democracy. Notably Glichon's trajectory towards Christianity begins at the point where the democratic implications of Christianity forcibly strike him. He asks Demetrius if it is true that Jesus made no distinction between aristocrats, slaves and even emperors. Demetrius replies that it was one of his greatest truths, to which Glichon pregnantly replies, 'No wonder they crucified him!' (the scene fades on the words, emphasising implications of race as well as class.). Here Glichon's Christianised black consciousness is presented as taking more reassuring directions than that of the scandalous support of the Soviet system and criticism of America of Paul Robeson, a high-profile figure in 1954 – he had just been awarded a Stalin Prize – whom Glichon parallels and realigns. Though limited, his further appearances are strongly marked. Firstly, before his conversion, he drives Dardanius's accomplices into the arena to their deaths at the hands of Demetrius. Then, Christianised, he rebukes Demetrius for lapsing from faith, and when Demetrius orders him not to see Peter again he refuses, an interesting moment of dignified black assertiveness. Then at the film's close (with Lucia all but forgotten) the fraternal pair of Demetrius and Glichon exit together at Claudius's command to take political rapprochement to the Roman Christians, though Claudius notably addresses only Demetrius – which ends the film on an (over) optimistic note of achieved (or soon to be achieved) racial unity, but with a hint of white/black hierarchy retained as the triumph of Christianity begins.

Coda

Victor Agonistes; or, justice done to an unconsidered star

BODY AND SOUL

In a recent episode of the English soap opera *Coronation Street*, two well-known middle-aged women characters were asked to take parts on a float in a local carnival. They were told it had a Roman theme which required them to play the parts of Vestal Virgins, and the scene ended with one of them dreamily fantasising about being carried off by Victor Mature. The choice of fantasy object is significant, for to many minds none of the other stars associated with the genre, not even Charlton Heston, is quite so indelibly linked with the Biblical Epic, none quite so much seen as a highly colourful fleshly paradigm of its glories and banalities. For this reason it seems apposite to devote the last chapter of this book to a reading of the 'body' of Victor Mature, the literal physical body on the screen and the corpus of his Biblical Epic roles (in *Samson and Delilah*, *The Robe*, *Demetrius and the Gladiators*), exploring through his outsize frame and agonistic features for a last time the crucial thematics of the genre.

MONUMENTALITY

Can this be hee,
That heroic, that renown'd
Irresistible Samson? Whom unarm'd
No strength of man or fiercest wildbeast
Could command. — Milton, *Samson Agonistes*

Epic films demand epic male stars, convincing in roles demanding the creation or defence of nations and religions, self-sacrifice and the victory of

the spirit over sexual temptation that mark civilisation's heroes of sublimation. Though the biblical genre has enough flexibility to accommodate
heroes like Robert Taylor, Steward Granger or Fredric March with meanings more commonplace than sublime, sublimity is the dominant rule,
whether resting on a charisma based on internal rather than physical
strength, as with Gregory Peck or Richard Burton, and invariably in the
Christ film, or whether it takes the form of the monumentality of physical
appearance, voice and gesture associated with, in particular, Charlton
Heston, Victor Mature, Kirk Douglas and Yul Brynner.

Primitive as the association between outward strength and moral force
may be, it has its undeniable appeal. The larger than life dimensions of the
stars who embody such qualities are an incontrovertible sign of the heroes'
origins as demi-gods, or, in secular myth, as the powerful father ruling
Freud's clans in *Totem and Taboo*. As the Epic reaches later chronologies,
urbanity tends to replace these more primitive analogies which function
most freely in the Old Testament epic, and critics, forgetting their force,
often exhibit lofty contempt, looking past the Herculean forms of these
actors and those in other genres related by their celebration of the heroic
male body, like the Tarzan or Swashbuckler films, for absent traces of the
psychological complexities of a Bogart or Tracy.

Clearly the primitive celebration of male force is also a celebration of
patriarchal power. Yet, beneath the superficial resemblances, these constructs of the he-man embody variations of masculinity as diverse as the
Olympians upon whom they are (Edgar Morin argues) distantly modelled.
Steve Reeves, the Arnold Schwarzenegger of his day, his iron pumped to
diastolic pressure bursting-point, was never more than a marginalised
Maciste, his gleaming glycerine-coated torso of no serious interest other
than as testimony to the nonconformist tastes of body-building cultists.
The idea of Reeves playing Moses, or even Samson, is absurd: the body,
uninformed by troubled spirit, is simply fetishistic spectacle. In comparison
the various Tarzans, Johnny Weissmuller, Lex Barker, Gordon Scott, are
more complex in their connotations: all hieroglyphs of physical perfection,
they are surrounded by an aura of pre-oedipal innocence, their jungle
mise-en-scène a prelapsarian Eden.

Like these heroes, Charlton Heston, the most epic of the 1950s male
stars, was similarly detached in *Ben Hur*, *El Cid*, etc. from sexuality. Heston
became synonomous with the lawgivers, the national heroes (such as
General Gordon in *Khartoum*), who placed duty before love and self-
sacrifice before self-indulgence. Even in his pre-epic days, his libidinal roles
seem awkwardly-suited. Heston, with what Michel Mourlet has hyper-
bolised as his 'eagle's profile, imperious arch of eyebrows . . . stupendous

strength of torso', embodied the Law of God and Moses not only literally in *The Ten Commandments* but also figuratively in *The Agony and the Ecstasy*, his Michelangelo formulating through his sculptures, frescos and paintings the rhetoric of the patriarchal law that elsewhere his mere presence asserts. Heston exemplifies the man who has conquered himself. In *El Cid* he is called 'the purest knight of all'. His chiselled features, high domelike forehead, tense, muscle-choked cheeks, flashing smiles revealing tightly-packed but orthodontically perfect teeth, are signs less of sexual readiness than the patriarch's eagerness to respond to honour and duty. So whereas Reeves is lost to narcissism, Barker and Weissmuller innocent of sexual desire and Heston austerely wary of its force, Victor Mature is the 1950s epic hero who represents the Titanic clash between the spirit and the flesh, a clash made all the more poignant by signs of flaws and frailties in his massive physique and face, his mannerisms and voice, warning of his propensities to voluptuous enslavement.

Whether bare-chested or besuited, Mature's fleshy frame, 6 feet 2 inches, over 200 pounds with 15 inch biceps, fills the screen with an outsize form: in suits he is box-shaped, even in 1940s and 1950s crime films finding meanings through identification with rugged mise-en-scènes, or by appeals to primitive cave-man echoes (since he was, memorably, a literal cave-man in *Man and His Mate*). Even in a modern thriller like *Dangerous Mission* he is associated with a figurative as well as literal landscape of avalanches, glaciers and storms, still being compared to primitive ancestors. Mature is a New World Adam, as Frank Sinatra's street Hoboken pronunciation of the name in *A Hole in the Head* as 'Matoor' emphasises, the anglicised '-ure' properly giving way to a New World demotic, for despite all the Old World roles Victor 'Matoor' remains attached to average American neighbourhood fantasies of grandeur. However pronounced, the name is charged with multiple heroic meanings. While 'Mature/Matoor' distances the persona from the innocence of a Weissmuller by its intimations of sexual 'Maturity', 'Victor' marks him out as the hero of the Hebrews, in Milton's *Samson Agonistes* 'The *victor* over all / That tyrannie or fortune can inflict'.

Many scenes expose the Mature character to physical danger, showing off his muscular prowess, but Mature is not one of Hollywood's graceful athletes. Though often expressing maximum pent-up energy, he has none of Burt Lancaster's or Kirk Douglas's fluid athleticism. In heroic mood, Mature is more statuesque, his great body a self-contained image of heroism. So that when this man kneels, renouncing the proud, erect stature of the hero, humility acquires additional pathos, as an early scene in *Demetrius* makes clear.

In the catacombs the Christians mourn the deaths of Marcellus and

Diana. Significantly, Demetrius, the man who in *The Robe* stood up to the Romans, the slave who rose from his abasement, now kneels, though only one knee touches the ground. The kneeling posture of a big man, already identified with heroism in many epic and non-epic roles, projects considerable pathos, compounded by the expression on Mature's face as he listens, with traces of tearfulness, to Peter's words about keeping faith. Analysis of Mature's sexual 'maturity', his almost invariable entrapments by sexuality (*The Robe* being exceptional), needs to recognise the duality of his mythic portrayals. He displays physical fearlessness (combat with men and animals), moral courage (the refusal to fight, as in *Demetrius*), and self-sacrifice (suffering the rigours of a persecuted faith). Yet it is in his compromises leading to mortal conflict between the laws of desire and of the super-ego that Mature's most distinctive contribution to the genre consists, a contribution which, however, can be properly assessed only if the sheer momumentality of physical presence is allowed to lose its exclusive grip over the definition of his ultimately complex persona.

AGONY

> Why was my breeding order'd and prescrib'd
> As of a person separate to God,
> Design'd for great exploits, if I must die
> Betray'd, Captiv'd, and both my Eyes put out,
> Made of my Enemies the scorn and gaze,
> To grind in Brazen Fetters under task
> With this Heav'n-gifted strength? — Milton, *Samson Agonistes*

While Mature's sheer physical size grounds his heroic monumentality, his face expresses the inner agonies of his various roles. Defamers of Mature's acting refuse to see more subtle effects within that combination of the overblown exotic and American demotic which the star projects, an attitude very much that of Robin Cross in his jokey picture-caption burlesque of the Biblical Epic, *The Bible According to Hollywood*. Here Victor Mature is given privileged treatment, especially in the chapter on *Samson and Delilah*, subtitled 'Never Give a Philistine an Even Break'. The subtitle encapsulates with witty superficiality what Hermann Broch and Milan Kundera describe less gaudily in their own analyses of kitsch, not just turning the ancient world of *Samson and Delilah* into modern comedy but mocking De Mille's version of the Book of Judges narrative for failing to liberate itself from

Hollywood's narrative, star and generic traditions. Cross's tone is one of a kitschy celebration of kitsch. If kitsch is not just a celebration of bad taste, of the triumph of the low over the high, the confusion of the aesthetic and ethical, but also, as Broch puts it, something at variance with true art in its failure to meditate on and illuminate the origins and meaning of existence, a flight from reality to a point ultimately of its very denial, its relevance to Mature's often-mocked persona seems obvious, though complex.

Not only, as in Cross's lampoon, is Mature frequently regarded as a kitsch object, he is also, in Susan Sontag's famous essay, further defined as 'camp', a term as difficult to pin down as kitsch but, as Sontag defines it, often turning on sexual ambiguity. We will shortly consider the triumph of the epicene and its appeal to different audiences in Victor Mature, but, as regards the theatricality of camp and its delight in self-conscious style, Sontag's identification of Mature with overwrought imitation of 'he-man-ness', insightful though it is, needs further definition.

In saying this, two connected things can be asserted against the simplest view of the actor: firstly, his iconic sexuality is often placed within a field of meaning where among the things it signifies are tension and stress: and secondly, parody and caricature being possible, it follows that the caricature image, in order to produce pleasure, must be apprehended as degrading something which is in reality more multi-faceted. Logically, if the object of parody was already absolute caricature, further reduction would be impossible (as one says, 'impossible to parody'). In fact Mature's excess constantly slips classification: too demotically American for outright 'otherness', he also signals the Mediterranean; too monumental for interiority, he projects the tortured soul; too self-conscious for realism, he is not predominantly associated with comedy. For all the force that camp and kitsch have to define the colourful palimpsest of his persona, once one reaches beyond the facile semiotics of bulk to the delineaments of a face potent with expression, various nuances of meaning, unlikely combinations of self-awareness, authenticity and vulnerability become evident, requiring analysis beyond jokes of the 'Samson's Hairobic Workout' kind.

The kinesic spectacle of Mature's features as, say, where he is forced to watch Lucia's rape in *Demetrius*, or when he first sees Jesus, or shrieks abuse at Marcellus during the Crucifixion in *The Robe*, is often framed in close-up either in alternation with or posed beside more placid features, further dramatising by contrast the hero's emotionalism. In *Demetrius* the features are those of Michael Rennie and Debra Paget. In the scene where he kneels beside Peter, the two are often in the frame together, the other character, as is often the case in such moments, doing most of the talking, freeing attention for the tremors of emotion that seismically jolt the land mass of

Demetrius's face. Here, as in the later scene where Peter visits Demetrius and Messalina and is rebuffed, the apostle's calm control of his emotions is mirrored in a face suffused with calm and in static unchanging gestures suggesting unmoveable faith. Even where Demetrius shouts at him in frustrated guilt and anger, Rennie's features remain as calm as his gestures, while Mature's lips contort themselves and writhe in bursts of speech interrupted by a characteristic bitter smile/grimace.

In the pre-fight saturnalia scene Mature and Debra Paget are posed in close-up near the opposite ends of the screen, forming a perfect symmetry as they face each other in profile. Paget's opaline, almost sleepwalking face, the essence of sexual innocence, plays against Mature's agonistically over-defined features as they signal a complex semiosis of love, involving tensions between semi-paternal, agapitic impulses towards a Madonna ideal and mixed desire and fear of the sexual, an embrace interrupted by Messalina, but not before Mature's features are fleetingly invested with a typical melancholy as if mourning their propensity to carnal enslavement.

But the difference between Mature's representation of interiority and Rennie's or Paget's is not just that they represent feeling under the control of calm but that their acting remains within the low-key constraints of realistic portrayal of emotions, whereas Mature's frequently advances beyond the boundaries of realism. This gigantism of emotion (nearly all the product of shifting features on a statically held head, his bodily gestures not being noticeably broad), transferring the huge thematics of the Epic to the moral landscape of his physiognomy, externalising the psychomachia in a mode where almost every gesture is frozen in absolute significance as in heroic paintings, requires audiences to view him and to respond to him if not through Brechtian modes of detachment then through other more mixed forms of distancing.

This element is too complex to be labelled self-parody, but is nevertheless part-defined by his off- and on-screen self-parodies – 'I'm not an actor and I have 60 films to prove it' – which reach a climax in his self-deprecatory role of the ageing film star in *After the Fox*. Mature's self-parodies are attractive not so much because they expose or ridicule his performance but because they faintly illuminate part of the complexity of his persona and style by their consistency with the presiding elements of anti-realism, iconicity and ludic sensibility within his image. Excess of histrionics in the service of realism leads to its subversion. The intensity of feeling he projects arouses pity and fear, but, by its stylised excess, invites not just an emotional but also a cooler, more intellectual response. Looking at Mature overdoing it may provoke derision but, whether in derision or in admiration, our mixed response to his screen portrayals pushes us to move beyond mere empathy into a distanced awareness of the artifice of all acting, and of all, even the most seductively realistic of art-forms. Mature and the Hollywood Biblical Epic, so well suited to each other in so many ways, complement each other also in their crude, pre-Derridean appeals to their own deconstruction.

ECSTASY

> I never see films where the man's tits are bigger than the woman's.
> — Groucho Marx on *Samson and Delilah*

Once the focus switches from lowest common denominators, audience response to Victor Mature is revealed as a complex question. Far from being defined by David Shipman's absurd dismissal ('you never get an inkling ... what he was thinking or feeling'), Mature's persona raises questions about star meanings and different levels of audience reception throughout the Hollywood cinema.

Serious writing about male stars tends either to treat the male pin-up as a *mauvaise foi* symbol of masculinity deflecting the threat of homosexual meaning or else, more straightforwardly, as a powerful endorsement of patriarchal prejudice. The first argument has been developed by, among others, Richard Dyer and Steve Neale. Analysing male pin-ups (inside and outside Hollywood), Dyer notes the over-provision of phallic symbols emphasising masculinity, commenting on a 'hysterically phallic portrait of the young Bogie', where Bogart is almost crowded out of the frame by tennis racquets, golf clubs and a Great Dane. In Mature's Biblical Epic films the equivalent manly paraphernalia is often gladiatorial or martial tackle. Yet, although these male-pursuit accessories may reinforce conventional notions of masculinity, other meanings created by the Mature persona develop in less obvious directions.

Consideration of Mature renders dubious Neale's view in 'Masculinity as Spectacle' that classical Hollywood unequivocally disavows male eroticism, not only because of homosexuality's threat but also because the female alone is defined as erotic. This second claim fails to consider the majority female heterosexual audience's desire for the erotic exhibition of the male star. Edgar Morin's work on stars, exploring the complexities of audience identification through distinctions between ego-ideals and objects of desire, provides a starting point for thinking about the realities of the cross-gender responses of identification, empathy and pleasure.

As an ego-ideal, Mature would have appealed to many 1950s men, not just as an obvious he-man but for more subtle, qualities, particularly the way he displays emotion without suggesting weakness. Equally, many women, if not actually identifying with Mature, would have empathised with his role in the films. As an object of desire, tall, massive and sensuously handsome, his box-office popularity proves his appeal to many women and (however theorised) to many men, regardless of sexual orientation. While recently there has been a deluge of crudely negative 'Big Bad Wolves' approaches to cinematic masculinity, a few feminist analyses have recognised the complexities of the male star, for example Pam Cook's analysis of De Niro in *Raging Bull*, Miriam Hansen's work on female responses to Valentino, or Norman Rodowick's exploration of similar questions in *The Difficulty of Difference*.

Hansen's notion of ambivalence, that even in a patriarchal cinema opportunities exist for women to 'violate the taboo on female scopophilia', and Rodowick's argument about the non-exclusivity to one sex of 'feminine' or 'masculine' responses, are highly appropriate to a discussion of Victor Mature, himself an unstable pattern of conventional and non-conventional, even subversive, masculinity.

As a star whose 1950s epic meanings were crossed by traces of earlier involvements in other genres, Mature embodied within the male ego-ideal construction of his epic roles 'subversive' meanings carried over from his 1940s Musicals and Films Noirs, genres known for their disruptions of conventions of sexual identity. So Mature brings to the epics echoes of the skirt-chasing frivolities of the Fox Musicals. 'O'Brien has gone Hawaiian', sings Betty Grable in *Song of the Islands*, while he becomes a victim of strange and tacky, effeminately colourful reversals of Irish whimsy and South Sea hula-hula revelry. A persona already curiously defined by his other gaudy Fox musicals was taken further along the road of shady, vulnerable masculinity in noir films like *Kiss of Death* and *Cry of the City*. Even as a cop, in *Cry of the City*, Mature falls prey to dubious morality. In *Kiss of Death* he is the stoolie who betrays his comrades to the cops.

In Ford's *My Darling Clementine* when Mature's Doc Holliday quotes from *Hamlet* the point is not so much one of detachment through Eastern learning from intellectually primitive Dodge or Tombstone, as to stress an affinity with theatricality and artifice, feeling and poetic sensibility. A star whose emotions were more than usually projected through the exaggerations of facial kinesics, he also gives the recitation a verbal emphasis signalling his partial alienation from the truly rugged world of, in this instance, Western, but elsewhere Roman or Hebrew virility. Dressed always in black, an effect, despite Wyatt Earp's (Henry Fonda) patronage of the 'tonsorial parlour', which dandifies him far in excess of the film's other men, he is described even by Earp as a 'nice lookin' fella', but is still, as in the Noir films, no stranger to cowardice and betrayal. Significantly, completing the drunken actor's quotation, he picks it up at a crucial point: '. . . undiscovered country . . . thus conscience doth make cowards of us all'.

The placing in quotation marks of Mature's image reaches its most flamboyant form in Sternberg's *The Shanghai Gesture*. Where in *My Darling Clementine* Earp directs the audience's gaze towards Mature as object of desire ('nice lookin' fella') – but since this is a Ford film in a way that stops well short of voluptuous over-indulgence – in *The Shanghai Gesture*, where the opposite may be expected, Mature is commented on by other characters as a beautiful specimen. Poppy's (Gene Tierney's) male escort defines his looks as 'marvellous', as the camera gazes in voyeuristically decadent celebration.

Like Valentino, defined by Hansen as a destabilisation of conventional masculinity, Mature is sometimes framed in ways that reverse the female/ object, male/agent patterns of spectatorship too simply theorised by many writers. In *The Shanghai Gesture*, Mature's Arabian in Madame Gin Sling's vice-den becomes noticeably self-conscious as he becomes aware of the gaze not only of Poppy's escort (playing with the permissible ego ideal/ impermissible object of desire boundaries of the male-on-male look) but of Poppy herself. Mature, not the female star, is explicitly the spectacle. Poppy insolently wonders whether he sleeps with his fez on. The remark's double entendre, invoking Freud's bisexual symbolism in *The Interpretation of Dreams* of hats as both male and female symbols, again draws attention to the presence of the epicene in Mature's sexuality.

Two spectators, male and female, watch Mature, both expressing delight. In a similar situation in the Theatre of Dagon in *Samson and Delilah* their reactions are predictably gender-based – the male: 'He still looks strong enough to kill a lion'; the woman: 'I wish I'd captured him'. Yet even here not everything is stable, for Delilah's peacock dress suggests an appropriation of the masculine, paralleling the great release of masochism as the passive Samson is tortured. In both scenes the spectators' object of desire is a curious mixture of male and female, with rugged frame and husky voice but also puce, tumescent lips like sliced plums, as fruity as those stuck by the cosmetics department on the faces of the Fox musical females with whom he starred. An ambivalent object of desire, he also arouses ambivalent sexual feelings in both male and female spectators, here represented on screen by Poppy and her escort. In other words, we are given not simply masculine and feminine spectators but a more complex representation of male and female spectatorship, in which varying responses, sexual and non-sexual, empathetic and antagonistic, may be aroused. Of course Poppy/Tierney's and Messalina/Hayward's gazes can be construed as negatively transgressive: women who appropriate the male privilege of the look must be defined as whores, femmes fatales or castrators. And so it proves in both cases. But while the look is being appropriated by the female (and, of course, the real-life female audience has no constraints on its gaze), the reality of that look draws attention to the vicissitudes of male/female responses as they lose some of their gender-specific constraints.

As the scene in *The Shanghai Gesture* reverses male power by giving the look to Poppy as well as to her escort, thus eroticising Mature through the gaze of a female as well as a male spectator, it highlights Mature's difference by tropes of foreignness. In his self-definition as 'Dr Omar of Shanghai and Gomorrah', Mature stresses the hetero (Gomorrah)/homo (Shanghai–Sodom?) erotic aura of his sexuality:

> My birth took place under a full moon on the sands near Damascus. My father was an Armenian tobacco dealer and was far away, and my mother, the less said about her the better. She was half French and the other half is lost in the dust of time. In short, I'm a thorough mongrel. I'm related to all the earth and nothing that's human is foreign to me.

The explanation of Dr Omar's origins is a metaphor for Mature's persona itself; a half-caste mongrel of sexuality, a man, for all his devotion to public duty, more luxurious, ready to surrender the will (recalling the Films Noirs) to the irrational dictates of sexual ecstasy, more ultimately decadent (recalling the musicals) than other epic heroes.

The epics rarely fail to dress Mature without exposing parts of his body. *The Robe* exceptionally distances him as far as possible from the sensuality with which he is so often identified, but his entanglement with Susan Hayward in *Demetrius* often includes moments that emphasise the sexual aura of partial displays of male nudity. This is especially so in the combat scenes where, within the rituals of hyper-aggressive masculinity, the softer, feminised elements of *The Robe* are surprisingly evident. For instance, prior to the first arena combat, a camera pan begins with a view of a voluptuous, Michelangelo-inspired statue of a naked Apollo. The pose is languid, like *The Dying Slave* or *David*, hands outstretched a little, head bowed, one leg bent. It is an image not so much of energy, power or violence as of feminine grace. The figure stands on wreaths of flowers further softening the image and displaying a male sexuality, not the embodiment of aggression, violence or even action but of erotic promise, of softened and sensuous contours, available to the gaze.

If the naked Apollo complicates the spectacle of the theatre of masculinity, the coupling of Victor Mature with Hedy Lamarr in a pastoral scene in *Samson and Delilah* again renders stable definitions of masculinity uncertain, showing that not only the female disrupts the order of patriarchal narrative and representation.

Though by the scene in which Samson surrenders to Delilah he has already been compared to a lion, both verbally and visually, his male physical strength is increasingly set against other qualities. In the wilderness, by a stream, once he has emerged from his swim, Samson and Delilah relax on the river bank. Like Delilah, Samson is only partly clothed. He and Delilah face the camera symmetrically. Before long he places his dagger in its sheath, a gesture appearing to vindicate the view that virile symbols in such scenes defuse passivity's threat to masculinity. Nevertheless, even if the dagger over-asserts the phallus's destiny, the architecture of Mature's body, his softly-curved torso, coupled in this film with the ambiguous symbolism of his hair, succeeds in demasculinising the '100 per cent' man that Lizabeth Scott calls him in *Easy Living* (Sparks, 1949).

Crude as his remark is, Groucho was right to notice that Mature's breasts, unhardened by pectoral discipline, move him towards the centre of the spectrum of sexual connotation. Like the abundant black hair and juicy lips, his breasts emphasise his capitulation to the senses. While his outsize frame emphasised the Biblical Epics' projection of masculinity then in circulation, his vulnerability to sexual compromise, 'Soften'd with pleasure and voluptuous life' (Milton on Samson), draws attention to the much debated 'crisis of masculinity', the feminisation of the male, and, ultimately, the rise of a less rigidified ideal of male sexual identity, to parallel, if not ultimately to break down, conventional norms.

Note on sources

For reasons of space the listings that follow are only of works cited in the argument of the text, or uncited but of primary relevance. The usual film-book practice of aggressively demonstrating theoretical credentials by including a vast general bibliography on the cinema has not been followed, and the list has also been abbreviated to the most immediately relevant in all other areas. For instance, as regards theological texts, Nineham's edition of St Mark is included because it is twice part of the argument, but other editions of the Gospels consulted are not listed. Citations are in order of consideration in the text.

INTRODUCTION

Leslie Halliwell, *Film Guide*, 5th edition (London, 1986). Gerald Kaufman, 'King Corn', *The Daily Telegraph*, 29 March 1989. Anne Edwards, *The De Milles: An American Family* (London, 1989). Phil Koury, *Yes, Mr De Mille* (New York, 1959). Christian Metz, *Psychoanalysis and Cinema: The Imaginary Signifier* (London, 1982). Joel Finler, *The Hollywood Story* (London, 1988), Cobbett Steinberg, *Reel Facts* (Harmondsworth, 1981). Foster Hirsch, *The Hollywood Epic* (New York, 1978). Derek Elley, *The Epic Film: Myth and History* (London, 1984). John Cary, *Spectacular! The Story of Epic Films* (London, 1974). Edward Edelson, *Great Movie Spectaculars* (New York, 1976). Jon Solomon, *The Ancient World in the Cinema* (London, 1978). Mike Munn, *The Stories Behind the Scenes of the Great Film Epics* (Watford, 1982). Michael Wood, *America in the Movies, or 'Santa Maria It Had Slipped My Mind'* (New York, 1978). Frank McConnell, *Storytelling and Mythmaking* (New York, 1979). Stephen Neale, *Genre* (London, 1980). Gilles Deleuze, *Cinema 1: The Movement-Image* (London, 1986). F. Nietzsche, 'The Uses and Abuses of History', *Untimely Meditations* (Cambridge, 1983). P. Berger and T. Luckmann, 'Sociology of Religion and Sociology of Knowledge', *Sociology and Social Research*, vol. 47 (1963). T. Luckmann, *The Invisible Religion* (London, 1967). John Neuhaus, ed., *Piety and Politics; Evangelicals and Fundamentalists Confront the World* (Washington, D.C., 1987). B. R. Wilson, *Religion in Secular Society* (London, 1966). Richard Niebuhr, *The Kingdom of God in America* (New York, 1959). Roy Eckhardt, *The Surge of Piety in America: An Appraisal* (New York, 1958). Martyn E. Marty, *The New Shape of American Religion* (New York, 1959). Will Heberg, *Protestant–Catholic–Jew: An Essay in American Religious Sociology* (1956). Hortense Powdermaker, *Hollywood, the Dream Factory* (New York, 1950). Paul Schrader, *Transcendental Style; Ozu, Bresson, Dreyer* (New York, 1972). Jacques Maritain, 'Religion and Culture', in *The Social and Political Philosophy of Jacques Maritain* (Garden City, 1965). Sigmund Freud, *The Future of an Illusion* (London, 1962). Kevin Jackson, ed., *Schrader on Schrader and Other Writings* (London, 1990). Sinclair Lewis, *Elmer Gantry* (Oxford, 1983). Max Weber, *Sociology of Religion* (London, 1965). Mircea Eliade, *A History of Religious Ideas* (London, 1978). Richard Maltby, '*The King of Kings* and the Tsar of All the Rushes', *Screen*, vol. 31, no. 2 (summer 1990). Bruce Barton, *The Man Nobody Knows: A Discovery of the Real Jesus* (Indianapolis, 1924). Donald Hayne, ed., *The Autobiography of Cecil B. De Mille* (London, 1960).

THE OLD TESTAMENT EPIC

Neal Gabler, *An Empire of Their Own: How the Jews Invented Hollywood* (London, 1989). Marshall Sklare, *America's Jews* (New York, 1971). Patricia Erens, *The Jew in American Cinema* (Bloomington, 1984). Lester D. Friedman, *Hollywood's Image of the Jew* (New York, 1982). Annette Insdorf, *Indelible Shadows: Film and the Holocaust* (Cambridge, 1989). Charles Higham, *Cecil B. De Mille* (New York, 1973). Louis Ginzburg, *The Legends of the Jews*, vols 3, 4, 6 (Philadelphia, 1909–38). Sir E. A. Wallis Bridges, trans and introduction, *The Queen of Sheba and Her Only Son Menyelek: Being the History of the Departure of God and His Ark of the Covenant from Jerusalem to Ethiopia . . .* (London, 1922). Mircea Eliade, *Patterns in Comparative Religion* (London, 1958). Michael R. Booth, *Victorian Spectacular Theatre 1850–1910* (London, 1981). Jeremy Maas, *Victorian Painters* (London, 1969). Robert Lang, *American Film Melodrama: Griffith, Vidor, Minnelli* (Princeton, N.J., 1989). Sigmund Freud, *Moses and Monotheism* and *Totem and Taboo* both in *The Origins of Religion* (Harmondsworth, 1980). F. Nietzsche, 'The Uses and Abuses of History', *Untimely Meditations* (Cambridge, 1983). Walter Coppedge, *Henry King's America* (Metuchen, New Jersey, 1986). James M. Cain, *The Postman Always Rings Twice* and *Double Indemnity* both in *The Five Great Novels of James M. Cain* (London, 1985). Ernest Hemingway, *The Snows of Kilimanjaro* (London, 1939). David Thompson, *A Biographical Dictionary of the Cinema* (London, 1975). Gabriel Josipovici, *The Book of God: a Response to the Bible* (London, 1988). Robert Alter, *The Art of Biblical Narrative* (London, 1981). Meir Sternberg, *The Poetics of Biblical Narrative* (Bloomington, Indiana, 1985). Sigmund Freud, 'A Special Type of Object Choice Made by Men', *On Sexuality: Three Essays on the Theory of Sexuality and Other Works* (Harmondsworth, 1977). Denis de Rougemont, *Passion and Society* (London, 1956). Jessica Benjamin, *The Bonds of Love: Psychoanalysis, Feminism and the Problem of Domination* (London, 1990). Joseph Heller, *God Knows* (London, 1985). Dan Jacobson, *The Rape of Tamar* (London, 1985). René Girard, *Deceit, Desire and the Novel: Self and Other in Literary Structure* (Baltimore, 1966). Tony Tanner, *Adultery in the Novel: Contract and Transgression* (Baltimore, 1981). Eduardo Moreno, *The Films of Susan Hayward* (Secaucus, N.J., 1979) for references to *Newsweek* and *Life*. J. J. Bachofen, *Myth, Religion and Mother-Right* (Princeton, N.J., 1967). Robert Briffault, *The Mothers* (New York, 1969). Adrienne Rich, *Of Woman Born: Motherhood as Experience and Institution* (London, 1977). Eve Kosofsky Sedgwick, *Between Men: English Literature and Male Homosocial Desire* (New York, 1985).

THE CHRIST FILM

Albert Schweitzer, *The Quest of the Historical Jesus* (London, New York, 1910). Robert Graves, *King Jesus* (London, 1946). Nikos Kazantzakis, *The Last Temptation* (London, 1988). Gerd Theissen, *The Shadow of the Galilean* (London, 1987) and *The First Followers of Jesus: a Sociological Analysis of the Earliest Christianity* (London, 1978). George Moore, *The Brook Kerith, a Syrian Story* (London, 1916). Mikhail Bulgakov, *The Master and Margarita* (London, 1988). A. Renan, *La Vie de Jésus* (Paris, 1924). D. F. Strauss, *The Life of Jesus Critically Examined* (Philadelphia and London, 1972). F. Nietzsche, *The Anti-Christ* (Harmondsworth, 1968). K. Kautsky, *Foundations of Christianity* (New York, 1953). Hugh J. Schonfield, *Passover Plot* (London, 1985). John M. Allegro, *The Sacred Mushroom and the Cross* (London, 1970). Carl Dreyer, *Jesus* (New York, 1972). New York Times reviews of *Intolerance* and *The King of Kings* in *The New York Times Film Reviews*, 6 vols, vol. 1 (1913–1931) (New York, 1970); for *Intolerance* see October 1916, p. 21; for *The King of Kings* see April 1921, p. 360. Charles Higham, *Cecil B. De Mille* (New York, 1973). Michael Baxandall, *Painting and Experience in Fifteenth Century Italy* (Oxford, 1972). Elisabeth Schussler Fiorenza, *In Memory of Her: a Feminist Reconstruction of Christian Origins* (London,

1983). Larry May, *Screening Out the Past* (Chicago, 1983). S. Higashi, *Cecil B. De Mille: a Guide to References and Resources* (Boston, 1985). J. Stevenson, ed., *A New Eusebius; Documents Illustrative of the History of the Church to A.D. 337* (London, 1957). Max Weber, *Sociology of Religion* (London, 1965). Leon Poliakov, *The History of Anti-Semitism*, vols 1, 4 (New York 1977). Mark Saperstein, *Moments of Crisis in Jewish–Christian Relations* (London, 1989). Susan P. Casteras, *Images of Victorian Womanhood in English Art* (London, 1984). Ann Douglas, *The Feminization of American Culture* (New York, 1977. Frances B. Nichol, *The Answer to Modern Religious Thinking*, quoted in Norman F. Furniss, *The Fundamentalist Controversy* (Hamden, Conn., 1963). D. H. Lawrence, *Hymns in a Man's Life* in *Phoenix II*, ed. Warren Roberts and Harry T. Moore (London, 1968). Roland Barthes, *Sur Racine* (Paris, 1963). Harold Bloom, *The Anxiety of Influence; a Theory of Poetry* (Oxford, 1973). Victor Perkins, *Movie*, vol. 9 (1983). Oscar Wilde, *Salome*, in *The Portable Oscar Wilde*, edited by Richard Aldington (New York, 1946). Gustave Flaubert, *Herodias* in *Trois Contes* (London, 1959). Leo Steinberg, *The Sexuality of Christ in Renaissance Art and in Modern Oblivion* (London, 1983). Paula Fredriksen, *From Jesus to Christ: the Origins of the New Testament Images of Jesus* (New Haven, 1988). Morton Smith, *Jesus the Magician* (Wellingborough, 1985). Henry Thoreau, *Walden, or Life in the Woods and On the Duty of Civil Disobedience* (New York, 1962). D. E. Nineham, *St Mark* (Harmondsworth, 1963). Stevens Interview, Felix Barber, 'Too Many Faces', *Evening News*, 8 April 1968. Fredric Jameson, *Signatures of the Visible* (New York, 1990). David Thompson and Ian Christie, eds, *Scorsese on Scorsese* (London, 1989). Kevin Jackson, ed., *Schrader on Schrader* (London, 1990). Robert Phillip Kolker, *The Cinema of Loneliness* (London, 1988). Jean Mitry, *Esthétique et Psychologie du Cinéma*, 2 vols (Paris, 1963, 1965). Pam Cook, *Monthly Film Bulletin*, vol. 55 (1988). Sigmund Freud, 'The Uncanny', *Standard Edition of the Complete Psychological Works*, 24 vols, London, 1940–68, vol. xvii. J. N. D. Kelly, *Early Christian Doctrines* (London, 1985). F. Nietzsche, *The Anti-Christ* (Harmondsworth, 1968). Frank Kermode, *The Genesis of Secrecy: on the Interpretation of Narrative* (London, 1979). Thomas De Quincey, 'Judas Iscariot', in *De Quincey's Collected Writings*, vol. viii, ed. David Masson (London, 1897). Jorge Luis Borges, 'Three Versions of Judas', *Labyrinths* (Harmondsworth, 1970). Edward W. Said, *Orientalism* (Harmondsworth, 1978). Geza Vermes, *Jesus the Jew* (London, 1983).

THE ROMAN/CHRISTIAN EPIC

Henryk Sienkiewicz, *Quo Vadis?* (London, ND). Lew Wallace, *Ben-Hur: a Tale of the Christ* (London, ND). Pär Lagerkvist, *Barabbas* (London, 1951). Anthony Burgess, *The Kingdom of the Wicked* (London, 1985). Gore Vidal, *Julian* (London, 1964). Hugo Montheilhet, *Neropolis* (Harmondsworth, 1988). Georg Lukács, *The Historical Novel* (London, 1962). Sigmund Freud, *Jokes and Their Relation to the Unconscious* (Harmondsworth, 1983). Robin Lane Fox, *Pagans and Christians* (Harmondsworth, 1988). Lloyd C. Douglas, *The Robe* (London, 1943) and *The Big Fisherman* (Cambridge, Mass., 1948). Edmund Wilson, *Classics and Commercials* (London, 1950). Frank McConnell, *Storytelling and Mythmaking* (New York, 1979). Charles Barr, 'Cinemascope Before and After', in *Film Theory and Criticism: Introductory Readings*, ed. Gerald Mast and Marshall Cohen (New York, 1974). Barry Salt, *Film Style and Technology: History and Analysis* (London, 1983). Richard Dyer, 'Four Films of Lana Turner', *Movie*, vol. 25. Ken Wlaschin, *The Illustrated Encyclopedia of the World's Great Movie Stars and Their Films* (London, 1979). Godfrey Hodgson, *America In Our Time* (New York, 1978). David Caute, *'The Great Fear': the Anti-Communist Purges under Truman and Eisenhower* (London, 1978). The Eisenhower inaugural address quoted in Peter Lyon, *Eisenhower: Portrait of the Hero* (Boston, 1974). Michael Grant, *Gladiators* (London, 1967). Melvyn Bragg, *Rich; the Life of Richard Burton* (London, 1988). Gerald Mast, ed., *The Movies in Our Midst* (Chicago, 1982), for quotes from the HUAC hearings. Pat McGilligan, *Backstory: Interviews with Screenwriters of the Golden Age* (Berkeley, 1986). Ben Witherington III, *Women in the Earliest Church* (Cambridge, 1988). J. P. V. D. Balsdon, *Life and Leisure in Ancient Rome* (New York, 1969). B. H. Warrington, *Nero: Reality and Legend* (London, 1969). Anthony A. Barrett, *Caligula: The Corruption of Power* (London, 1969). J. P. V. D. Balsdon, *The Emperor Gaius* (New York, 1976).

VICTOR MATURE

Sigmund Freud, *Totem and Taboo*, in *The Origins of Religion* (Harmondsworth, 1986). Edgar Morin, *Stars* (New York, 1960). Michel Mourlet, 'In Defence of Violence', reprinted in *Stardom: Industry of Desire*, ed. C. Gledhill (London, 1991). Robin Cross, *The Bible According to Hollywood* (London, 1984). H. Broch, *Poesía e investigación* (Barcelona, 1974). Milan Kundera, *The Unbearable Lightness of Being* (London, 1984). Susan Sontag, 'On Camp', in *Against Interpretation* (New York, 1969). Victor Mature, *The Hollywood Reporter*, 31 October 1949, quoted in *The Hollywood Reporter, the Golden Years*, ed. T. Wilkerson and M. Borie (New York, 1984). David Shipman, *The Great Movie Stars: 2. The International Years* (London, 1972). Steve Neale, 'Masculinity as Spectacle', *Screen*, vol. 24, no. 6 (Nov.–Dec. 1983). Richard Dyer, 'Don't Look Now – the Male Pin-Up', *Screen*, vol. 23, nos 3–4 (Sept.–Oct. 1982). Pam Cook, 'Masculinity in Crisis?' *Screen*, vol. 23, nos 3–4 (Sept.–Oct. 1982). D. N. Rodowick, *The Difficulty of Difference: Psychoanalysis, Sexual Difference and Film Theory* (London, 1991). Miriam Hansen, 'Pleasure, Ambivalence, Identification: Valentino and Female Spectatorship', *Cinema Journal* vol. 25, no. 4 (summer 1986). Laura Mulvey, 'Afterthoughts on "Visual Pleasure and Narrative Cinema" Inspired by *Duel in the Sun* (King Vidor, 1946)', *Framework*, nos 15–17 (summer 1981). Sigmund Freud, *The Interpretation of Dreams* (Harmondsworth, 1975).

Index *of films, directors, authors, actors and sources*

Acts of the Apostles, The, 117, 156, 199
Acts of Pilate, The, 101
After the Fox, 232
Agony and the Ecstasy, The, 229
Aimée, Anouk, 59
Aldrich, Thomas Bailey, 43
Alexander, Mrs C. F., 123
Alexander, Shana, 1
Alexander the Great, 214
Allegro, John M., 99
Allen, Woody, 39
Alter, Robert, 79
Althusser, Louis, 22
Altman, Robert, 150
Androcles and the Lion (Erskine), 177, 188, 190, 219
Angeli, Pier, 59, 188–9
Annie Hall, 39
Anno Domini (Cooper), 7, 178, 200
Arnold, Matthew, 126
Around the World in 80 Days, 5
Augustine, Saint, 202, 220
Augustine of Hippo (Rossellini), 100, 170, 218

Bachofen, J. J., 50, 69
Back Street, 76
Baker, Carroll, 148
Barabbas (Fleischer), 177, 178, 180, 185, 186, 190, 200, 217, 219
Barber, Felix, 148
Barker, Lex, 228
Barr, Charles, 207
Barthes, Roland, 126, 127
Barton, Bruce, 22–4
Baxandall, Michael, 102
Bellini, 102
Bellow, Saul, 39
Bells of St Mary's, The, 5, 17–20
Ben-Hur (Niblo), 5, 39, 177–9, 181, 183, 194, 224
Ben-Hur (Wallace), 178, 187, 193, 200, 201
Ben-Hur (Wyler), 5, 7, 61, 177, 182, 193, 194, 202, 228
Beresford, Bruce, 2, 6, 41, 55, 58
Berger, P. and Luckmann, T., 13

Bergman, Ingrid, 18, 19
Bergryd, Ulla, 53
Beyond a Reasonable Doubt, 75
Bible: In the Beginning, The (Huston), 6, 53, 59, 64
Big Country, The, 77
Big Fisherman, The (Borzage), 6, 177, 180
Bloom, Harold, 127
Bogart, Humphrey, 134, 135, 228
Bond, Ward, 18
Bonfire of the Vanities, The, 39
Booth, Michael R., 61
Borges, J. L., 160
Borgnine, Ernest, 190
Born on the Fourth of July, 157
Borzage, Frank, 6, 177, 180
Bosch, Hieronymus, 163
Boston Strangler, The, 185
Botticelli, Sandro, 102
Bowie, David, 103
Boyd, Stephen, 194
Boys from Brazil, The, 78
Bragg, Melvyn, 214
Brandauer, Klaus Maria, 203
Bresson, Robert, 15, 17
　Journal of a Country Priest, 15, 17
　Pickpocket, 15, 17
Briffault, Robert, 69
Brigham Young, 18
Broch, Hermann, 230–1
Brynner, Yul, 40, 47, 51, 52, 228
Bucholz, Horst, 99
Bulgakov, Mikhail, 99
Buñuel, Luis, 66, 100, 119, 120
　Viridiana, 66
　La Voie Lactée, 119
Burgess, Anthony, 178, 179, 200
Burton, Richard, 183, 190, 199, 208, 209, 214, 215, 216
Burton, William, 121
Bushman, Francis X., 194

Cain, James M., 75
Calderón, 143
Capra, Frank, 19

Cast a Giant Shadow, 39
Casteras, Susan P., 123
Chandler, Jeff, 193
Chapman, Edythe, 45
Chosen, The, 39
Chronicles, Books of, 47
Cleopatra (Mankiewicz), 64, 178, 215
Cohn, Harry, 34
Colbert, Claudette, 188, 192
Collins, Charles, 123
Collins, Joan, 66
Conte, Richard, 140
Cook, Pam, 234
Coreggio, 16, 135
Corinthians, Epistles to the, 113, 198, 232
Coulouris, George, 131
Cregar, Laird, 143
Crosby, Bing, 18–19
Cross, Robin, 230–1
Crossfire, 37, 38, 40
Cry of the City, 234
Cumming, Dorothy, 110
Curtis, Tony, 131, 191
Curtiz, Michael, 5, 42

Dafoe, Willem, 117, 156, 157
da Messina, 163
Damn Yankees, 143
Dangerous Mission, 229
Daniel, Book of, 136
Daves, Delmer, 5
David and Bathsheba (King), 5, 40, 50, 51, 60,
    70–90, 220
Da Vinci, 142, 148
Davis, Bette, 38
Dayan, Moshe, 40
Dean, James, 133
De Bosio, Gianfranco, 47, 55, 58, 60
De Carlo, Yvonne, 131
Deleuze, Gilles, 11, 12, 64
Demetrius and the Gladiators (Daves) 5, 177,
    178, 180, 187, 188, 190, 192–4, 203,
    217–27, 229–32, 236
De Mille, Cecil B., 2, 3, 4, 5, 9, 10, 12, 15, 22,
    23, 35, 42, 44–7, 54, 57, 60, 62, 63, 98,
    99, 100, 101, 102, 103, 104, 105, 106,
    108, 109, 110–26, 127, 130, 133, 135,
    138, 140, 152, 153, 160, 178
  Cleopatra, 178
  The Godless Girl, 115
  Manslaughter, 42
De Niro, Robert, 234
De Quincey, Thomas, 159–61

Derek, John, 40
De Rougemont, Denis, 85
Derrida, Jacques, 233
Dieterle, William, 185
Dix, Richard, 45
Doré, Gustave, 44, 100, 118, 119
Dostoievsky, F., 158
Dyce, William, 118

Exodus, Book of, 44, 46, 47
Exodus (Preminger), 39, 40, 202

Fall of the Roman Empire, The (Mann), 6, 182,
    204
Farouk, King, 87
Fellini, F., 178, 204, 205
Ferrer, Jose, 131, 140
Findler, Joel, 5
Flaubert, Gustave, 132
Fleischer, Richard, 185
Fonda, Henry, 234
Ford, Henry, 122
Fox, Robin Lane, 201
Freud, Sigmund, 2, 7, 15, 20, 46, 47, 50, 58,
    79, 122, 155, 228, 235
  The Future of an Illusion, 15
  The Interpretation of Dreams, 235
  Jokes and their Relation to the Unconscious,
    203
  Moses and Monotheism, 46–7, 58, 122
  *A Special Type of Object Choice Made by
    Men*, 87–90
  Totem and Taboo, 228
  The Uncanny, 154
Friedman, Lester D., 37
Fromm, Erich, 218

Gabler, Neal, 33, 34
Gabriel, Peter, 164
Gardner, Ava, 73
Garr, Teri, 3, 60
Genesis, Book of, 224
Genn, Leo, 192
Gentleman's Agreement, 36, 37, 38
Ghost, 8
Gill, Brendan, 1
Gitai, Amos, 41, 43
Godfather, The (Coppola), 18
Gospel According to Matthew, The (Pasolini),
    8, 53, 100, 104, 116, 160, 225
Gospel of Mary Magdalene, The, 101
Grable, Betty, 234
Granger, Stewart, 190

Grant, Michael, 217
Graves, Robert, 98
Greatest Story Ever Told, The (Stevens), 1, 6, 98, 99, 100, 104, 106, 109, 139–48, 149, 224
Great Sinner, The, 78
Griffith, D. W., 4, 12, 16, 17, 24, 35, 43, 49, 50, 111, 116, 117, 124
  Birth of a Nation, 62, 124
Griffith, Hugh, 7, 202
Grünewald, 163
Gunfighter, The, 71

Halliwell, Leslie, 1
Hamlet, 234
Handel, G. F., 148
Hansen, Miriam, 234
Harareet, Haya, 201
Hardwicke, Sir Cedric, 59
Hawkins, Jack, 195
Hayden, Sterling, 210
Hayward, Susan, 75, 85, 87, 188, 217, 220, 221
Hayworth, Rita, 185
Heaven Can Wait, 143
Heberg, Will, 13
Hebrews, Epistle to the, 199
Heller, Joseph, 79, 80
Hemingway, Ernest, 76
Hepburn, Audrey, 77
Herbert, John Rogers, 122
Hershey, Barbara, 109
Heston, Charlton, 7, 10, 64, 142, 227, 228, 229
Higashi, S., 117, 118
Higham, Charles, 42
High Noon, 6
Hodgson, Godfrey, 225
Hole in the Head, A, 229
How the West Was Won, 6
Humoresque, 36
Hunt, Holman, 118, 126
Hunter, Jeffrey, 100, 117, 128, 135, 157
Hussey, Olivia, 116
Huston, John, 6, 20, 53, 59
  Wise Blood, 20, 167

Iliad, The, 10
I Married a Communist, 211
I Want to Live, 220, 222
Inherit the Wind, 21
Intolerance (D. W. Griffith), 4, 5, 12, 16, 37, 42, 61, 62, 101, 116, 117, 124, 149

Isaiah, Book of, 142
It's a Wonderful Life, 19
Ivanhoe, 36, 39
Ives, Charles, 125

Jacobson, Dan, 80
Jesus Christ Superstar, 39
Jesus of Montreal (Arcand), 98
Jesus of Nazareth (Zeffirelli), 104, 116
John, Gospel According to, 113, 134, 138, 144, 160, 168
Josephus, 46
Josipovici, Gabriel, 79
Jourdan, Louis, 77
Joy, Leatrice, 45
Judges, Book of, 230, 231
Judith of Bethulia (D. W. Griffith), 4, 39, 43, 49, 50
Jung, Carl, 134
Justice, James Robertson, 80

Kauffmann, Stanley, 1
Kaufman, Gerald, 2
Kautsky, Karl, 99
Kazantzakis, Nikos, 17, 107, 109, 111, 128, 150, 154, 161, 167
Keitel, Harvey, 161
Kelly, Gene, 21
Kermode, Frank, 159
Kerouac, Jack, 139
Kerr, Deborah, 187, 188, 189, 190, 214
Keys of the Kingdom, The, 77
Khartoum, 228
King, Henry, 5, 35, 70–90
  Captain from Castile, The, 70
  Carousel, 71
  Jesse James, 70
  Love is a Many Splendoured Thing, 71
  Snows of Kilimanjaro, The, 71, 73, 76, 77
  Song of Bernadette, The, 4, 5, 70, 72
  Tol'able David, 70, 72, 73
  Wilson, 71, 72
King and I, The, 52, 58
King David (Beresford), 2, 6, 41, 51, 58, 60
King of Kings (Ray), 6, 98, 100, 101, 103, 108, 109, 127–38, 157
King of Kings, The (De Mille), 2, 4, 5, 9, 22, 23, 37, 98, 100, 101, 103, 108, 109, 125, 138, 154, 160, 196
Kings, Book of, 47, 48
Kiss of Death, 244
Kolker, Robert, 151
Koster, Henry, 5, 48

Koury, Phil, 2
Kramer, Stanley, 21
Kubrick, Stanley, 6, 11
    A Clockwork Orange, 11, 65
Kundera, Milan, 230

Lacan, Jacques, 22
Laffan, Patricia, 188
Lagerkvist, Pär, 185, 186
Lamarr, Hedy, 237
Lancaster, Burt, 20, 47, 229
Landi, Elissa, 188, 189
Land of the Pharaohs, 178
Lang, Robert, 68
La Rocque, Rod, 45
Last Days of Pompeii, The (Schoedsack), 5,
    177, 181, 191, 194, 217
Last Days of Sodom and Gomorrah, The
    (Aldrich), 40, 42, 54, 56, 57, 58, 59, 65,
    67
Last Temptation of Christ, The, 4, 6, 8, 14, 17,
    62, 98, 100, 103, 104, 105, 107, 108,
    109, 116, 149–68
Laughton, Charles, 203
Lawrence of Arabia, 6
Le Roy, Melvyn, 5
Leviticus, Book of, 53, 54
Life of Brian, The, 100
Lindbergh, Charles, 38
Lindfors, Viveca, 49
Logan, Jacqueline, 114
Lollobrigida, Gina, 47, 68
Lukács, Georg, 50
Luke, Gospel According to, 110, 145

McAvoy, May, 201
McCallum, David, 140
McCarey, Leo, 19
McConnell, Frank, 10, 207
McKenna, Siobhan, 108
Macomber Affair, The, 76
Macpherson, Aimée Semple, 20
Macpherson, Jeanie, 42
Magnificent Seven, The, 141
Malamud, Bernard, 39
Malcolm, Derek, 2
Maltby, Richard, 22, 23, 24
Man and His Mate, 229
Mandingo, 185
Mangano, Silvana, 186
Mantegna, 147, 148
Man Who Shot Liberty Valance, The, 168
March, Fredric, 188, 190

Maritain, Jacques, 15
Mark, Gospel According to, The, 111, 145
Marshall, William, 224, 225
Martin, John, 63
Marty, Martin E., 13
Marx, Groucho, 233, 237
Marx, Karl, 22
Massey, Raymond, 82
Matthew, 150
Matthew, Gospel According to, The, 122, 145,
    156, 160
Mature, Victor, 40, 220, 227–37
May, Larry, 117
Mayer, Louis B., 34
Mayo, Virginia, 195
Meadows, Jane, 84
Mencken, H. L., 21
Metz, Christian, 3
Michelangelo, 79, 135, 236
Mildred Pierce, 76
Millais, J., 123
Miller, Arthur, 79, 211
Miller, Henry, 51
Milton, John, 11, 98, 143, 155, 227, 229,
    230, 237
Miracle Worker, The, 20
Mississippi Burning, 157
Mr Skeffington, 37, 38, 40
Mitchum, Robert, 20
Mitry, Jean, 151
Moby Dick, 78
Montheilhet, H., 179, 200, 203
Moore, George, 98, 167
Moore, Henry, 15
Moore, Kieron, 84
Moore, Mickey, 110
Morin, Edgar, 228, 233
Moses (De Bosio), 47, 55, 58, 60
Mourlet, Michel, 228
My Cousin Rachel, 215
My Darling Clementine, 234, 235

Naldi, Nita, 45
Neale, Steve, 8, 10, 11, 12, 233
Neff, Hildegarde, 77
Newman, Paul, 40, 195
Newton, Robert, 219
Nichol, Frances, B., 124
Niebuhr, Richard, 13
Nietzsche, Friedrich, 11, 12, 17, 50, 53, 99,
    133, 140, 146, 155, 158, 167, 168, 190,
    213, 224
Night of the Hunter, The, 20

Nineham, D., 144
Noah's Ark, 5, 42
Noerdlinger, Henry, 62
Novarro, Ramon, 29
No Way to Treat a Lady, 39

Olivier, Sir Laurence, 190
Omen, The 78
Once Upon a Time in America, 39
Origin of Species, The, 21
Osborne, John, 215

Paget, Debra, 188, 221, 231, 232
Palance, Jack, 190
Paradine Case, The, 77, 78
Paris, Texas, 167
Parks, Larry, 211
Pasolini, Pier Paolo, 8, 53, 100, 104, 108,
    116, 150, 152, 160
  Medea, 164
  Oedipus Rex, 164
Paul, 113, 163, 167, 168, 191, 198
Pavan, Marisa, 68
Peck, Gregory, 40, 70, 76–81
Perkins, Victor, 129
Pius XII, Pope, 82
Platoon, 157
Pleasance, Donald, 143
Plummer, Christopher, 204
Plutarch, 214
Poitier, Sidney, 224
Postman Always Rings Twice, The, 75
Powdermaker, Hortense, 13
Poynter, Sir Edward John, 64
Prodigal, The, 47, 48, 57
Pudovkin, V., 4

Quo Vadis? (Le Roy), 5, 9, 177–84, 187, 188,
    190, 196, 198, 200, 204, 205, 219
Quo Vadis? (Rossi), 178, 197, 203

Racine, Jean, 36
Rains, Claude, 38
Raphael, 16, 102
Ray, Nicholas, 6, 98–100, 103, 105, 106,
    108, 109, 127–40, 143, 149, 152, 156,
    160, 161, 164
  Bitter Victory, 134
  In a Lonely Place, 134–5
  Johnny Guitar, 134–5
  On Dangerous Ground, 134
  Rebel Without a Cause, 133
  The True Story of Jesse James, 128

Wind Across the Everglades, 134
Reeves, Steve, 228
Reisenfeld, Hugo, 125–6
Rembrandt, 85
Renan, A., 99
Rennie, Michael, 231–2
Repo Man, 167
Ribera, D., 135
Robe, The (Koster), 5–7, 128, 153, 159, 177,
    178, 182, 183, 187, 188, 190, 191, 193,
    194, 196, 199, 201, 203, 206–16, 220,
    227, 230, 231, 236
Roberts, Theodore, 45
Robinson, Jay, 211
Rodowick, Norman, 234
Roman Holiday, 77
Rose-Marie (1936), 65, 66
Rose-Marie (1954), 65, 66
Roth, Philip, 39
Ryan, Robert, 40

Said, Edward, 165
Saigon, 157
Salome (Dieterle), 128, 177, 179, 180, 185,
    193, 194, 201
Samson and Delilah (De Mille), 2, 5–7, 40, 46,
    50–1, 54, 57–8, 61, 64–5, 227, 235–7
Samuel, Book of, 84
Sanders, George, 51–2
Satyricon (Fellini), 178, 204, 205
Schildkraut, Joseph, 112, 115
Schildkraut, Rudolph, 120
Schoedsack, Edward B., 5
Schonfield, Hugh J., 99
Schrader, Paul, 8, 14, 15, 16, 17, 109, 150,
    155, 161
  American Gigolo, 15, 17
  Hardcore, 15, 150
Schwarzenegger, Arnold, 228
Schweitzer, Albert, 98–9
Scorsese, Martin, 6, 8, 14, 98–100, 104–5,
    108–9, 116, 130, 135, 149–68
  Cape Fear, 20, 78
  Raging Bull, 14, 141
  Taxi Driver, 14, 17, 150, 151
Scott, George C., 59
Scott, Gordon, 228
Scott, Lizabeth, 237
Sergeant Rutledge, 225
Shakespeare, William, 79
Shanghai Gesture, The, 235, 236
Shaw, Bernard, 219
Sienkiewicz, H., 178, 187, 189, 192, 195–7,

200, 218
Sign of the Cross, The (De Mille), 4, 5, 177,
    178, 184, 186–8, 190–3, 196, 198–200,
    203–4, 217–18
Sign of the Pagan, The (Sirk), 178, 192–3
Silver Chalice, The, 177–8, 181, 188–90,
    195–6, 200
Simmons, Jean, 188–9, 199, 215–17
Simon, John, 1
Sinatra, Frank, 229
Sklare, Marshall, 36
Smith, Morton, 138
Sofaer, Abraham, 200
Solomon and Sheba (King Vidor), 6, 47–8,
    50–2, 54–8, 64–5, 67–9
Song of the Islands, 234
Sontag, Susan, 231
Spartacus (Kubrick), 6, 7, 178, 182–3, 188,
    191–2, 194, 196, 217, 219, 224–5
Spellbound, 74
Spellman, Cardinal, 34
Spielberg, Steven, 3, 8, 61
    Close Encounters of the Third Kind, 3, 8, 60
    E.T., 8
Stevens, George, 1, 6, 98–100, 104–5, 109,
    139–48, 152, 156, 160–1
    Shane, 141
Stewart, James, 19
Story of Ruth, The, 43, 48, 50, 65
Strauss, D. F., 99, 103, 111
Strode, Woody, 219, 224, 225
Stud, The, 66
Sun Also Rises, The, 70
Superman, 8
Sweet, Blanche, 44

Taylor, Robert, 188, 190, 210
Ten Commandments, The (De Mille, 1923), 4,
    5, 12, 35, 42–6, 60, 64–5, 118
Ten Commandments, The (De Mille, 1956), 3,
    5–7, 10, 15, 35, 42, 44, 46–7, 51–2,
    54–5, 57–62, 67, 118, 224, 229
Theissen, Gerd, 98, 120, 142
Thesiger, Ernst, 212

Thompson, David, 78
Thoreau, H. D., 141–2
Thring, Frank, 131
Tierney, Gene, 235–6
Tirso de Molina, 36
Tissot, James, 101, 118–9
Torrance, Ernest, 110
Tracy, Spencer, 228
Trotti, Lamar, 72
Turner, Lana, 51, 221
Twain, Mark, 197

Ustinov, Peter, 7, 203

Valentino, Rudolph, 234–5
Van Eyck, 157
Vidal, Gore, 179
Vidor, King, 6, 35, 47–8
Von Sydow, Max, 102, 117, 128

Wagonmaster, 18
Walker, Alexander, 2
Walston, Ray, 143
Walthall, Henry B., 44
Warner, H. B., 23, 24, 102, 117, 119, 123
Wayne, John, 147–8
Weber, Max, 22, 111, 114
Weissmuller, Johnny, 228
Welles, Orson, 128–9, 134, 137
Whitman, Stuart, 49
Whitman, Walt, 206
Wild At Heart, 157
Wilde, Oscar, 132
Williamson, Bruce, 1
Wilson, B. R., 13
Wilson, Edmund, 206
Winters, Shelley, 148
Wood, Michael, 9–12
Wyler, William, 5, 7, 201

Yordan, Philip, 137

Zeffirelli, Franco, 104, 116, 160